the state and the poor

This book is the product of a Faculty Study Group of the Institute of Politics in the Kennedy School of Government, Harvard University.

the state
and the poor

SAMUEL H. BEER
RICHARD E. BARRINGER
Editors

WINTHROP PUBLISHERS, INC.
Cambridge, Massachusetts

©1970 by **Winthrop Publishers, Inc.**
17 Dunster Street, Harvard Square
Cambridge, Massachusetts 02138

contents

v

preface

Considering how much time has been spent studying poverty on a national scale, it is surprising how
little is known about its incidence in particular
states. In this book, for the first time to our knowledge, a group of scholars have collaborated to apply
their several disciplines to poverty as a major problem of a specific state government: Massachusetts.

The strength of this approach lies in its focus on
a particular state. Countless books have been written about poverty as a national problem and what
the federal government ought to do about it. The
authors of this book do not deny the fact of federal
leadership and in many ways ask for its further
exercise. The need for an intermediate tier between
the localities and Washington is obvious, however,
and has inspired a good deal of writing about the
proper role of state government in general. Yet the
states vary so greatly in the nature of their problems and in their capacities to cope with them that
these general discussions must have limited useful-
ness. If the academic expert is to offer advice that
will be helpful to a state government, he must look
at the problem in terms of the realities of that state.

The reader who is unknowing of poverty might

best begin by looking at the case studies that John Myer has appended to his chapter on housing. These reports, laconic, factual, and in no way exaggerated, vividly call to mind what poverty means in the everyday life of individuals and families. If at any point in his perusal of this sometimes demanding book the reader begins to wonder what the point of it all is, he will do well to turn to those case studies, which portray in concrete, human terms the reality of the blight that we are trying to relieve and, if possible, to eradicate.

√ The concern of this book, however, is not to paint a picture of poverty, but to say what state government can do about it. In their respective chapters the authors have used their specialized academic knowledge to examine some of the main aspects of the problem in Massachusetts and to propose lines of government action for attacking them.

With respect to each aspect of the problem, the authors have sought to present carefully thought-out, thoroughly researched, and professionally designed proposals on which programs and legislation can be based. These proposals are a good deal more than "bright ideas" merely deserving further consideration. At the same time, they are less than detailed schedules of action constituting statutes or other programmatic formulations. They represent the service to government that the academic specialist is equipped to perform: not himself to govern, but to make available to those directly concerned with government the perspective on a problem that flows from expert knowledge.

The authors hope that what they have written will prove useful to legislators and governors, to candidates, office-holders and members of the interested public, to writers of editorials, speeches, and position-papers, to civil servants, task forces, and pressure groups. Their work is strictly nonpartisan and they would happily exchange recognition for influence. Their hope is for maximum feasible plagiarism by actual or aspiring policy-makers.

A brief guide to the topics taken up in each chapter may help the reader.

Basing his analysis upon the findings of the succeeding chapters, Samuel Beer in an introductory chapter summarizes the case for a comprehensive state anti-poverty program. He sets forth the objectives of such a program and the priorities by which they could be achieved, relating these proposed changes to the new role that the state is already assuming in the federal system.

In a pioneering effort, David Birch and Eugene Saenger, Jr., present answers to some basic factual questions, giving special attention to the

trend in numbers of poor and their location in Massachusetts. Following
this exposition of the nature and extent of the problem, Michael Piore's
chapter takes up the fundamental question of how government action
can help the dependent poor become self-supporting. He explains the
failure of manpower programs as a whole in recent years and, basing his
recommendations on this analysis, suggests practical steps the state can
take to make its effort in this field more effective.

The next six chapters take up activities of the state that alleviate the
effects of poverty in the fields of public assistance, education, health,
housing, and transportation. Since these activities also help the poor
achieve independence, the authors, with varying degrees of optimism,
frame their recommendations with an eye not only to the alleviation but
also to the reduction of poverty.

Charles Schottland describes the Massachusetts welfare programs
against a national background, makes constructive criticisms of recent
federal proposals, and suggests a series of substantial reforms in the
present state system. In their chapter on public education, David Cohen
and Tyll Van Geel, while examing critically the role of the state in educational leadership, give their main attention to the question of state aid to
poor school districts, a topic as important as it is complicated. They show
how far the present system goes toward its professed goal of "equalization" and indicate what further steps should be taken. Even more controversial and hardly less complicated is the question of medical care.
Having shown the long-run forces that are transforming the whole structure of health care services, Gerald Rosenthal points out what the state
can do to control costs and make adequate services accessible to all.

The problem of housing is considered from two angles. Bernard Frieden
shows how the magnitude of our housing deficiencies makes it imperative
that the state assume a far greater role in seeing that the supply is
correspondingly increased. John Myer and John Perkins, both architects,
supplement this analysis with an examination of the impact of housing
on the quality of life of poor families and on their efforts to cope with their
social and physical environment. While the relation of the previous fields
of policy to the problems of poverty is well recognized, only recently has
the importance of transportation been perceived. John Wofford develops
the opportunities and responsibilities of state government in this field.

After looking at the problem of poverty from the perspective of these
special fields of government activity, the authors turn to more general
considerations. In his chapter on planning, Basil Mott shows not only how
planning is related to the current effort to "modernize" state government

in Massachusetts, but also what should be done to make this crucial function of state government more responsive to the needs of the poor.

It would be irresponsible to suggest the new programs proposed in this book without facing the questions of how much they will cost and how the money to pay for them is to be found. In her chapter on finance, Ann Friedlaender deals forthrightly with these questions, basing her recommendations upon a close analysis of the incidence on poor and nonpoor of the fiscal structure as a whole. She also puts the state's effort into perspective by compiling, for the first time, an overall budget, including all sums spent on poverty programs in Massachusetts by all levels of government. In the epilogue Richard Barringer suggests the need for a new, more inclusive antipoverty strategy which will involve the interests of all the poor and build programs upon the interests they have in common with the rest of society.

A word on how the book was written. It is the product of a faculty study group sponsored by the Institute of Politics in the Kennedy School of Government at Harvard. Richard Barringer organized the study group early in 1969 and subsequently became its executive director. Samuel Beer was chairman of its proceedings, and Paul Abrams performed the indispensable task of keeping its record. The origins of the study group lay in a series of informal springtime meetings among friends and colleagues with a common interest; and its impetus, in their continuing motivation and heightened interest. Tentative discussion meetings thus became planning sessions in which the structure of the study group was established and a program of research sketched out. The intent at this early stage was to prepare the papers in this book (and possibly others) as a series of monographs for release individually throughout the election year 1970. Only later did the possibility and desirability of publishing them as a single volume become apparent.

The preliminary research for each chapter was conducted during the summer of 1969 under the decentralized but coordinated direction of the contributing authors. The study group then met weekly in full session during the fall to consider first drafts of each paper and requirements for its further research. Subsequent drafts of each were then reviewed and finalized in smaller sessions throughout the winter of 1970. So while the authors bear final responsibility for their respective chapters, a wide circle of critics and commentators contributed generously and significantly to planning the book and to shaping its ideas. This book is also their book, and we wish here to acknowledge their help.

Participants from the academic community of the Boston area included Paul Abrams, Alan Altshuler, Francis Bator, Vincent Ciampa, Peter Doeringer, Martha Derthick, Otto Eckstein, Rashi Fein, Nathan Glazer, Charles Haar, John Kain, Francis Larkin, Sidney Lee, Frank Michelman, Richard Musgrave, Hugh Tilson, Lloyd Ohlin, Samuel Popkin, Richard Rowland, Raymond Vernon, Adam Yarmolinsky, and Alonzo Yerby.

Others who contributed comment and criticism included, from the private sector, Hans Loeser and Harry Durning; from Boston city government, Hale Champion, former head of the Boston Redevelopment Authority, and David Davis, director of the Office of Public Service; from the executive branch of state government, Donald Dwight, Commissioner of Administration and Finance, and Robert Marden, Director of the Office of Program Planning and Coordination; from the legislative branch, Speaker David Bartley, Senate President Maurice Donahue, and Senator John Parker. While a Fellow of the Institute of Politics John Gardner, chairman of the National Urban Coalition, helped the project to get started.

Funds from the Institute of Politics and grants from Urban America, Inc., and the Carnegie Corporation covered expenses. The responsibility for what is said in this book, of course, rests with the authors and editors, not with these donors, with the Kennedy School, or with Harvard University.

Thanks, too, to James J. Murray III and Winthrop Publishers, Inc., for expeditious handling of the manuscript.

S.H.B.

R.E.B.

Cambridge, Massachusetts
March 1970

the state and the poor

SAMUEL H. BEER

introduction: poverty and the state

The central thrust of the proposals in this book is that the state of Massachusetts ought to establish a comprehensive antipoverty program. This program would include activities bearing on the problems of the poor in the various agencies concerned with public assistance, health, housing, education, jobs and training, transportation, and so on. Its purpose would be not only to increase the state's antipoverty effort but also to make this effort more successful by subjecting it to more effective planning and control. Our discussion, therefore, culminates with the proposal in the chapters on finance and planning of a poverty budget which would make possible a clear and deliberate allocation of resources among the complex of antipoverty programs and between them as a whole and other large demands on state government.

If such a comprehensive antipoverty program is to be established, it must rest upon a clear understanding of the condition it seeks to alleviate and reduce. This chapter therefore begins by considering what is meant by poverty—the question of defi-

Samuel H. Beer is professor of government at Harvard University.

1

nition. It then turns to the human embodiment of the problem, the various groups of poor people whom the antipoverty program would try to help. Having looked at these broad dimensions of the problem, we then consider the general strategy of attack on it that is implied by the proposals of this book—the ordering of priorities. The final topic is the impact that our proposals would have upon state government and its relations with local governments and with the federal government. It appears that they would add to and fit in with major new responsibilities that the state is already rapidly acquiring.

Dimensions of the problem

DEFINITIONS

Absolute or relative poverty?

The problem with which we are concerned is suggested by such phrases as: "a minimum level of living consistent with health and decency"; "standards . . . sufficient to permit families to acquire the consumption items needed to maintain life at a level of decency"; "an income sufficient to obtain food, shelter, clothing, and other basic items of consumption needed to maintain family life at a level of decency and dignity" (chapter 4).

As we see from Charles Schottland's discussion, expert opinion differs on what concrete meaning to give these phrases. The "Orshansky" standard used by the Social Security Administration draws the poverty line at an income of $3,335 for a family of four, almost exactly what Massachusetts AFDC provides. Schottland, however, suggests that Massachusetts welfare payments should be increased by 30 to 50 percent. This would raise the AFDC payment for a family of four from $3,338 to somewhere between $4,339 and $5,007. The higher figure, incidentally, is almost exactly the family-income figure—$4,496 in 1967 dollars—used by Birch and Saenger to define the group they are concerned with.

Underlying these differences over where to draw the "poverty line" are not only technical and empirical questions, such as the relation of kinds and quantities of food to health, but also differences of value relating to the meaning of "decent," "reasonable," "adequate." Such differences of value become even more important to the problem of definition when we extend presently accepted meanings of poverty backward in time. As Stephan Thernstrom has remarked, "Certainly if we projected backward to mid-nineteenth century America some contemporary 'poverty line'—$3,000 annual income in 1960 dollars or whatever—every workingman (and virtually all people in middle-class jobs, for that matter) would appear desperately poor."[1]

There are two important implications. In the first place, poverty by nineteenth-century standards has been reduced to minor proportions. This secular decline of poverty is characteristic of the American economy. As Thernstrom says, speaking of more recent times, "wherever the line is drawn—$3,000, $4,000, or wherever—an ever-smaller fraction of the American population falls below that line." So also Birch and Saenger, using a poverty line of $3,000 (adjusted for inflation) find that between 1950 and 1967 the percentage of poor families in Massachusetts has fallen dramatically from 35 percent to ten percent. In this basic sense, the long-run trend in the United States and in Massachusetts is toward the elimination of poverty.

In the second place, however, the prevailing definition of poverty clearly has changed greatly since the middle of the nineteenth century. People who then thought of themselves as comfortable would be regarded as poor by today's standards. The meanings of "decent," "adequate," "basic" change radically over time.

We find on the one hand a long-run decline in poverty as measured by any fixed standard, but on the other hand a parallel trend toward an ever rising standard in the public mind. These facts must be recognized in our approach to the poverty problem. We must supplement any fixed standard with a measurement that will not confuse such future changes in valuation but that will periodically cause us to reassess our conventional and accepted judgments. With such a relative definition of poverty, Birch and Saenger begin their analysis. "Poor people," they observe, "are those who have the *least* opportunity." These authors, therefore, take as one operational definition of poverty "those families whose incomes are lower than 80 percent of all families in the Northeast region. In short, the lowest 20 percent.

If we try to move directly from this definition to a statement of the goals of antipoverty policy, difficulties arise, as these authors immediately point out. Since there will always be a lowest 20 percent, the problem of poverty, so defined, can never be solved or even reduced.

---

[1]"Poverty in Historical Perspective," in Daniel P. Moynihan (ed.), *On Understanding Poverty* (New York: Basic Books, Inc., 1969), p. 162.

For the administrator who wishes to be able to measure the performance of a program, this standard fails to provide a yardstick. For the officeholder seeking to display the achievements of his "war on poverty," it affords no platform.

Yet, as their analysis shows, the relative definition has its utility. They use it, in the first place, to put the poverty problem in Massachusetts into comparative perspective. By starting from a 20 percent poverty line for the Northeast region (in 1960, a family income of $3,675), they find that Massachusetts is slightly better off than the region as a whole. This comparison can be made from decade to decade to see whether this state's proportion of the less-well-off is rising or falling.

Birch and Saenger also use the relative definition in their analysis of the locational distribution of the less-well-off groups between central city, suburb, and rural areas. Their striking and unexpected findings are that over time a substantial "suburbanization" of the poor is taking place. While their initial definition was relative—the lowest 20 percent —they supplement this approach with a fixed or absolute standard which sets the poverty line at $3,000. By both standards they confirm the trend toward suburbanization of poverty.

This dispersion of the poor, reflecting in large part an actual movement from the central city to the suburbs, is a finding of major importance for public policy. In contrast to popular impression, it means that the central cities of Massachusetts are not tending to become the exclusive home of the poor, walled up in ghettos, amid ever increasing pressures and problems. On the contrary, the suburbs and other areas outside the central cities are accounting for more and more of the poor, with all this means for an increasing need for relevant services and a sharper understanding of the nature of this typically "urban" problem.

The relative definition of poverty, like other definitions, has its value, but it must be properly used. As we have just noted, this means in conjunction with some more fixed or absolute standard. Such a standard will not be simple; nor can we expect to find universal agreement among all groups and all schools of experts. But in the end we must accept the dictum of common sense that poverty is a measurable deficiency of consumption opportunities, such that if the deficiency were made good for any individual or group, his or their poverty would no longer exist. Starting from this proposition, we see that the opportunity to make good such deficiencies has been presented to American society by historical circumstances that emerged only in recent decades.

In the course of human development, problems sometimes are solved and the concerns to which they gave rise in the public mind subside. The notion that poverty is a problem that can be solved is supported by a unique historical fact of recent times. During the past generation the United States, like various other advanced countries, crossed a major threshold in the development of its economy. This was the transition to a stage of unprecedented productive power. New terms were found necessary to describe this new stage: "affluence" (Galbraith), "economic maturity" (Rostow), "integrated society" (C. E. Black). In the light of this transition, poverty came to be looked on in a new light. Of previous periods of history, Galbraith wrote: "poverty was the all-pervasive fact of that world. Obviously it is not of ours. Here today the ordinary individual has access to amenities—food, entertainment, personal transportation, and plumbing—in which not even the rich rejoiced a century ago."[2] The implication is clear: poverty, an objective condition, roughly quantifiable, was formerly the lot of nearly everyone, has now been transcended by most, and could be eliminated for all.

It is in the context of the recognition of affluence that the new consciousness of poverty has arisen. Given an economy powerful enough to produce and distribute to the vast bulk of its members so high a standard of material well-being, the existence of groups that fall below this level is as intolerable as it is perplexing. Such new productive powers call for a new remedial effort. No doubt the poverty line will continue to be the subject of disagreement on both technical and normative grounds. But as affluence has appeared for the first time in history, so is it possible to conceive of poverty as appearing for the last time. This means that our fundamental guide in antipoverty policy-making must be an absolute definition.

Poverty or inequality?

One reason some people are uneasy with a fixed or absolute definition of poverty is that what troubles them is not so much poverty as inequality —not deprivation but "relative deprivation." As many of the chapters of this book show, programs designed to serve one purpose may also serve the other. Measures for the relief of poverty are up to a point measures of equalization. Yet the two concepts are distinct, refer to quite different states of fact, and should be distinguished when policy is being made and remedial programs of government action designed.

The definition of the poor as the lowest one-fifth of the population

[2] J. K. Galbraith, *The Affluent Society,* 2nd edn., revised (Boston: Little Brown & Co., 1969), p. 2.

ranked by income is useful to a person concerned with inequality. It provides a focus for determining how the income of a nation or a state is divided among various strata. It sets one on the road to saying whether the lowest stratum is getting a larger or smaller slice of the pie than in the past and how its slice compares with that of other strata. National figures suggest that over time there is no pronounced trend toward more equal distribution but that the lowest stratum continues to get about the same portion of a pie that is continually growing larger.[3]

Another formulation that has won a good deal of support draws the poverty line at 50 percent of the median income.[4] Half the population would, of course, be above and half below the median, but there could be great variations in the number who had less than half this income. People who accept this definition usually make the goal of policy an increase in the incomes of those below the line to the point where they would be at or above the 50 percent line. In this way they propose to attack poverty by lessening the income spread among the lower strata of the population and indeed among the population as a whole.

Such an index would shift upward with economic growth. It would, however, provide a standard by which antipoverty efforts could be evaluated and would make conceivable a solution of the problem—that is, a condition in which no one had less than half the median income. Thus, if the median income were $10,000, and a tenth of all families had incomes between zero and $5,000, the problem would be solved if these lower incomes were brought up to $5,000—that is, half the median.

This proposal is usually discussed as a standard of poverty, yet it is essentially concerned with equality and inequality. That is obvious from the fact that, according to this standard, no matter how high the income of the lowest group might be, if it were less than half the median income, it would have to be raised. Even more telling is the fact that the standard can be satisfied just as well by reducing the amount of the median income as by raising the income of the lower groups. Thus heavy taxation of the upper levels of income (for whatever purpose) could so reduce the median that even the lowest group would no longer be "poor."

---

[3]Thernstrom, "Poverty in Historical Perspective," p. 171.

[4]Victor Fuchs, "Toward a Theory of Poverty," in *The Concept of Poverty,* First Report, Task Force on Economic Growth and Opportunity (Washington, D.C.: U.S. Chamber of Commerce, 1965), pp. 71–91.

A major objection to equality as a goal of public policy is that, as just illustrated, it can be as well satisfied by reducing the advantages of the haves as by increasing the advantages of the have-nots. To be sure, the strategy of the antipoverty effort will be redistributionist, providing for the poor by taxing the well-to-do, because, in short, that is where the money is. But this effect on the well-to-do is only incidental to the strategy which aims at improving the lot of the poor without regard to how that may affect the rich and the super-rich.

These generalities are of crucial importance in framing specific programs of government action. A concern with poverty will lead to programs providing a certain level of material security. These programs will also mean a degree of equalization. Yet since the objectives of thorough-going equalization and of the antipoverty effort are quite different, at some point the two rationales lead to sharply divergent lines of public policy. David Cohen's discussion of public education illustrates this possibility.

In Massachusetts, the system of state aid to school districts has as its express statutory aim "to promote the equalization of educational opportunity in the public schools of the state and the equalization of the burden of the cost of school support to the respective cities and towns." How far does the commitment to equalization go, according to this language? "To promote" is not to "to achieve" and judging by past behavior the legislative intent may well be to go some way toward educational equality of opportunity but not all the way.

Cohen's analysis of the actual effects of state aid shows just how far it does go toward equalization. His conclusion is that "the state equalization program ... does a relatively ineffective job of eliminating expenditure differences among school districts that tax themselves at the same rate but vary in property tax base." Moreover, his method makes it possible for decision-makers and voters to assess accurately the effects of further schemes of state aid and so, if they choose, to show a greater commitment to educational equality of opportunity. As he points out, the present system of state aid could be extended to the point at which it did actually achieve, rather than merely promote, such equalization.

On the other hand, his analysis also provides the groundwork for a policy based solely on an antipoverty criterion in contrast with a thorough-going policy of equalization. With regard to state aid to school districts, this approach would mean putting a floor under the school expenditures of every district, leaving additional expenditure up to the taste and politics of the locality. To know what this floor would be we should need to have a standard defining what is meant by a "poor district"—a kind of Orshansky line for communities.

Informed by such a standard, one of the alternative systems of state aid considered by Cohen would be acceptable as part of the antipoverty effort. Involving further centralization of educational finance, it would include a statewide per-pupil minimum for every district and additional grants conditioned on need, both wholly financed by the state, plus such further expenditures as local authorities might wish to support from local taxation. Such a scheme would involve continuing inequalities among districts. It would, however, satisfy the antipoverty criterion. Also, although largely financed by the state, it would allow local authorities to spend on education according to taste, to this extent preserving liberty against central control and uniformity. Like other solutions, it would not satisfy everyone. We cannot expect to find ideal solutions to the conflicts of these three competing values of modern government—security, equality, and liberty.

Equality is a legitimate and familiar objective of public policy in particular spheres and as a comprehensive ideal. It is, however, different from the antipoverty objective. If we are to have a comprehensive antipoverty effort that is operationally coherent, this distinction must be maintained.

CLASSIFYING THE POOR

Poverty is plural. The poor are not a class with a coherent and homogeneous set of interests. They consist of a great many groups with quite different traits and needs, unified not by a positive purpose or function but by a common deficiency. Classification of the groups to be assisted is therefore necessary for a comprehensive poverty program. As we will see in this book, the various antipoverty activities must be conducted by the functional agencies of state government, such as welfare, housing, health, and so on. Normally the program designed to help a particular category of poor people will involve the activities of more than one agency. These separate activities should be restrained from the bureaucratic tendency to become ends in themselves. This means that each must be looked at as part of a program and that this program must be judged by its effect upon the relevant group of poor. If the state is to design effective programs and if it is to be able to evaluate their performance, it must have a clear idea of the categories of poor people the programs are to serve.

Categories of the poor

The *elderly poor* make up an obvious category with distinctive traits and problems. Using a $3,000 poverty line and 1960 data, Birch and Saenger show that by far the largest category of poor families—some 40 percent—have heads of households over 65, these being largely elderly couples whose children are no longer at home. They seem to be concentrated in the suburbs although some evidence shows a tendency in recent years for older families to remain in the central cities while younger ones are moving to the suburbs.

It should be realized that Birch and Saenger are counting families. If we count individuals, the proportions are rather different. Looking at the welfare figures for 1969, we see that although almost exactly the same number of people received Old-Age Assistance as families received AFDC, the latter group included almost four times as many people. With regard to both categories of poor, the Massachusetts profile is very much that of the nation as a whole. In the state as in the nation, about one percent of the population is on Old-Age Assistance and something over three percent depend on AFDC. As Schottland points out, the characteristics of people who receive OAA and AFDC in Massachusetts are similar to those of recipients in the United States as a whole.

Likewise, the AFDC program in Massachusetts, as in the nation, is the most expensive public assistance program, the fastest growing, and the most controversial. Beginning in the thirties as a very narrowly defined program for the "deserving poor," AFDC has become primarily a means of support for *broken homes.* In Massachusetts eight out of ten of the families are headed by females, a circumstance giving a distinctive character to the problems of this category of the poor. In view of popular misconceptions, it should be emphasized that only 20 percent are nonwhite.

As set forth by Schottland, public assistance categories include the relatively small numbers of *blind and disabled* and those on general relief. As he also points out, only a few people on public assistance are employable; his estimate is 10,000 adults among those now on AFDC. He does not, therefore, find a significant category of *employable adults* among the poor on welfare.

A developed antipoverty program will also direct its attention to people not on welfare. Certainly one category worthy of programmatic attention is the *working poor.* While they may on occasion be partially or wholly dependent on public assistance, they are adults who normally support themselves, although on low and undependable earnings. Characteristic would be the persons employed in what Michael Piore has described as the secondary labor market. This group would be the target for the manpower program component of the antipoverty effort even more than people already on welfare. Still another group that it might be useful to distinguish would be *unemployed youth,* as under existing OEO programs.

A developed antipoverty policy would thus be based on a classification of the poor including such groups as the elderly poor, members of broken homes, the disabled poor, employable adults, the working poor, and unemployed youths. The problems of each group are sufficiently different to justify distinctive programs, although, of course, there would be overlap in the sense that similar activities, such as manpower training, might apply to more than one group. Using this approach it would be possible to know what resources were being allocated to each program and to evaluate the extent to which a program achieved its objective—for example, providing more adequate nursing care to the elderly or reducing unemployment among young people from poor households.

Location of the poor

Other lines of classification cut across these categories. Birch and Saenger show why we need to know the distribution of the poor by area as well as category. This distribution would give us an idea of the different "mix" of poverty groups in different areas and jurisdictions. It would tell us whether, for instance, the poor typically found in suburbs are sufficiently different in social characteristics from those in central cities and rural areas to require a radically different system of social services. This could have implications for local governments in those areas and for such questions of state administration as regionalism. The locational analysis also brings out the presence of "pockets of poverty." In the Birch-Saenger data Fall River and New Bedford stand out as areas having a concentration of poor families some fifty percent higher than that of other metropolitan areas, including Boston. Piore suggests that the secondary labor market is an important factor in the peculiar economy of this area which needs to be attacked on a regional basis.

Transient versus chronic poor

Another distinction that is important for the organization and evaluation of the antipoverty effort is the distinction between those who remain among the dependent poor year after year, in contrast with those whose dependency is less continuous. As Schottland points out, for a large number of cases—perhaps 50 percent of those on AFDC—welfare is "a revolving door." For them only minimal services are needed and their stay on dependency is only temporary. It is this group that comes to mind when we read that the average time a person spends on AFDC in Massachusetts is only one year and ten months. In contrast are the "hard-core" poor, roughly about 30 percent of AFDC cases, or some 15 to 20 thousand families.

To make this distinction is not to say that the transient poor have no long-term problems. Many are marginal families, living on the border-line of dependency and from time to time falling back on public assistance. Yet it clearly is necessary to distinguish a group whose problems are deeper and more persistent. As Schottland indicates, this group of "chronic" poor requires far more attention than the other groups, an intensive and coordinated effort of a number of social services. There is no easy answer to the question how to set these families, in particular the children, on the road to self-supporting independence. But if, as Schottland recommends, the business of welfare payment is separated from the delivery of services, more professional manpower will be available for the effort.

The ordering of priorities

If the Commonwealth is to deal effectively with the problems of poverty, it must make certain choices.

AN ANTIPOVERTY PROGRAM

The first is whether it will have an explcit, institutionalized antipoverty program. The theme of this chapter is that it can and should have such a program. At present large expenditures are made on problems of poverty, but they lack the direction and control of a program.

On the basis of figures for fiscal 1968, Ann Friedlaender finds that all governments, federal, state, and local, spend more than one billion dollars on a wide range of antipoverty purposes in Massachusetts.[5] Of this total, the state government raises 37 percent and spends 53 per-

[5]See the first table in her chapter, "Fiscal Prospects."

cent. This is a great deal of money, but it does not constitute an antipoverty program or antipoverty budget. As she points out, Massachusetts presents its budget in terms of departments or agencies, rather than functions; hence, it is very hard to find out what is being spent on any particular program. Her own effort to make such a calculation is pioneering. For the first time, we have an idea of the resources being devoted to the various categories of antipoverty effort, such as health, education, welfare, and so on, and the total effort being made by each level of government.[6] With the state spending over $600 million (according to 1968 figures; the amount would be substantially greater for fiscal 1970), the need for the direction and control provided by an explicit poverty program and poverty budget is obvious.

INCREASED RESOURCES

A second crucial choice is what resources to allocate to the antipoverty effort and in particular whether to spend more and how much more. A poverty budget would give us the tools for making this choice. Otherwise, the state, as at present, will make this choice by a series of ad hoc and unrelated decisions. A poverty budget would enable us to confront the question as a deliberate choice.

Friedlaender describes some of the competing demands on resources. Without any change in present state spending programs and state taxes, a growing revenue gap will develop, amounting to $75 million in fiscal 1971. Theoretically, this could be met by a decision to reduce the standards of spending in some of these programs, but this is not the kind of choice that governments often make. If such an alternative were to be pursued, our skepticism of the effectiveness of some of the manpower training programs—which, incidentally, are very expensive—would recommend them as candidates for restraint.

Among other demands is the need for relief of the property tax, which could usefully absorb $200 million in increased local aid. As David Cohen points out, pressures are growing for the state to take over all costs of public education. Even more pressing are the vast costs of the fight on environmental pollution, a cause that is rapidly gaining support in Massachusetts as in the nation.

Fully aware of these competing demands, the authors of this book nevertheless strongly support substantial increases in antipoverty ex-

---

[6]See the antipoverty budget in the appendix to "Fiscal Prospects."

penditures. An increase in the money incomes of the poor is the first priority. Schottland suggests that the level of public assistance be raised for all categories by 30 to 50 percent. A 50 percent increase would raise the grant to a family of four from $3,338 to $5,007 and, on the basis of 1969 figures, would add about $125 million to the state budget. With Schottland we recommend and hope that the federal government will relieve the state of its welfare burden. With Friedlaender we may doubt that this is likely to happen. One must expect that the burden of such increases as we propose would fall largely on the state.

Next in priority comes a very substantial, indeed massive, increase in the state's housing effort. The actual amount would be much influenced by future federal efforts and by developments in the private market. Yet Bernard Frieden's estimate—$8 to $22 million a year for ten years—indicates the order of magnitude. Close to housing in importance comes transportation. The stress on this area of poverty problems is new, yet it is clear from John Wofford's analysis that like properly located housing, new programs in transportation can be of crucial assistance in giving job-seekers access to the areas where the new jobs are. As for the net additional cost to the state of all our antipoverty proposals in the immediate future, it would probably total $100 million and might come to $150 million.

AN INCOME MAINTENANCE SYSTEM

A third choice is forced on our attention as soon as we begin talking about increasing the money incomes of the poor by public payments. Should we try to maintain the present system of categorical assistance, or turn to a system of outright income maintenance? This problem and the choice it involves are discussed by both Schottland and Piore. The problem arises when the increase in the public grant gets to the point where it is as remunerative as lower-paying jobs and hence begins to attract people away from that kind of employment to public assistance. A categorical system gives protection against this phenomenon since the elderly, the disabled, and husbandless women with children to raise are not likely to be working under any circumstances. This protection does require, however, that the categorical conditions be policed, so that, for instance, husbands working for a low wage do not find it better to desert their families so they can be eligible for public help. Such policing is rapidly being scaled down, because of its ineffectiveness, its humiliation of clients, and its waste of professional manpower. Yet without such a control, necessary improvements in welfare standards can tend to break up homes and draw people away from self-supporting independence.

The other approach is to drop the categories and say that anyone, working or not, will get a grant sufficient to bring his income to a certain level. The trouble with income maintenance, in this simple form, is that it provides a disincentive to work, since any income from earnings is deducted from the grant—in effect, a 100 percent "tax" at the margin. For the same reason, if a person were working at a low-paying job, he would have a positive incentive to quit and rely on his guaranteed income for the same level of upkeep.

These effects can be remedied by graduating the "tax," so that the grant is reduced by less than earnings, thus enabling the recipient to realize some net gain from taking or keeping employment. Schottland makes such a proposal in the form of a scale of "incentive earnings." This arrangement, however, as he points out, would be very expensive (unless the poverty line defining the guaranteed income were very low). For if the scheme is to be effective in encouraging people to work and, what is more important, not to give up jobs they already hold, the "tax" must be graduated gently. This means continuing to make grants to people with total incomes well above the poverty line. The more effective the system in encouraging people to become and remain employed, the larger will be the number of people receiving grants under the system and the higher its cost to the taxpayer.

The income maintenance system offers very real advantages to society and to the poor. Moreover, if Massachusetts were to adopt such a system it might set an example and show the way to the national government, thus demonstrating that the states can still sometimes act as laboratories of social experimentation. On the negative side, we must consider that an income maintenance system would impose a very great additional financial burden on the state. Even more important, a policy with so great an impact on the labor market and economic growth of the whole country surely should be determined and directed by the national government, not by state government. We do not know, for instance, at what point and to what extent increases in such public grants would distort the normal movement of manpower by attracting labor to the more generous state. For both financial and economic reasons, therefore, the main burden of developing an income maintenance system had best be left to the federal government.

GREATER FISCAL REDISTRIBUTION

A fourth major choice centers on the question of income redistribution. Intrinsically, public support of those without income will be redistributive, taking from those who have to provide for those who have not. Yet the weight of the tax burden can vary greatly, bearing heavily either upon the working poor themselves, and upon other less-well-off groups, or upon the upper-income groups who are better able to pay. The crucial question, however, is the progressivity, not of taxes alone, but of the whole fiscal structure, including taxes and expenditures, and including state and local taxes, since both sorts are ultimately authorized by the state. In an analysis of major importance to the antipoverty effort, Friedlaender makes such an evaluation. Moreover, since, as we have seen, the definition of poverty must include not only money income but also available public services, she accordingly includes in poverty expenditures both income transfers and certain specific public services benefiting the poor (see her Table 11–5).

The net incidence of taxes and benefits in Massachusetts is distinctly progressive. If we look at the tax burden as offset by benefits (transfers and special services), we see that a family at the $10,000–$15,000 level pays a percentage of its income almost twice that of a family at the $4,000–$5,000 level. Yet there are some incongruities. Families with incomes as low as $2,000 to $4,000, instead of being net beneficiaries, are net losers, paying more into the system than they are getting from it in income transfers and special services. This would support Friedlaender's general recommendation that the regressivity of the tax structure be diminished. While the structure of state and local taxes in Massachusetts is less regressive than the average for the United States at the very lowest levels of income, the percentage of family income paid in taxes rises above the national average at levels of income still within the poverty range and remains at about the same level for the other higher income groups. One may well feel that it is not only unfair but also counterproductive to burden in this degree families who are so clearly within the concerns of the antipoverty effort. Substantial reversal of the regressivity of the fiscal effort at these levels of income is clearly called for.

The issue of redistribution comes forward even more sharply if we consider possible new taxes, a question that will become more pressing in the future whether the new money is to be used for antipoverty programs, the fight against pollution, relief of the property tax, or other purposes. Friedlaender offers three alternative tax programs, showing for each the burden it imposes on various income classes. In choosing among tax plans, however, the state must consider economic efficiency —for example, the effect on industrial location—as well as progressivity. Friedlaender's analysis shows, first, that the state indubitably can raise additional and indeed vast amounts, if it chooses to do so; and, second, that without disregarding economic efficiency, substantial progressivity in the distribution of the burden of new taxes can be achieved (see Friedlaender's Plan A, in Table 11–9).

STRONGER PLANNING AND CONTROL

A final choice in this ordering of priorities is one upon which all the others depend for success. This is the choice of a new order of planning and control in state government. Massachusetts has not been unresponsive to the needs of the poor. Relative to other states, its welfare payments are close to the highest in the country. It has shown itself willing to tax and to spend on poverty problems at an increasing rate. But it has been woefully inadequate in defining what it is trying to do, keeping track of how the money is spent, and evaluating the effect of its expenditures.

Control is a matter of preventing waste. But, even more important, control is necessary if the programs being financed are to solve the problems which presumably gave rise to them. A problem cannot be solved or a public need met merely by spending money. The central operation in problem-solving is the working out of a pattern of human behavior that will tend to produce the desired condition. To bring into existence this pattern of human behavior—this new agency of government, or system of services—will take money, and in the antipoverty field usually a great deal of money. But the mere spending of a great deal of money will not solve problems. It can make matters worse. Medicaid, a well-intentioned, but ill-conceived response to a major need of the poor, is a leading example of how this can happen. Against the increase in services it has provided the poor, one must weigh the inflation of medical costs that afflicts everyone, including the near-poor who do not benefit by Medicaid, and the political reaction which in some states has resulted in cutting off large groups of needy from further eligibility. In this field, control—the kind of constraint that Rosenthal sketches—will help not only the taxpayer but also the beneficiaries of Medicaid and other less-well-off groups.

It is not unusual to hear knowledgeable persons report that the state budget is "out of control." Methods of assessing results have lagged so far behind growth in size and complexity of operations that it is often impossible for members of the executive and legislative branches to ascertain just what a given expenditure has accomplished. Lack of adequate information and control also afflicts the attempts of central budgeting, and in particular of the Governor, to shape the allocation of money among various fields and subfields in such a way as to reflect a clear sense of priorities.

The chapter on planning is especially concerned with this problem. But the need for control also informs the whole set of proposals made in this book. As a major step toward this end, we strongly support the development of a system of program budgeting. This device is no panacea. But it does encourage government to ask the right questions: What are we trying to do? What are the conditions we are trying to change? Which activities of which agencies are supposed to help with this problem? What is the overall cost? What evidence have we that the program has made progress?

It is hard to overemphasize the importance of better planning and control as a priority of the antipoverty effort. The needs of the poor justify and require larger expenditures, as we have recommended. Yet judging by recent experience, finding the money for increased antipoverty expenditures has not been an insuperable problem. Although the poor are only a small minority of present-day society, political support for growing antipoverty programs has been forthcoming in the community and at the state house. Far more difficult has been the task of making this effort and these expenditures effectively achieve their objectives. The main governmental problem is not political or financial but administrative.

The role of state government

The fact that we are writing a book about state government is no excuse for falling in love with the subject and imagining that it is the *beau idéal* of American political organizations. The authors have not hesitated to criticize the performance of the state of Massachusetts and to recognize the limitations on what it can realistically be expected to do.

On the other hand, they would agree that compared with other states and with what is possible for fallible human beings, Massachusetts is a well-governed polity. Moreover, they have been hopeful enough to suggest a large number of specific, concrete opportunities for more effective antipoverty action by the government of the state. Nor do these proposals merely reflect hope. They flow from a realistic assessment of the actual trend of events, which is continually leading the government of Massachusetts to assume new functions and wider responsibilities.

Such a view of the future of state government contradicts the expectations of many observers. These observers see the typical American state as squeezed between the powers of the federal government and the problems of the cities. They find the cities carrying the main burden of present-day problems, of which poverty is a principal instance, and judge the states to have failed to respond to the "urban crisis." In their eyes, the future, therefore, would seem to lie with a "direct federalism," linking Washington and the cities, bypassing state capitols, and including an ever larger portion of the flow of activity between center and periphery, while the states waste away for lack of useful function.

A quite contrary view of the future sharing of power among the three levels of government follows from the proposals of this book. Since this view was not decided on in advance but emerged from the separate work of individual authors, we may appropriately sum it up by reviewing some of their conclusions. It will help bring out the general character of the role they assign the state if we think of the functions of government as coming under three headings: providing the resources, determining how they are used, and converting them into specific activities: in other words, the functions of finance, of planning and control, and of delivery of services.

NEW FUNCTIONAL RESPONSIBILITIES FOR THE STATE

Public assistance

In the field of welfare there can be no doubt that the thrust of our proposals would be to pass on more power and responsibility to Washington. This is continuous with the tendencies of state-federal relations since the passage of the Social Security Act in 1935. We would like to see the financing of public assistance taken over wholly by the federal government. This is not simply a financial matter. As Charles Schottland observes, the old federal-state partnership in this field is no longer effective. Expert opinion is turning away from the categorical system and toward a system of income maintenance. But, as we have seen, the impact of income maintenance upon interstate and interregional economic flow is so great that the basic powers of planning and control must be in the hands of the national government.

This does not mean that the state will retain no function in the field of welfare. On the contrary, a major reason for federalizing the financial aspect is to release the energies of the state to concentrate on providing a more effective system of services. These services have a poor record of performance. Recently the state has taken over from the cities and towns the task of delivering them. If the state can now take the further step of withdrawing from the business of payment and its attendant problems of determining eligibility, it will be able to direct its professional manpower to more appropriate and important tasks, such as dealing with the problems of the chronic poor.

Housing

The new sharing of power and responsibility proposed by Bernard Frieden for the field of housing is radically different. He would by no means oppose an influx of new federal money. But he doubts this is likely and, moreover, feels that in certain important respects the state can do a more effective job than the federal government. At the same time, he is disillusioned with the record of local housing authorities. His main theme, therefore, is that the state take a much greater role in the field, planning, directing, and financing a massive new housing program. The crucial demand is for a deliberate and forceful housing policy that would concentrate action not only in the provision of houses but also in related fields such as highway location, antidiscrimination policy, and building codes. If necessary, he would have the state itself step in as houser of last resort. John Myer's proposals would add further to the responsibilities of the state in this field. Certainly the thrust of the basic strategy of those authors is sharply contrary to "direct federalism."

Public health

In contrast with the welfare and housing proposals, those relating to public health and education do not involve large increases in expenditure. Rosenthal's analysis of public health problems makes better accessibility of medical services its theme. In this field, the federal government already finances the larger part of the cost through Medicare and Medicaid. Although the Medicaid program has increased the services provided to poor people in Massachusetts, it has otherwise been very disappointing. Immensely expensive, the program has failed to use its great financial leverage to restrain spiraling costs and to promote easier and wider access.

Following the approach toward comprehensive health planning suggested by the recent federal Partnership for Health Act, the state could remedy these deficiencies by using powers it already possesses, in particular its control over hospital licensing and reimbursement of medical costs. Massachusetts does not, like some states, take an important role in directly providing public health services. It does, however, have the powers crucial to more effective planning and control. Rosenthal recommends that these powers be used not only to increase accessibility, but also to impose effective restraints upon the soaring costs of medical services.

Under these proposals, rather like those for welfare but unlike those for housing, funding would continue to come very largely from Washington. Yet the federal-state "partnership" would be retained and the role and activity of the state greatly strengthened. As under the housing proposals, the state would extend its powers of planning and control. It would not, however, move further into the delivery of services, which would remain with local private and municipal institutions and agencies.

Public education

The proposals we have so far reviewed express considerable faith in the efficacy of state government. David Cohen's analysis of the record in education should reduce any undue buoyancy. His examination of the way the Department of Education has handled one of the principal antipoverty programs, the compensatory education programs under Title I of the Elementary and Secondary Education Act of 1965, is instructive. In a searing analysis, he shows how the department has failed to such an extent in its task of evaluation that it is impossible "to determine whether any particular Title I project in the state—or, for that matter, the entire state program—met any of the program's goals."

Cohen is as convinced of the need for more effective planning and control by the state as are the authors of the proposals for housing and public health. He is more skeptical, however, that under present circumstances the state can provide the leadership so evidently needed. The unusual power of localism in the field of education imposes exceptional restraints on state action and his major proposal—a more equitable distribution of state aid to school districts—would surely arouse strong local resistance. One way—perhaps the only way—of overcoming this resistance is for the state to assume all the costs of education. Such a step is being seriously discussed in several states and has been put forward for consideration in Massachusetts. If it were adopted here, we could expect that the resulting greater financial responsibility would enlarge the effective authority of the Department of Education. Both in what has been attempted in recent years, such as the Willis-Harrington reforms, and in what is being currently proposed, we can detect the drift toward a greater role for state government in relation to local government even in the field of public education.

In terms of our threefold classification of government functions—finance, planning and control, delivery of services—the proposals of this volume would mean a greater responsibility for state government in regard to the first function, financing the antipoverty effort. In significant instances they would also involve the state further in the performance of the third function, the direct delivery of services. Obviously, however, their main thrust is to widen the state's role in deciding how resources are to be used and seeing that they are so used—the crucial function of planning and control.

NEW AREAL RESPONSIBILITIES FOR THE STATE

This brief review not only points to a functional development of the state's role. It also reveals the growing power of the state relative to local governments—the increase in its areal responsibilities, to use Arthur Maass' descriptive adjective.[7] As the authors describe what is happening and what ought to be done, they hardly suggest that state government is withering away, or that it will be superseded by "direct federalism." On the contrary, with regard to intergovernmental power, the most striking indication is that responsibility and power are shifting from local government to state government, from city hall to the state house.

Fiscal prospects

This hypothesis accords with Ann Friedlaender's analysis of the flow of money. In a striking statistic she shows that the federal contribution to the antipoverty effort in this state is 62.2 percent, the state contribution 37.0 percent, and the contribution of local governments only 0.7 percent. These figures relate to the unit of government that levies the taxes that go to pay for the antipoverty programs. They show that the share borne by the cities and towns is negligible, while the share of the state government is very large. This money, of course, is often actually spent by local governments, although the source is federal and state

[7]Arthur Maass, ed., *Area and Power: A Theory of Local Government* (Glencoe, Ill.: The Free Press, 1959), Part I, "Division of Powers: An Areal Analysis."

funds. Yet even as a channel of expenditures, the role of the state is large relative to local government, the state accounting for 53.3 percent of all antipoverty expenditures, while local governments account for only 14.3 percent.

Judging by the experience of Massachusetts in the antipoverty field, it would seem that the intermediate tier of American government is acquiring responsiblities that formerly rested with local governments. The cities and towns have their large and growing burdens, as their soaring property taxes prove. But it must be recognized that these do not result primarily from the poverty problem, since antipoverty expenditures are financed almost entirely by the state and federal governments. Apart from educational expenditures, which in the near future may also be shifted entirely to the state, the cities and towns bear the financial burden of maintaining the physical fabric and preserving law and order, while the state and federal governments raise the money for social programs.

"Direct federalism" is no illusion, as we can see if we look at the disposition of federal antipoverty money in Massachusetts. According to 1968 figures, a little more than half these funds are spent directly by the federal government on antipoverty programs, while the remainder goes to the state and to local governments. Of this remainder, local governments as a whole receive not much less than the state—42.9 percent as compared with 57.1 percent. Here we see the result of the growing contacts of Washington with city and other local governments in recent years. But although "direct federalism" is important, we need to see it in perspective. Even in the antipoverty field, state government receives a larger share than local governments. Moreover, if we look at federal grants-in-aid as a whole, the overwhelming position of the state in the intergovernmental flow of funds appears. In 1968 less than 15 percent of federal grants to governmental units went to local governments—some $57.9 million in contrast with $367.0 million to the state. While many of the innovative programs of recent years have been channeled directly to the cities, massive sums for traditional functions such as welfare, education, and highways were directed to the state.

We have seen the large role of the state in antipoverty expenditures and in providing resources for the antipoverty effort. In view of the frequent attacks upon state government for being "unresponsive," it is necessary to recognize the immense financial effort of Massachusetts in recent years, if we are accurately to assess the future role of the state. Between 1950 and 1968, state expenditures for all purposes more than quadrupled, rising from $433 million to $1,775 million. Federal money helped, but state taxes more than kept pace, increasing from $233 million to over one billion dollars. This increase meant that the tax burden per person rose from $49.03 to $190.34. To be sure, the economy was booming during these years. Yet the increase in fiscal effort was substantial. While state taxes took 3.1 percent of total personal income in Massachusetts in 1950, by 1968 the figure had risen to 5.4 percent. This was higher than the figure for New Jersey (3.7%) and Connecticut (4.3%) and lower than that for Michigan (6.5%) and Wisconsin (7.5%). Looking toward the future, we see that the state budget (including trust funds), which at present hovers around two billion dollars, will probably increase by another $820 million by 1976.

When we compare state and local tax burdens, we again see the trend to increasing responsibilities for state government. Traditionally, the state tax burden has been considerably less than the total tax burden of local governments. In recent years this gap has closed rapidly as the state tax burden, which was equal to 61 percent of the local tax burden in 1961, rose to 92 percent of it by 1968.

A shift of power and responsibility to state government would seem to be the natural political consequence of recent economic and social development. Urbanization continually extends the network of interdependence and the interlocal flow of social costs. The problems of the central cities affect the welfare of the suburbs, while suburbanites who use the city for work and recreation escape the more onerous burdens of municipal taxation. Some observers have thought that developments of this sort would produce a new plane of jurisdiction in the form of metropolitan government, and proposals of this sort have often been made for Boston and its suburbs. As Friedlaender points out, however, since such problems afflict not only Boston and its environs but also similar metropolitan areas throughout the state, a more general approach at the state level would be not only pragmatically more effective, but also politically more feasible.

While metropolitanism will probably be bypassed in Massachusetts, as it has been generally in the United States, the economic and social developments that have made it a plausible alternative are creating a statewide political base for action by the state. In the light of the "suburbanization of poverty" we can more readily understand why the welfare system should have been made wholly a state responsibility. The further spread of such "urban" problems will help create the political support necessary if the new responsibilities proposed in this volume are to be assumed by the government of the state.

FEDERAL LEADERSHIP

The state's role is being enlarged by a shift of responsibilities from local government. There is also a good deal of talk about decentralizing power from Washington. Can we look forward to a growth of state government, nourished by a flow of power from above as well as below?

We have already taken note of the predominant position of state government as a receipient of federal money in Massachusetts. President Nixon's Family Assistance Plan might add $15 to $65 million more to these funds. Outright revenue-sharing could raise the sum by at least another $40 million (see Friedlaender's Table 11–7). The Administration's plans to decentralize the federal manpower programs would significantly add to the state's powers in an area of economic importance and substantial expenditure. In these and similar ways, the state's role in the American system of government may be enlarged by a shift of money, power, and function from Washington as well as from City Hall.

Yet it should be observed that, judging by the way the authors of this volume see the facts and the opportunities, we cannot expect vast measures of decentralization to the state. The growing interdependence that tends to centralize government within the state has similar consequences for the nation. Basic public policies in crucial spheres, therefore, will remain federal—for instance, maintaining economic equilibrium, promoting economic growth, managing the labor market, redistributing wealth among groups and regions. The authors of this book recognize the deep foundations of "federal leadership" and in numerous and significant instances call on it for further action. Even if and as the state develops its new role, Washington will remain not only the source of major finance, but also the principal center of innovation with regard to antipoverty programs.

Yet Federal leadership does not preclude an important and distinctive role for state government. Economic and social development will surely continue to enlarge the areal functions of the state, shifting responsibilities from local to state government. At the same time, the state will probably expand and develop those functions of planning and control that are particularly appropriate for the intermediate tier of the federal system. Such new areal and functional responsibilities will still further increase the state's fiscal burdens. Although this burden is heavy, Massachusetts can afford to do its share in financing an adequate antipoverty effort. Finding the money is a political rather than an economic problem. The major question is administrative and bureaucratic: can Massachusetts provide the personnel and create the organizations necessary to make such an antipoverty effort effective?

DAVID L. BIRCH and EUGENE L. SAENGER, JR.

the poor
in Massachusetts

Who are the poor in Massachusetts? How many are there? What kinds of people are they? Where are they? Where are they moving to? These kinds of questions will be addressed in this chapter. Taken together, the answers to these questions pose a challenge to the other authors of this book. It is their job to suggest how the state is to respond.

An immediate and terribly difficult question arises: Who is poor? It would be convenient to brush the issue aside and simply assert that poor people are people who don't have very much money. "Much" could be defined in terms of some minimum requirements with adjustments for family size, age, inflation, region, and so on. But the issue

David L. Birch is associate professor of business administration in the Harvard Graduate School of Business Administration. Eugene L. Saenger, Jr., is a candidate for the M.B.A. in the Harvard Graduate School of Business. George Sheehan and Clement Perkins were of particular assistance in assembling the data for this paper. Cornelia Lehmann and Janis Daisey in turn collected, organized, and presented it with great pains and care. Raymond Vernon and Adam Yarmolinsky contributed thoughtful, sometimes imponderable questions concerning concepts and approach.

cannot be put to rest that easily. In private conversations, Adam Yar-molinsky captured an additional dimension quite nicely when he defined a poor person as "one who is prevented from using his or her energies to make the kind of contributions to society for which society is willing to offer a decent reward." While Yarmolinsky's definition makes meas-urement somewhat awkward, it highlights the *relative* nature of poverty. The poor are the ones who, for various reasons, are not participating fully in society. As a consequence, their rewards are not decent relative to the rewards received by others. They are the ones at the bottom of the heap.

When we try to quantify this concept of relativity in income terms, we are led to a measure that defines "the bottom of the heap." Somewhat arbitrarily, we have decided that by bottom we mean the lowest 20 percent. More specifically, unless we indicate otherwise, a poor family is one whose income is lower than that of 80 percent of the families in the Northeast (that is, Maine, New Hampshire, Vermont, Rhode Island, Connecticut, New York, New Jersey, Pennsylvania).

Several factors were considered in selecting the Northeast as the basis for comparison. A large area was desired because it was more likely to exhibit stable trends, over a period of time, to which Massa-chusetts could be compared. The area could not be so large, however, that it led to the comparison of quite different kinds of people in differ-ent situations. After considerable investigation, we found that income distributions for the northeastern states were reasonably similar in 1960, but that there were significant differences between the Northeast and other regions, particularly the South. The Northeast was thus the largest area that could be considered. Fortunately, within the Northeast there are no great variations between states or between rural and suburban areas within states. The Northeast thus qualified as our standard.

Obvious psychological difficulties are associated with a "bottom 20 percent" definition. First, it includes people who are not, in the lay sense, "in poverty"—that is, they are not starving or severely lacking in some basic human need. Their inferior *share* of things, not their total deprivation, distinguishes them from others. The reader will have to accustom himself to this distinction as he reads this chapter.

More bothersome still is the notion, implicit in the "lower 20 percent" definition, that a group of poor will always exist no matter how hard we may strive to ease their burden. Practically speaking, of course, this has always been the case. St. Matthew noted that "ye have the poor always with you." Nineteen hundred years later we face the same problem, and though we may wish otherwise, the poor are not likely to disappear during the next ten years. More likely, in the foreseeable future, there will always be a group at the bottom demanding services and money from the state. For policy-formulation and decision-making purposes, therefore, it is most important to identify who constitutes this bottom group and where they are located.

While our "bottom 20 percent" approach should aid the politician in drawing up social programs, it clearly is not useful to him when he is campaigning. On the speaker's platform, he needs an absolute standard against which to measure progress. No elected official wants to be told that, during his administration, the number of poor families (the bottom 20 percent) grew substantially. He would rather point to the large number of families which were "pulled over the line." In deference to his predicament, therefore, we will try in this chapter to analyze the shifts in poverty under a fixed dollar standard, adjusted for inflation.

It is worth noting at the start that, although the differences between the relative and the absolute standards are philosophically profound, operationally it makes very little difference which definition is used. The trends in the location and composition of the poor are so strong that they prevail under any reasonable definition.

The chapter begins with a detailed description of the poor as they existed in 1960, the last year for which extensive data were collected. Next, piecing together what scraps of information are available, we trace trends through the postwar era. Finally, we set forth related developments in jobs, housing, education, age, and race. Weaving all these threads together, we conclude that rapid shifts are taking place, both in the characteristics and in the location of the poor, and that these shifts pose a very real challenge to the Commonwealth of Massachusetts.

The poor in 1960

Massachusetts in 1960 was populous and dense, and its population was comparatively wealthier than that of surrounding areas and of the nation. In 1960, 233,900 Massachusetts families, 18 percent of her 1,292,000 families, were poor. That is, 18 percent of Massachusetts' families had incomes below $3,675, a figure established on the basis of the poorest 20 percent of families in the Northeast as a whole. Table

2–1 shows that this percentage of poor was 1.9 points below that of the Northeast and 1.4 points below that of New England. Massachusetts' average density was twice that of the Northeast, three times that of New England, and more than 12 times that of the nation as a whole.

The median income of all Massachusetts families in 1960 was very close to that of all families in both New England and the Northeast. It was, however, 11 percent greater than the median family income for the United States and 40 percent greater than that of the average southern family.

Comparative data on population, density, number and percentage of poor families, and median family income are presented in Table 2–1.

URBAN AND RURAL

Massachusetts was also an extremely metropolitan state. At the time of the 1960 census, 88.1 percent of the state's poor families lived within ten Standard Metropolitan Statistical Areas (SMSAs). These areas contained 84.15 percent of Massachusetts' population, six percent more people than lived in SMSAs in all northeastern states and 21 percent more than lived in SMSAs throughout the nation. Table 2–2 shows that the state's metropolitan areas were almost nine times as dense as its rural areas. Rural areas contained 11.9 percent of the state's poor families and 15.5 percent of its population. The concentration of poor families (poor families per 100 families) was two points lower for rural areas than for metropolitan areas. Though population size and density and number of poor families are nearly six times greater in metropolitan areas than in rural areas, the concentrations of poor are similar.

Clearly, however, the rural poor were numerous in 1960. Although the two areas with the highest concentration of poor were metropolitan, the next six areas highest in concentration of poor were all rural. Table 2–3 presents comparative data on population and income for each of the 22 metropolitan and rural areas in the state, ranked by percentage of poor families within each area. New Bedford and Fall River are the two metropolitan areas that have high concentrations of poor families. These areas are dominated by central cities whose textile industries have been declining for decades. The result has been that these SMSAs have seen less population and economic growth in recent years than any other metropolitan area in the state. But the next six areas are rural, sparsely populated, and relatively unindustrialized.

Table 2-1 State and regional comparisons of population and family income for 1960

	Population	Mean density pop. per sq. mile	Number of families (000)	Median family income	Number of Poor families (000)	Poor families per 100 families
Massachusetts	5,149	655	1,292	$6,272	233.9	18.1
New England	10,509	167	2,654	6,128	520.2	19.6
Northeast	44,678	273	11,474	6,191	2,294.7	20.0
South	54,973	63	13,512	4,465	—[1]	—
United States	179,323	51	45,128	5,660	—	—

Source: See note at end of chapter for sources of data in tables.
[1] Not applicable, given relative definition of poverty.

Table 2-2 Distribution of poor families in metropolitan and rural areas of Massachusetts in 1960

	Metropolitan (SMSA)	Rural (non-SMSA)
Population of Massachusetts (000)	4,321	798
Percentage of Massachusetts population	84.5	15.5
Percentage of Massachusetts poor [1]	88.1	11.9
Mean density (per sq. mi.)	1,449	165
Number of poor families (000)	196	27
Poor families per 100 families	19.44	17.3

Source: U.S. Bureau of the Census.
[1] Insufficient data make it impossible to locate 4.75% of the state's poor by metropolitan or rural areas. They have been arbitrarily allocated in proportion to the known poor.

CITY AND SUBURB

In 1960 the central cities of Massachusetts' ten SMSAs accounted for 39.6 percent of the state's *metropolitan* population. Massachusetts had a greater percentage of its population within metropolitan areas than did the Northeast or the nation, but it had a far smaller percentage of its metropolitan population in central cities than these areas did (Table 2-4).

In 1960 the distribution of poor families within metropolitan areas was almost equally divided between the central cities and the suburbs. (Table 2-5). The central cities had just over 54 percent of the metropolitan poor. Nearly 40 percent of the state's poor families were living in the suburbs in 1960.

Table 2-3 Population and Distribution of poor families in 22 areas of
Massachusetts in 1960

Area	Metro/ rural	Popu- lation (000)	Density (pop. per sq.mi.)	No. of poor families (000)	Percentage of state's poor	Poor families per 100 families
New Bedford[1]	M	143	1008	9	3.76	31.79
Fall River	M	128	1112	9	3.85	29.67
Dukes-Nantucket	R	9	61	0	.09	26.89
Plymouth County	R	48	136	2	.77	26.25
Franklin County	R	55	78	1	.60	24.80
Essex County	R	77	415	4	1.60	24.52
Hampshire County	R	39	93	1	.40	22.28
Worcester County	R	170	191	6	2.50	22.03
Lawrence-Haverhill	M	186	1130	10	4.27	21.90
Worcester	M	329	693	15	6.41	2.190
Fitchburg-Leominster	M	90	539	4	1.73	21.80
Bristol County	R	124	411	5	1.98	21.20
Lowell	M	164	1093	8	3.42	21.11
Middlesex County	R	90	336	2	1.05	20.69
Brockton	M	150	921	6	2.56	20.00
Pittsfield[1]	M	77	585	3	1.28	19.96
Springfield-Holyoke	M	490	969	22	9.40	19.65
Boston	M	2595	2626	111	47.44	18.07
Berkshire County	R	66	82	4	1.56	17.35
Norfolk County	R	43	393	1	.33	16.56
Barnstable County	R	70	178	2	.87	5.43
Hampden County	R	7	28			

[1]Income data are not available for part of the area.

Table 2-4 Distribution of metropolitan populations in Massachusetts, the
Northeast, and the U.S. in 1960

	Mass.	N.E.	U.S.
Population in metropolitan areas	84.5%	78.0%	62.9%
Metropolitan population in central cities	39.6	46.0	51.7
Metropolitan population in suburbs	60.4	54.0	48.3

BOSTON

In 1960 no other metropolitan area could approach Boston in number of poor people. (Table 2-3). The Boston SMSA was the largest in

Table 2-5 Distribution of poor families in central cities and suburbs of
Massachusetts in 1960

	Central cities	Suburbs
Population (000)	1,724	2,627
Metropolitan population	39.4%	60.6%
Mean density	4,834	993
Number of poor families (000)	107	89
Metropolitan poor families	54.6%	45.4%
Massachusetts poor	48.1%	39.9%
Poor families per 100 families	24.8	15.4

Table 2-6 Distribution of Poor Families in the Boston SMSA in 1960

	Central city	High-density suburbs	Low-density suburbs
Population (000)	697	1,530	367
Mean density	16,146	4,583	600
Poor families (000)	41	63	7
Boston SMSA poor	36.8%	56.6%	6.6%
State poor	17.5%	26.9%	3.1%
Poor families per 100 families	24.9	16.2	12.0

the state and accounted for almost half of the state's poor families. Its
central city accounted for 38 percent of the state's central-city poor,
and its suburbs accounted for 79 percent of the state's suburban poor.

In order to examine the Boston SMSA more closely, we divided the
suburban towns within its limits by their median density (1,875) and
then grouped them to provide three areas for analysis: the central city,
the high-density suburbs, and the low-density suburbs.[1] In Table 2-6
we provide comparative population and income statistics for its three
subdivisions.The high-density suburbs of the Boston SMSA housed

[1]The division of Boston's suburbs by high and low density produced the following two
groups in 1960: *high density*—Arlington, Belmont, Beverly, Braintree, Brookline,
Cambridge, Chelsea, Dedham, Everett, Hull, Lynn, Malden, Marblehead, Medford,
Melrose, Milton, Nahant, Natick, Needham, Newton, Norwood, Peabody, Quincy,
Reading, Revere, Salem, Saugus, Somerville, Swampscott, Wakefield, Waltham, Wa-
tertown, Wellesley, Weymouth, Wincester, Winthrop, Woburn; *low density*—Ashland,
Bedford, Burlington, Canton, Cohasset, Concord, Danvers, Dover, Duxbury, Framingham, Hamilton, Hanover, Hingham, Holbrook, Lexington, Lincoln, Lynfield, Manches-
ter, Marshfield, Medfield, Middleton, Millis, Norfolk, North Reading, Norwell,
Pembroke, Randolph, Rockland, Scituate, Sharon, Sherborn, Sudbury, Topsfield, Wal-
pole, Wayland, Waltham, Weston, Westwood, Wilmington

twice as many people as the central city and four times as many as the low-density suburbs. These denser suburbs had 50 percent more poor families than the central city and nine times the number in the remaining suburbs. Taken as a group, the high-density suburbs of the Boston SMSA had nearly the same population and density as the aggregated central cities of the state (see Table 2–5). Physically, then, the distinction between central city and suburb in the Boston SMSA has become somewhat blurred. Politically, of course, it remains a very real distinction, and therein may lie a source of difficulty.

We cannot, of course, talk about the location of the poor without examining what sorts of people they are. Are they old or young, black or white? What sorts of work do they do? One thing is clear: they are mostly white. Only 5.1 percent of Massachusetts' poor families in 1960 were black. Thus, the poor in Massachusetts do not live primarily in black ghettos. For black people, however, the problems associated with low income are far more prevalent, as we can see in Table 2–7. Among nonwhites the incidence of poverty is much higher: 30.5 percent, contrasting with 12 percent among whites.

Many of the other social pathologies frequently associated with low income are in evidence in Table 2–7. Predominance of female heads of household, absence of wage-earners, and heavy reliance on manufacturing and retail trade for jobs are all present. One relatively unusual characteristic of Massachusetts' poor is their age. By far the largest number of poor families have heads of household who are over 65. Many of these older families are, in fact, elderly couples whose children are no longer at home. Almost 60 percent of all poor families in Massachusetts have no children under 18. The focus in this chapter on poor *families* may thus distort somewhat the distribution of poor *people*. If, for example, poor black families tend to be younger and have more children, then the proportion of poor people who are black will be somewhat greater than five percent.

Unfortunately, no detailed data exist to show the characteristics of the poor by geographical areas. Scraps of evidence, bolstered by non-systematic observation, suggest that in 1960 many of the elderly were concentrated in the suburbs and many of the younger poor couples, particularly the black ones, were concentrated in the cities. A close look at the 1970 census will be required, however, before these sorts of conjectures can be put forth as assertions.

Wherever the poor may be, it is obvious that different classes of poor people have different needs and problems, and any realistic attempt to

Table 2-7   *Distribution of Poor Families and Percentage of Families That Are Poor by Selected Characteristics in 1960[1]*

	Percentage of families		Percentage of families that are poor
	All families	Poor Families	
Total	100	100	12.4
Age of Head			
Under 35	22.5	20.8	11.5
35–44	23.9	13.3	6.9
45–64	38.2	25.0	8.2
65 & over	15.4	40.9	33.0
Sex of head			
Male	89.1	69.7	9.7
Female	10.9	30.3	34.7
Children under 18			
None	42.8	59.4	17.3
1–3	48.1	34.7	8.9
4 or more	9.1	5.9	8.0
Earners in family			
None	6.6	42.1	79.3
One	44.4	44.0	12.3
Two	36.8	12.9	4.4
Three or more	12.2	.9	.9
Color of family			
White	97.9	94.9	12.0
Nonwhite	2.1	5.1	30.5
Employment by industry			
Construction	8.2	8.8	n.a.
Manufacturing	38.9	27.9	n.a.
Retail trade	11.8	18.6	n.a.
Services	9.9	14.7	n.a.
Public administration	6.0	2.3	n.a.
Other	25.2	34.7	n.a.

[1]In this table, a poor family is one whose income is less than $3,000. The cutoff for the lower 20 percent, in contrast, was $3,675 in 1960.

attack poverty must take these differences into account. Economic development and manpower efforts are not likely to touch the 40 to 50 percent of Massachusetts poor who are retired. Programs designed only for black families miss 95 percent of the poor. Funds earmarked for the cities miss well over half the poor. The challenge is to design a very flexible overall program that can somehow work with local governments to respond to the specialized needs of the particular poor who happen to be within their boundaries.

SUMMARY

In summary, it is useful to view the poor in Massachusetts in terms both of their number and of their concentration. A study of concentration alone tends to overlook the number of poor families in the suburban and rural areas of the state. Boston and the other central cities have large concentrations of poor, but the number of poor in suburban and rural areas is greater. Similarly, while black neighborhoods may contain high concentrations of poor families, the great majority of Massachusetts' poor are white. Perhaps the dominant characteristic of the state's poor is their age; well over half are elderly couples with no young children. The evidence suggests that different communities have very different kinds of poor people. The elderly tend to live in some areas; in others live the young mothers receiving Aid to Dependent Children. This diversity poses an enormous administrative challenge to any statewide program or policy.

Trends in population and poverty

Between 1950 and 1967 population in Massachusetts grew more slowly than it did in the Northeast or the nation. By 1967 Massachusetts' population was 5,434,000, an increase of 15.8 percent over the 1950 mark. This was considerably less than the 21.6 percent population growth in the Northeast and nearly half the 30.8 percent national growth. There has been a gradual decline in the portion of Massachusetts population that is poor, even on a relative scale (Table 2-8). On any absolute scale, of course, declines in the number of poor families have been quite dramatic, as we shall see shortly.

URBAN AND RURAL

While the nation clearly shows a trend toward urbanization—increase in the metropolitan share of total population—the reverse is true in the Northeast and in Massachusetts (Table 2-9). This phenomenon is simply explained. As the population in Massachusetts and the Northeast increases, finding adequate living space in the dense metropolitan areas becomes more difficult. Growth thus takes place in the rural areas, which will soon have to be considered quasi-metropolitan whether or not they are included in an SMSA. Such growth results in rising percentages of population and increased density in rural areas, while densities remain about the same in the metropolitan centers.

The number of poor families in metropolitan areas has remained relatively stable from 1950 to 1967 (Table 2–9). Since total population has increased, the percentage of the state's poor families living in metropolitan areas has fallen from 88.9 in 1950 to 83.3 in 1967.

Table 2–8 *Trends in population and number of poor families in Massachusetts, 1950–1967*

	1950	1955	1960	1967
Population (000)	4,691	4,838	5,150	5,434
Number of poor families (000)	220	224	234	246
Poor families per 100 families	18.8	18.5	18.1	18.1
Percentage of Northeast poor	10.9	10.3	10.2	10.1

Table 2–9 *Trends in population and distribution of poor families for metropolitan and rural areas in Massachusetts, 1950–1967*

	1950	1960	1967
Metropolitan			
Total population (000)	4,016	4,351	4,525
Population in metropolitan areas	85.4%	84.5%	83.3%
Mean density	1,537	1,449	1,507
Number of poor families (000)	201	196	205
Poor in metropolitan areas	88.9%	88.1%	83.3%
Poor families per 100 families	20.2	19.4	18.1
Rural			
Total population (000)	685	798	907
Population in rural areas	14.6%	15.5%	16.7%
Mean density	141	165	186
Number of poor families (000)	25	27	41
Poor in rural areas	11.1%	11.9%	16.7%
Poor families per 100 families	14.6	17.3	18.9

During this same period, the "poverty cutoff"—the family income below which 20 percent of families in the Northeast fall—rose from $2,120 in 1950 to $3,675 in 1960 and $4,950 in 1967.[2] Although the majority of poor still live in metropolitan areas, by 1967 the highest

[2] The 1950 and 1960 data on family income are derived directly from census publications. The 1967 data are derived primarily by calibrating the cumulative income distributions of the state, the SMSAs, and the central city against the Northeast

incidence of poverty was in the rural areas of Massachusetts. The per-centage of poor people living in rural areas grew by more than five points between 1950 and 1967. Along with increases in population and density, the number of rural poor families has grown by nearly 50 percent in the period. The concentration of poor families in rural areas has increased, between 1960 and 1967, to 18.9 per hundred families. This figure is greater than the same measure for central cities in that year.

CITY AND SUBURB

The percentage of metropolitan population living in Massachusetts' central cities is falling. While 46 percent of the metropolitan population lived in the central city in 1950, this figure had dropped to 36 percent by 1967 (Table 2–10). This drop was accompanied by declines in absolute population and in density during the same period.

Massachusetts has usually had a smaller share of her metropolitan population living in central cities than has either the Northeast or the nation. From 1950 to 1967 the trend in all three areas was toward a decline in the share of population in the central city, but, as could be expected, Massachusetts' figure was about ten points below that of the other two regions. This low share is a result of the relatively high den-sity of Massachusetts' central cities, the relatively thorough develop-ment of the suburban areas that surround them, and the early date (around 1920) at which Boston stopped annexing suburban towns.

The suburbs, as expected, have had great population growth—33 percent—in the years from 1950 to 1967. Mean density has grown 25 percent in the same period. While the national trend is for greater suburban growth, Massachusetts is far ahead of the averages for both the Northeast and the nation. By our *relative standard, there has been a decline* in the number of poor families in central cities, and by 1967 this number had dropped to 91,000 from 136,000 in 1950. The

distribution in 1960, and, assuming that the relationships between distributions re-main constant, reconstructing the 1967 state distributions based on the actual 1967 Northeast income figures and the 1967 population estimates published by the Cen-sus Bureau. This procedure was then cross-checked by building up the same data from estimates provided by *Sales Management Magazine*. While the results checked quite closely, they are certainly no substitute for the 1970 data when they become available, and the results strongly indicate the need for a detailed, intermediate checkpoint every five years, if only on a sample basis.

Table 2-10 Shifts in population by metropolitan-rural and central
city-suburban in Massachusetts, the Northeast, and the U. S.,
1950–1968

	1950	1960	1968
Massachusetts			
Population in metropolitan areas	85.43%	84.50%	83.31%
Population in rural areas	14.57	15.50	16.16
Metropolitan population in central cities	46.09	39.60	35.51
Metropolitan population in suburbs	53.91	60.40	64.49
Northeast			
Population in metropolitan areas	n.a.	78.0%	76.1%
Population in rural areas	n.a.	22.0	23.9
Metropolitan population in central cities	n.a.	46.03	44.15
Metropolitan population in suburbs	n.a.	53.97	55.85
United States			
Population in metropolitan areas	56.07%	62.9%	64.6%
Population in rural areas	43.93	37.1	35.4
Metropolitan population in central cities	58.48	51.67	45.51
Metropolitan population in Suburbs	41.56	48.33	54.49

percentage of metropolitan poor living in the central city has fallen
much faster than the percentage of metropolitan population living
there. The concentration of poor families has declined from its 1960
peak of 24.8 per hundred families to 23.0 per hundred. By 1967 less
than half the metropolitan poor were living in central cities (Table 2–
11).

Many poor families have located in the suburbs as part of the population growth there. The number of poor families in suburban areas has
grown by about 75 percent, from 65,000 in 1950 to 114,000 in
1967. More than 55 percent of the metropolitan poor now live in the
suburbs, and the concentration of poor in these areas has grown substantially since 1960.

All of this analysis is based on a relative concept of poverty. The poor
are those who have the least opportunity—the bottom 20 percent.
Fortunately, Massachusetts is doing so much better than the rest of the
Northeast that even on a relative scale the percentage of families who
are poor is declining.

Using a fixed dollar cutoff, of course, the number of poor and their

THE POOR IN MASSACHUSETTS

Table 2-11   Trends in central city and suburban population and distribution
of poor families for Massachusetts, 1950–1967

	1950	1960	1967
Central City			
Population	1,851	1,724	1,585
Metropolitan			
population in central cities	46.1%	39.6%	35.5%
Density	5,190	4,834	4,440
Number of poor families (000)	136	107	91
Metropolitan poor in			
central cities	67.7%	54.6%	44.5
Poor families per 100 families	21.2	24.8	23.0
State poor in central cities	60.2%	48.1%	37.0%
Suburbs			
Population	2,165	2,627	2,878
Metropolitan population			
in suburbs	53.9%	60.4%	64.5%
Density	818	993	1088
Number of poor families (000)	65	89	114
Metropolitan poor in suburbs	23.3%	45.5%	55.5%
Poor families per 100 families	18.5	15.4	15.6
State poor in suburbs	28.7%	40.0%	46.3%

relative significance are dropping far more rapidly. Taking the commonly used 1960 poverty line of $3,000 as a yardstick, and adjusting for inflation, we can see (Table 2–12) that the number of families falling below this absolute cutoff has decreased sharply from 411,000 in 1950 to 137,000 in 1967. As we have indicated, however, the geographical distribution of the poor is virtually unaffected by the change in definition.

Regardless of which standard is used, the suburbanization of the poor has become very pronounced in recent years. The question is: where did the suburban poor come from? Evidence about the process by which suburbanization took place is far sketchier than evidence documenting its existence. As we piece the scraps together, though, a fairly clear pattern emerges. First, the age of the poor suggests that many suburban families became poor (in the income sense) simply because the family head retired. Many elderly couples own and have paid for their homes, and their low income levels do not necessarily indicate extreme hardship. A retired couple with no children and minimal expenses for shelter and transportation can get by on $3,000 a year, particularly if the couple spends capital or is partly supported by children. They will not be comfortable, but they can get by.

Some of the suburban poor, young or old, may well have come from rural areas in search of jobs. A significant number, however, have probably migrated from the central cities. It is impossible to trace the movement of individual families, but the absolute declines both in total population and in the number of poor in the central cities, coupled with the rapid growth of both categories in the suburbs, suggest some movement. The suggestion is even stronger when the movements of people are sorted out in more detail. In Boston, for example, between 1955 and 1965 the total population declined by 108,000 or roughly 15 percent. This decline, however, reflected a gain of 63,000 births and a net migration out of the city of 172,000 people, or 24 percent of the total population. In other words, 172,000 more people moved out than moved in. The total number of people who actually moved away was, of course, higher still—say 35 or 40 percent. Thus at least one out of every three people who lived in Boston in 1955 had moved out by 1965.Looking at the age distribution of Boston's lost population from 1960 to 1965 (Table 2–13) we get a clearer picture of who is leaving: mainly young couples and their young children. While we have no direct evidence that any of these young people are in fact poor, trends in jobs, educational opportunity, and housing (presented in the next section) suggest that incentives for moving would certainly be greater for a young poor couple than for an older one. The demographers tell us that poorer, less well-educated families tend to move shorter distances. It is not unreasonable to conjecture, therefore, that a significant number of the poor families leaving Boston are poor young couples seeking better jobs. Furthermore, it is likely that these couples moved short distances into adjacent suburbs, accounting in part for the growth in the number of suburban poor families.

Pulling all these threads together, we can attribute the growth in suburban poor to a number of factors. Many suburban families entered the ranks of the poor simply because the family head retired. Some of the poor came from rural areas in search of jobs. In addition, large numbers of poor families appear to have left the central cities, and their destination has most likely been an adjacent suburb. When related trends in jobs, educational opportunity, and housing are examined, we may well wonder that this movement of poor families from central city to suburb has not taken place more rapidly.

Table 2–12 *Trends in the distribution of poor families using a 1960 cutoff of $3,000, adjusted for inflation[1]*

	1950	1960	1967
Massachusetts			
Poor Families (000)	411	146	137
Poor Families per 100 Families	35.0	12.6	10.1
Metropolitan			
Poor Families	363	128	114
Poor Families per 100 Families	36.2	12.7	10.1
State Poor	88.3%	87.6%	83.2%
Rural			
Poor Families	48	18	23
Poor Families/100 Families	28.1	11.6	10.0
State Poor	11.7%	12.4%	16.8%
Central City			
Poor Families	241	70	53
Poor Families/100 Families	52.1	16.2	13.4
Metropolitan Poor	66.4%	54.8%	46.5%
Suburbs			
Poor Families (000)	122	58	61
Poor Families/100 Families	22.6	10.1	8.3
Metropolitan Poor	33.6%	39.6%	53.5%

[1]The resulting cutoffs are: 1950—$2,420; 1960—$3,000; 1967—$3,510.

Table 2–13 *Changes in Population Age in Boston, 1960–1965*

Age	1960	1965	Change
Under 5	66.0	53.9	−18.3%
5–14	105.6	97.2	−8.0
15–19	52.8	42.4	−19.7
20–35	142.5	119.7	−16.0
35–45	84.5	73.8	−12.7
45–65	160.8	145.7	−9.4
Over 65	85.6	83.7	−2.2
Total	697.2	616.3	−11.7%

SUMMARY

The poor in Massachusetts are becoming suburbanized. The notion that they are somehow restricted by their low incomes to central-city ghettos or to failing farms is not supported by the data. Absolute declines in the number of poor in the cities have been matched by significant increases in suburban areas and in the surrounding countryside. This redistribution of the poor is evident, regardless of which definition of poverty is used.

In order to explain these shifts, we must examine related trends in jobs, education, housing, age, and race.

Related trends: jobs, education, housing, age, race

Massachusetts has experienced a marked shift in the location of both her population and her poor. In order to judge the strength and probable future course of the shift, we must understand better the context in which it is occurring.

Although we cannot examine all social and economic characteristics of the state in depth, we may look briefly at some related trends which strongly suggest that the shift of poor families will continue at the same rate, and perhaps accelerate.

JOBS

The share of metropolitan area jobs located in the central cities of Massachusetts is declining (Table 2–14). In all cases the share of metropolitan area jobs found in the central city dropped between 1954 and 1963. The decline is steady and gives every indication of continuing. While shifts in the Boston SMSA are greater than those in other SMSAs, the declining trend is present in every central city in the state.

The change in share of jobs is attributable both to absolute jobs declines in the central cities and to strong growth rates in the suburbs. Central-city employment in retail trade, wholesale trade, and manufacturing declined. Only selected service jobs grew in the central city (Table 2–15). The same nine-year period saw a substantial absolute increase in the number of jobs located in the suburbs in all four categories of employment (Table 2–15). There were significant annual increases in retail and wholesale trade jobs and in selected services employment. Even manufacturing jobs were growing in number by almost 2 percent each year.

As the jobs have moved from the central city, families have had a strong incentive to move closer to them. Absolute declines in the number of central-city jobs and absolute growth in the number of suburban jobs, combined with the problems of commuting from the central city

Table 2-14   Metropolitan area jobs in Massachusetts central cities,
              1954-1963

	1954	1958	1963
All central cities			
Retail trade	59.34%	53.75%	47.47%
Wholesale trade	72.63	67.36	58.94
Manufacturing	53.25	49.45	46.96
Selected services	64.19	63.35	57.41
Boston			
Retail trade	49.35%	43.28%	36.32%
Wholesale trade	68.01	61.33	51.22
Manufacturing	33.94	30.33	28.14
Selected services	57.76	58.65	52.14
Other central cities			
Retail trade	78.65%	74.52%	67.68%
Wholesale trade	87.02	85.62	79.99
Manufacturing	74.77	70.93	68.27
Selected services	80.66	75.51	72.06

Table 2-15   Average annual change in number of metropolitan area jobs in
              Massachusetts' central cities and suburbs, 1954-1963

	Central cities	Suburbs
All SMSAS		
Retail trade	-1.67%	4.16%
Wholesale trade	-1.30	7.02
Manufacturing	-.94	1.98
Selected services	2.10	6.46
Boston SMSA		
Retail trade	-2.63%	4.50%
Wholesale trade	-2.31	6.71
Manufacturing	-1.47	1.53
Selected services	2.52	6.00
Other SMSAS		
Retail trade	-.51%	7.55%
Wholesale trade	1.17	9.50
Manufacturing	-.67	3.45
Selected services	1.34	9.01

to outlying suburban jobs via mass transportation systems, have
created the need and motivation to leave the central city. Need and
motivation are particularly great for the poor because they depend

upon the kinds of jobs that are declining fastest in the central city and because they must pay the relatively high cost of commuting if they take on suburban jobs.

HOUSING

Wealthy families were the first to move into the suburbs. They preferred and could afford to live in open, less densely settled land. In 1960 the median family income for suburban families was $7,110, almost $1,400 more than that for central-city families. The median family income in low-density Boston suburbs was $7,726, almost $500 more than that for high-density suburbs, and more than $2,000 more than the median family income in the Boston central city (Table 2–16).

As wealthy families move farther and farther into the suburbs in search of open spaces, the housing stock they leave behind ages and eventually is divided up into apartments and offered on a rental rather than an ownership basis. This process opens up an increasing stock of relatively inexpensive housing to the poor in the suburbs. This trend is most clearly demonstrated in Boston's high-density suburbs, where 73 percent of the housing units were built before 1939, 37 percent are already apartments, and 34 percent are available for rent. In the absence of a massive renewal effort, all these percentages are likely to continue to grow with the passage of time.

EDUCATION

Educational opportunities for children are greater outside the central cities (Table 2–17). Expenditures per student are highest in rural areas. This is probably a result of demand for better education in these areas by new residents moving into them, high costs of transporting children to school, and general diseconomies of small scale. The next highest expenditures are in the suburbs, and the central cities spend the least, per pupil, on education.

Median education is measured for everyone over 25 years of age, and consequently it will be low in rural areas, despite high expenditures, because these areas are in the process of catching up. Median education can be expected to rise significantly in rural areas in the coming years.

Educational achievement is highest in the suburbs. In the Boston

Table 2-16 *Distribution of income and status of housing stock in Massachusetts in 1960*

	Central cities	Suburbs	Rural
Median family income	$5,754	$7,110	$5,863
Houing built before 1939	84.4%	60.2%	76.1%
Housing multi-unit	64.4	20.4	34.6
Housing renter-occupied	55.9	24.0	39.3
Housing sound	84.2	89.9	85.7
Housing vacant	3.5	1.9	3.2

	Boston central city	Boston high-density suburbs	Boston low-density suburbs
Median family income	$5,700	$7,282	$7,726
Housing built before 1939	90.7%	73.3%	48.1%
Housing multi-unit	83.6	36.8	8.6
Housing renter-occupied	72.7	34.1	16.6
Housing sound	87.7	91.2	90.8
Housing vacant	3.9	1.5	2.1

	Other central cities	Other suburbs
Median family income	$5,758	$6,523
Housing built before 1939	83.9%	59.7%
Housing multi-unit	62.8	17.6
Housing renter-occupied	54.5	22.4
Housing sound	83.9	88.5
Housing vacant	3.5	2.0

SMSA, median education in the low-density suburbs is greater than that in the high-density suburbs, which in turn is greater than that for the central city. Achievement is also higher in the other suburbs in the state than it is in the other central cities. Just as wealthy families are attracted by better educational opportunities, so too are poor families.

RACE

Some poor urban families are better able to respond to the attraction of the suburbs than others. Historically, poor, urban, nonwhite families have been less able. Nonwhites were thus largely concentrated in the central cities in 1960. Of the Boston central-city population in 1960, 9.8 percent was nonwhite, compared to .68 percent

Table 2-17 Educational expenditures and achievement in Massachusetts in 1960

	Central cities	Suburbs	Rural
Per-student expenditures	$447	$527	$555
Median education (years)	10.1	11.9	10.7

	Boston central city	Boston high-density suburbs	Boston low-density suburbs
Per-student expenditures	$528	$549	$579
Median education (years)	11.2	12.0	12.5

	Other central cities	Other suburbs
Per-student expenditures	$440	$489
Median education (years)	10.1	11.2

Table 2-18 Nonwhites in the total population of Massachusetts 1960

Total	
State	2.40%
All central cities	5.20
All suburbs	.90
Rural	1.30
Boston	
Boston central city	9.80%
Boston high-density suburbs	.68
Boston low-density suburbs	.81
Other	
Other central cities	1.70%
Other suburbs	.50
Rural	1.04

in the high-density suburbs and .81 percent in the low-density suburbs (Table 2–18).

A critical question is whether blacks have been participating in the migration away from the central city in search of better jobs. This question is very difficult to answer with confidence for Massachusetts, since no statewide census has collected data on race since 1960.

Nationwide, the indications are that blacks began moving into suburbs in significant numbers beginning around 1965. The growth rate of blacks in suburban communities rose sharply between 1966 and 1968 (Table 2–19). Other evidence suggests that during this same

Table 2-19 Average annual rate of change in white & nonwhite population in all U.S. metropolitan areas

	1960–1966	1966–1968
White		
Central city	-.03%	-1.0%
Suburbs	3.0	2.0
Nonwhite		
Central city	3.4%	1.0%
Suburb	.7	8.0

interval black population in central-city ghettos was declining by 8.9 percent each year. This movement can be attributed in part to intensive civil-rights activity during the Kennedy and Johnson administrations. It is probably also due partly to the sharp increase in black buying power. Black incomes rose far more rapidly than white incomes during the 1960s (Table 2–20), and while they have yet to reach parity, the gap between black and white is closing fast.

In Massachusetts there is some evidence that blacks are moving out of central-city ghettos and that some of this movement has extended into suburban communities and rural areas. According to the newspapers, Little City Hall mayors in Mattapan and Brookline report a great deal of tension as blacks begin to move into their communities in large numbers.

Since 1965 the state has been required to collect data on race for each school system. While school-age population is not a very accurate measure of total population, the results are at least consistent with our conjecture that blacks are moving out. Suburban school systems in 1968 show substantially greater percentages of blacks than did the corresponding suburban populations as a whole in 1960. Furthermore, the percentages grew from 1965 to 1968 (Table 2–21).

Relatively few blacks live in Boston's suburbs (the national average was about 5 percent in 1968), probably because of historically low concentrations of blacks in Massachusetts' central cities. Central cities are frequently used as way-stations by blacks in search of better jobs. Central-city percentages of black across the nation average 20 percent. Massachusetts' percentage in 1960 was only half of that, and as a result, its central cities provided a much smaller pool of potential black migrants. There is some indication that this may be changing, however (Table 2–21). The Boston school system is now nearly 30 percent black, and the proportion appears to be growing rapidly. Other central-

Table 2-20 *Median family income, by race of head, for all U.S. metropolitan areas (1967 dollars)*

	1967	1959	Change, 1959–67
Metropolitan areas			
White	$8,993	$7,493	20%
Negro	5,670	4,339	31
Percentage of white income	63%	58%	(X)
Central cities			
White	$8,294	$7,160	16%
Negro	5,623	4,397	28
Percentage of white income	68%	61%	(X)
In metropolitan areas of 1,000,000 or more			
White	$8,524	$7,579	12%
Negro	5,822	4,848	20
Percentage of white income	68%	64%	(X)
In metropolitan areas under 1,000,000			
White	$8,084	$6,795	19%
Negro	5,284	3,560	48
Percentage of white income	65%	52%	(X)
Suburban rings			
White	$9,497	$7,791	22%
Negro	5,857	3,985	47
Percentage of white income	62%	51%	(X)

Table 2-21 *Black school enrollment in Massachusetts, 1965 and 1968*

	1965		1968	
All central cities	12.9%	(33,661)	14.6%	(39,464)
All suburbs	1.3	(8,414)	1.7	(11,642)
All rural	1.0	(1,264)	1.2	(1,781)
Boston central cities	25.7	(23,919)	29.2	(27,449)
Boston suburbs	1.4	(5,500)	1.9	(8,080)
Other central cities	5.7	(9,742)	6.8	(12,015)
Other suburbs	1.2	(2,914)	1.4	(3,562)

city school systems are showing significant gains as well. If Massachusetts is at all like other metropolitan states, we can expect that its suburban black population will grow substantially during the next ten years. This trend should begin to show in the 1970 census.

The pattern of black suburban settlement will probably not be uniform. Most recent data suggest that suburban blacks tend to live in clusters, and that the suburban averages mask large differences in concentration. We can rank the suburban and rural school systems in Massachusetts by percentage of blacks in 1968, for example (Table 2–22), and find that relatively few school systems account for the bulk of the suburban black population. Many of these school systems, particularly those on Cape Cod, have had significant black populations for some time, and only a few are experiencing sharp inward migrations.

AGE

As we saw earlier, younger families are settling in the suburbs while older families tend to remain in the central cities (Table 2–23). In 1960 the median age of the suburban population was lower than that of the central-city and rural populations. Within the Boston SMSA, the low-density suburbs had the lowest median age and the highest percentage of its population under 21 years, indicating that the population in this area was composed of younger families.

The percentage of the population over 65 years of age is rising in the central city and falling in the suburbs. Within the Boston SMSA the trend was most pronounced. The percent of the population over 65 grew in both the central city and the high-density suburbs and declined in the low-density suburbs.

SUMMARY

The attractions of suburban living—better schools, better housing, and easier access to a growing number of suburban jobs—have drawn a large segment of Massachusetts' population. While the old and the nonwhite have been less able to respond to these attractions, younger couples— black and white—appear to be doing so now. The strength of the job trends and the availability of rental housing in the inner suburbs suggest that, if anything, suburbanization of the poor and the black will accelerate.

Conclusion

The number of poor in Massachusetts appears to be decreasing relative to the Northeast as a whole, and it is certainly decreasing on an absolute scale. The concentration of poor families has been dropping since 1950.

The poor are concentrated in metropolitan areas, but they are dispersing rapidly with the population as a whole. The number and concentration

Table 2-22   *Blacks in suburban and rural school systems, 1968*

Rank	School system	Black	Rank	School system	Black
		Suburban			
1.	Cambridge	15.9%	5.	Lynn	4.7%
2.	Brookline	7.5	6.	Medford	4.0
3.	Lincoln	7.4	7.	Chicopee	3.5
4.	Chelsea	4.9	8.	Newton	3.1
		Rural			
1.	Mashpee	34.7%	14.	Rochester	6.7%
2.	Carver	17.6	15.	Tisbury	6.3
3.	Marion	15.7	16.	Martha's Vnyrd.	5.9
4.	Oak Bluffs	15.6	17.	Nantucket	5.8
5.	Ayer	14.5	18.	Freetown	4.4
6.	Harwich	14.2	19.	Lancaster	4.2
7.	Falmouth	9.1	20.	Duxbury	4.1
8.	Truro	9.0	21.	Plimpton	4.0
9.	Barnstable	8.3	22.	Mattapoisett	3.8
10.	Bourne	8.2	23.	Plymouth	3.2
11.	Shirley	7.8	24.	Sharon	3.0
12.	Wendell	7.3	25.	Hancock	3.0
13.	Otis	6.8	26.	Bridgewater	3.0

Table 2-23   *Massachusetts population by age group and area, 1960*

	Under 21 in 1960	Over 65 in 1960	Median age in 1960
All central cities	36.2%	12.6%	33.7
All suburbs	40.2	9.2	31.4
Rural	38.0	11.7	32.7
Boston central city	66.3	12.3	32.9
Boston high-density suburbs	61.7	10.5	32.9
Boston low-density suburbs	58.2	7.9	28.5
Other central cities	63.6	12.6	33.8
Other suburbs	59.7	9.3	31.2

of poor families in the suburbs are both increasing rapidly. Today more poor people live in the suburbs of Massachusetts than live in its central cities. The number of poor families living in rural areas is also growing.

Other trends are encouraging the continuation of this dispersal. The growing number of jobs in the suburbs and the availability of land in low-density neighborhoods in the suburbs are chief among these influences. Different groups are affected in different ways by these trends. Thus, unlike the wealthy and the white, the poor, the nonwhite, and the aged are less able to respond to the attractions of the suburbs. Yet today they are starting to respond in greater numbers.

If political boundaries were of no consequence, shifts across them would be of no consequence. Practically speaking, however, we all recognize that federal program funds are allocated to political entities whose representatives are elected by constituencies.

In view of this reality, the shifts described in this chapter pose two major kinds of problems for politicians and planners in Massachusetts and in Washington. First is the problem of ensuring equal assistance for all poor people, wherever they may be found. In particular, the places where the poor have been living are much more accustomed to assisting them than the places to which the poor are moving. By what process will the delivery of direct services—welfare, health, public housing —be reallocated?

The second problem is more subtle. To what extent will the state government encourage or discourage the dispersal of the poor—intentionally or otherwise—through its policies on housing, transportation, education, and the other functional areas into which it is divided? What is the effect of rent control, for example, or of a town-by-town quota for low- and moderate-income housing, or of highway construction, or of state aid to education? Must the state's role increase as the poor cross local boundaries at a greater rate? And how is an internally consistent policy to be achieved?

It is far beyond the scope of this chapter to answer such questions, but the analysis presented here certainly raises them and, we trust, poses something of a challenge to those who struggle to find the answers.

Finally, the inadequacy of the data upon which this chapter must be based points up a glaring deficiency in the Massachusetts planning process, at least so far as the poor are concerned. It is easy to explain why past data have been inadequate—but there can be no excuse for not capitalizing on the 1970 census data when they become available. Since many of the 1970 census data will be collected and stored in machine-readable form, with modest initiative the state could request and obtain special tabulations that are of interest to it.

With regard to the poor, it would be extremely helpful for planning purposes to know what kinds of poor people are living in which areas.

In particular, it would be helpful to know, at a minimum, for each city and town, the distribution of families by age of the head of household, by race, and by income group.In addition, it would be useful to know (1) the employment by industry, (2) the unemployment rate, and (3) the average family size for each group so defined.

These data could be obtained easily if they were requested now, while the Census Bureau is planning for the distribution of the 1970 data. We recommend strongly, therefore, that the state organize itself immediately to take advantage of the Census Bureau's increased ability to respond to special requests. We must know who and where the poor are before we can adequately assist them in coping with their difficulties.

Sources of data in the tables

The following publicatons of the U.S. Bureau of the Census were used: *Seventh Census of the United States: 1950; Eighteenth Census of the United States: 1960; Current Population Reports: Population Estimates*, 1956, 1968; *Current Population Reports: Consumer Income*, 1956, 1968; *Census of Business: Retail Trade-Area Statistics, Census of Business: Wholesale Trade-Area Statistics*, and *Census of Manufactures: Area Statistics*, 1954, 1958, and 1963; *Current Population Reports: Special Studies*, Series P–23, No. 27. The following Massachusetts publications were used: Department of Commerce and Development, *SMSA, County, City, and Town Monographs*, 1968–1969; Secretary of the Commonwealth, *The Decennial Census: 1965;* Department of Education, *Annual School Census*, 1965–1968.

MICHAEL J. PIORE

jobs and training

In this chapter, concerned with the impact of state manpower policy upon the problem of poverty in Massachusetts, the term "manpower policy" encompasses those activities of state government that directly affect the operation of the labor market. For practical purposes, it includes those policies and procedures that, on the federal level, fall within the purview of the Secretary of Labor. Of particular interest are the state employment service, manpower training programs, equal employment opportunity, and occupational licensing and entry restrictions.

"Manpower policy" is frequently used in a much broader sense to include all activities that affect the willingness or ability of individuals to obtain a living through gainful employment. In this chapter, the ramifications of this broader concept of manpower

Michael J. Piore is associate professor of economics at Massachusetts Institute of Technology. The chief research assistant was Bertram Shlensky; he did most of the field work upon which the chapter is based. Additional assistance was provided on public welfare by Andrew Sum, on employment discrimination by DonCosta Seawell, and on occupational licensing by Eric J. Wallach.

policy are recognized only to the extent of examining institutions that link the school system and the system of public assistance to the labor market. The limited perspective which this affords will, we hope, be broadened by other chapters in this book.

The state is probably not the most appropriate level of government at which to formulate and execute manpower policy to aid the poor. Present arrangements for the manpower component of the poverty program, which bypass the state in favor of a direct link between the federal government and local organizations, are most consistent with the political and economic contexts in which the programs must operate. The political pressures of the poverty problem are felt more keenly in federal and local governments than in the state house. Economically, the poor and near-poor tend to operate within a labor market encompassed by the boundaries of a city or a county. Expanding the geographic limits of employment opportunity is an important policy option, but it is unlikely—and, to eliminate poverty, probably not necessary— that such limits can be enlarged beyond the confines of a metropolitan area. The fate of the work force within these local markets is often determined by broader economic forces like industrial production and level of unemployment, but such forces tend to be national or regional in character. They can seldom be controlled by a single state alone.

However appropriate its present role, the state's responsibilities in manpower appear to be increasing. In this respect, our study comes at a critical juncture. The Nixon Administration, it is now apparent, is attempting to strengthen the role of state government in manpower policy. The administration-sponsored Manpower Training Act of 1969 (H.R. 13472, S. 2838) proposes to channel through the state government most of the funds now allocated directly to local organizations; and it attempts to do so in a way that will provide an incentive to the governor to develop a manpower planning capability and a coordinated manpower strategy. The Secretary of Labor has, in fact, begun to exercise his considerable discretion under existing legislation to move in this direction. The state already exercises nominal control over related programs in education, welfare, public employment service, and equal employment opportunity. It has tended to abrogate authority in all of these areas to federal and local governments, but the moves required to assert control are largely administrative in character, consistent with existing legislation. The philosophic commitment of the Republican party to state government and the party's relative strength at the state level suggest that changes in the federal role in these other areas are likely to reinforce the pressures generated by the new manpower act.

In a sense, we address ourselves to the question how, from the viewpoint of reducing poverty, the state ought to exercise the power it is being pressed to assume. This chapter is directed specifically at the problems of Massachusetts. Much of the analysis, however, is generally applicable to northern states that have large pockets of urban poverty.

Our analysis embodies a somewhat unorthodox view of the manpower problems of the poor. That view is summarized, and its limitations explored, in the first part of this paper. The second part discusses the substance of state manpower policy. The third considers the issues raised by the Nixon administration's proposals for manpower reorganization.

The labor market and poverty

The central tenet of the analysis is that the role of employment and of the disposition of manpower in perpetuating poverty can be best understood in terms of a dual labor market. One sector of that market, which I have termed elsewhere the primary market,[1] offers jobs which possess several of the following traits: high wages, good working conditions, employment stability and job security, equity and due process in the administration of work rules, and chances for advancement. The secondary sector has jobs that are decidedly less attractive, compared with those in the primary sector. They tend to involve low wages, poor working conditions, considerable variability in employment, harsh and often arbitrary discipline, and little opportunity to advance. The poor are confined to the secondary labor market. Eliminating poverty requires that they gain access to primary employment.

The factors that generate the dual market structure and confine the poor to the secondary sector are complex. With some injustice to that complexity, they may be summarized: First, the most important characteristic distinguishing primary from secondary jobs appears to be the behavioral requirements they impose upon the work force, particularly that of employment stability. Insofar as secondary workers are barred from primary jobs by a real qualification, it is generally their inability to show up for work regularly and on time. Secondary employers are far

---

[1]See Michael J. Piore, "On-The-Job Training in the Dual Labor Market," in Arnold Weber, *et al., Public-Private Manpower Policies* (Madison, Wisc.: Industrial Relations Research Association, 1969), pp. 101–132.

more tolerant of lateness and absenteeism, and many secondary jobs are of such short duration that these do not matter. Work skills, which receive considerable emphasis in most discussions of poverty and employment, do not appear a major barrier to primary employment (although, because regularity and punctuality are important to successful learning in school and on the job, such behavioral traits tend to be highly correlated with skills).

Second, certain workers who possess the behavioral traits required to operate efficiently in primary jobs are trapped in the secondary market because their superficial characteristics resemble those of secondary workers. This identification occurs because employment decisions are generally made on the basis of a few readily (and hence inexpensively) assessed traits like race, demeanor, accent, educational attainment, test scores, and the like. Such traits tend to be statistically correlated with job performance but not necessarily (and probably not usually) causally related to it. Hence, a number of candidates who are rejected because they possess the "wrong" traits are actually qualified for the job. Exclusion on this basis may be termed *statistical discrimination.* In addition to statistical discrimination, workers are also excluded from primary employment by *discrimination pure and simple.*

Discrimination of any kind enlarges the labor force that is captive in the secondary sector, and thus lowers the wages that secondary employers must pay to fill their jobs. Such employers thus have an economic stake in perpetuating discrimination. Since it limits the supply of labor in the primary sector and raises the wages of workers who have access to job there, primary workers also have a stake in discrimination. Discrimination pure and simple is not generally of economic value to primary employers, since it forces them to pay higher wages without obtaining corresponding economic gains. In statistical discrimination, however, the higher wages are compensated by the reduced cost of screening job candidates, and here primary employers share the interest of secondary employers and primary workers in perpetuating such discrimination.

Third, the distinction between primary and secondary jobs is not, apparently, technologically determinate. A portion—perhaps a substantial proportion—of the work in the economy can be organized for either stable or unstable workers. Work normally performed in the primary sector is sometimes shifted to the secondary sector through subcontracting, temporary help services, recycling of new employees through probationary periods, and the like. Nor is the primary-secondary distinction necessarily associated with a given enterprise. Some enterprises, most of whose jobs constitute primary employment and are filled with stable, committed workers, have subsections or departments with inferior job opportunities accommodated to an unstable work force. Secondary employers generally have a few primary jobs, and some have a large number of them. Nonetheless, despite a certain degree of elasticity in the distribution of work between the primary and secondary sections, shifts in the distribution generally involve changes in the techniques of production and management and in the instututional structure and procedures of the enterprises in which the work is performed. The investment necessary to effect these changes acts to strengthen resistance to antipoverty efforts.

Fourth, the behavioral traits associated with the secondary sector are reinforced by the process of working in secondary jobs and living among others whose life-style is accommodated to that type of employment. Hence, even people initially forced into the secondary sector by discrimination tend, over a period of time, to develop the traits predominant among secondary workers. Thus, a man who works in a world where employment is intermittent and erratic, tends to lose habits of regularity and punctuality. Similarly, when reward and punishment in the work place are continually based upon personal relationships between worker and supervisor, workers forget how to operate within the impersonal, institutional grievance prodecures of the primary sector. When such workers do gain access to primary jobs, they are frustrated by the system's failure to respond on a personal basis and by their own inability to make it respond on an institutional basis.

Finally, among the poor, income sources other than employment, especially public assistance and illicit activity, tend to be more compatible with secondary than with primary employment. The public assistance system discourages full-time work and forces those on welfare either into jobs that are part-time or into jobs that pay cash income which will not be reported to the social worker or can be quickly dropped or delayed when the social worker discovers them or seems in danger of doing so. The relationship between social worker and client builds upon the personal relationship that operates in the secondary sector, not on the institutional mechanisms that tend to operate in the primary sector. Illegitimate activity also tends to follow the intermittent work pattern prevalent in secondary employment, and the attractions of such activity, as well as life patterns and role models it presents to those not themselves involved but associating with people who are, foster behavioral traits antagonistic to primary employment.

The dual market interpretation of poverty has some central implications: the poor do participate in the economy; the manner of their participation, not the question of participation as such, constitutes the manpower problem of the poor; and their current mode of participation is ultimately a response to a series of pressures—economic, social, and technical—playing upon individuals and labor market institutions. This suggests that a distinction can be drawn between policies that are designed to alleviate the pressures which generate the dual market structure and those that attempt to attack the problem directly by moving individuals from secondary to primary employment. The latter policies combat prevailing pressures but leave intact the forces that generate them. The second part of this chapter draws heavily upon this distinction. The thrust of the argument is that in concentrating upon training, counseling, and placement services for the poor, manpower policy has overemphasized direct approaches, and that more weight should be placed upon policies which affect the environment in which employment decisions are made and the pressures which the environment generates. Among such policies are antidiscrimination policy, occupational licensing reform, and the structure of public assistance.

Analysis of the dual labor market suggests a further implication: because the "poor" do participate in the economy, certain groups are interested in that participation and how it occurs. Policies aimed at moving the poor out of the secondary market work against the intersts of these groups and therefore are in danger of being subverted by them. This danger is a major reason for concentrating on indirect approaches that are not susceptible to the same kind of subversion; in fact, because such approaches alleviate the pressures generating the dual market structure, they reduce the resistance to policies that move directly against that structure. The dangers to which existing institutions subject programs designed to move the poor directly out of the secondary market are twofold. The new institutions created by these programs can be rejected by the prevailing economic system and isolated off to one side; a program, for example, would then recruit workers for training in skills that are little utilized in either the secondary or the primary market. Alternatively, the new institutions may be captured by the prevailing economic system and used to facilitate its operation; for example, neighborhood employment offices may recruit secondary workers for secondary jobs, and training may be provided in primary employment to workers who would have gotten it anyway in establishments that would have financed it themselves. The central problem in the design of direct approaches to manpower programs is to organize them in such a way that they can resist this twofold threat of rejection on the one hand and capture on the other. It is to this problem that the third part of the chapter is addressed.

These conclusions follow directly from the dual market interpretation of the poverty problem but they are not uniquely dependent upon it. The dual labor market is one of a class of theoretical constructs which views poverty in the United States in terms of a dichotomy in the economic and social structures. Such a dichotomy is implicit in the concept of a "culture of poverty" and in the expression of public policy goals associated with poverty in terms of an income cutoff. Most such views of poverty entertain the idea that the dichotomy is a product of forces endogenous to the economy (or, more broadly, the society as a whole). It follows that attempts to eliminate poverty will tend to run counter to the natural operation of the economy, and that they will be resisted by existing institutions and are in danger of rejection. To say all this is perhaps to say simply that if poverty were easy to eliminate, it wouldn't be around in the first place. But it does at least identify as a certain problem in the program design the task of equipping the institution which works with the poor to withstand the rejection pressures.

What the dual labor market interpretation implies that is not implicit in other dichotomous interpretations is that the poor are separated from the nonpoor not only in the negative sense of exclusion from activities and institutions to which the nonpoor have access, but also in the positive sense that they have economic value where they are; that, in other words, *there are groups actively interested in the perpetuation of poverty.* It is this interest that makes new institutions created to work with the poor in the labor market subject to threats of capture as well as of rejection.

The major alternative to the dual labor market interpretation as a foundation for manpower policy is one that associates poverty either with the inability to find work or with full-time work at low wages. This interpretation of poverty emphasizes, on one hand, the high incidence of unemployment and the relatively low rates of labor force participation among the poor and, on the other, the number of people employed full-time, all year round, at low-paying jobs. Unlike the dual labor market interpretation, this interpretation often focuses attention upon people who are incapable of productive employment in any realistic sense and whose poverty is thus beyond reach of manpower policy. This group includes, for example, many aged people, people with serious physical handicaps and mental and emotional disorders, and small children in families headed by the old and the handicapped.[2] The dual market interpretation implies that, beyond these people, what appears statistically to be an unemployment problem results largely from the attempt to classify and interpret the experience of the secondary market by means of statistical categories applicable to the primary labor market. Thus, for example, measured unemployment and labor force participation rates in poor neighborhoods are distorted by number of individuals who are unemployed because of instability of jobs, unwillingness to work a continuous five-day week, illegal or quasi-illegal jobs, support by family members not classified as such by the survey, and the like. The second group of poor which the dual labor market interpretation tends to slight (the full-time, full-year, but low-wage workers) could not be separately identified for Massachusetts. This group is large nationally, but it is concentrated in the South and in agriculture.[3]

The dual labor market provides a convincing interpretation of the realities of labor markets in black urban ghettos. The combination of high measured unemployment rates and bitter complaints of narrow employment opportunity, on the one hand, with high turnover rates and persistent employer complaints of labor shortage, on the other hand, cannot be reconciled with a conventional unemployment interpretation but are readily comprehended with a two-sector model in which the sectors are also consistent with autobiographical and sociological descriptions of urban ghetto life.

The constraints of the present study did not permit a rigorous investigation of each poverty group, but an attempt was made to assess the applicability of the model outside the black ghettos of the state capital. This assessment led to the conclusion that the dual labor market was the most meaningful framework in which to analyze the manpower problems of the state's poor, with certain qualifications.

[2] A small proportion of the people in these groups can be helped to work. There are programs designed to do this; we did not investigate them.

[3] See, for example, Vera C. Derrella, "Low Earners and Their Incomes," *Monthly Labor Review,* 90, No. 5 (May 1967), 37–40. This study indentifies full-time, full-year workers with 1965 income under $2,500. Further, a third of this group is in agriculture and half lives in the South.

Within Boston, it was generally felt by those working in manpower programs that the model is somewhat less applicable to the white ethnic poor than to the black poor. It appears that a larger proportion of the white ethnic poor are simply locked into low-wage jobs that do not possess the combination of debilitating characteristics typical of low-paying black employment. On the other hand, many of these ethnic white workers do not think of themselves as poor and resent efforts to treat them as such.

Outside the Boston area, we visited four communities: Springfield, the Berkshire area, Lowell, and New Bedford. Poverty in Springfield closely resembles that in Boston. It has a large black component whose problem is readily encompassed by a dual market model; the remaining poverty is concentrated among white ethnic groups that have a greater proportion of poor in low-paying, stable jobs than is true in the black community but a lesser consciousness of their own poverty. Poverty in the Berkshire area is rural, closely tied to low agricultural incomes and a scarcity of alternative employment opportunities. Here, a conventional employment model is more appropriate than the dual market model, and an emphasis upon the dual market model slights the area's manpower problems. The rural character of the Berkshires, however, makes it atypical of Massachusetts' poverty in general.

The third community, Lowell, was selected because it was though to typify the "depressed area" problem generated by the decline of the shoe and textile industries in the older industrial centers of the state. Such depressed areas have been thought in the past to present the archetypal employment problem, one that can be solved only by out-migration or growth of new industry. But, surprisingly, poverty in Lowell appeared better understood in terms of the dual market model derived from the black ghetto. The high measured unemployment rate was apparently attributable to instability of jobs and workers in the secondary sector composed of the remaining textile and shoe plants. The labor force in this sector comprised recent migrants, largely from Puerto Rico and southern and eastern Europe (with some French Canadians and southern blacks), a great many of whom were trapped in secondary jobs by their inability to speak English. Measured unemployment was apparently inflated by the practice of workers' dropping out of the effective work force in order to draw unemployment insurance as soon as they had established eligibility and by the irregular attachment to the labor force of migrants who returned home periodically. The migration was itself indicative of the tightness of the labor market, and the effort of low-wage employers to recruit workers for their jobs was apparently an important spur to in-migration, especially among the Puerto Ricans. Employment programs in Lowell were under intense pressure to serve the secondary labor market.

Employment in Lowell benefits from proximity to the growing electronics industry around Route 128, and it can be argued that Lowell is therefore not typical of the state's depressed areas. The New Bedford labor market was added to the study to compensate for any distortion which Lowell might have introduced. New Bedford is clearly less prosperous than Lowell, Springfield, or Boston: unemployment is higher, incomes are lower, and concern about lay-offs and declining industry surface more frequently in discussions. Nonetheless, in New Bedford as in other cities, manpower problems center around the quality of jobs. Despite high reported unemployment, job vacancies in the textile, garment, and rubber industries, all of which possess many secondary jobs, are difficult to fill; employers are encouraging Puerto Rican migration and lobbying in Washington for an increase in quotas for Portugal and Cape Verde, the traditional sources of New Bedford migrants. It is more difficult in New Bedford than in other parts of the state to identify primary jobs that might provide alternatives to secondary employment, and in this respect New Bedford might be characterized as a depressed area. But clearly the expansion of secondary industry, which is the prescription emerging from the conventional depressed area model, is not a solution to the problem. The garment industry, a major source of secondary jobs is, in fact, a newly expanding sector of the New Bedford economy.

The substance of manpower policy

Manpower policies may be divided into two groups: those that attempt directly to move secondary workers into primary jobs, and those that operate indirectly to change the pressures operating upon individuals and institutions and determining the costs and payoffs to various labor market arrangements. The manpower programs associated with the War on Poverty are of the first type, and we shall now discuss the substance of these programs. Then we will discuss several policies affecting the environment in which workers and managers make labor market decisions: structure of public assistance, occupational licensing policy, and antidiscrimination policy. The last two policies operate primarily upon employer decisions; the structure of public assistance tends to achieve its impact primarily through its effect upon the labor force. The last part of this section deals with policy for depressed areas.

THE "NEW MANPOWER" PROGRAMS

The "new manpower" programs have their roots in the Area Redevelopment Act of 1961 and the Manpower Development Act of 1962, through which most are still governed, but the present orientation of these programs dates from President Johnson's announcement of the War on Poverty in 1964. The programs consist largely of training, counseling, and job development, although some ancillary services are often provided in the process and a certain amount of what is called "training" is more than public employment or subsidized private employment. The organization of these programs is discussed in the next part of the chapter. The concern here is with their substance.

It was argued in the preceding section that the central task of manpower policy is to move secondary workers into primary jobs. My own assessment of the "new manpower" programs is that in this regard they have been for the most part unsuccessful. A great deal of their energy is expended in facilitating the movement of the poor within the secondary labor market. Most of the jobs are the kind that program participants can and were getting on their own. The programs, in other words, have been captured by the existing market institutions.

The relatively few primary employment opportunities also fail to achieve the goals—at least the *enunciated* goals—of the programs. Such opportunities are going largely to people who are already qualified for primary employment when they enter the program. Some of these people would eventually have gotten primary jobs on their own. The remainder benefit not from the services provided by the program but from pressures upon employers to hire the disadvantaged with which the programs are in one way or another associated but for which they are not responsible. The most important of these pressures are those generated by federal equal employment opportunity activities. Riots in the black ghetto have also been important both as a generalized spur to the civic conscience of the business community and as a specific threat to the property of individual employers. The jobs opened by these pressures would probably go to some other "disadvantaged" worker were the new manpower agencies not around to supply applicants.

The implication of this discussion is that were the "new manpower" programs—and in fact the "old" programs as well— eliminated tomorrow, the poor would suffer no great loss. In terms of the service they are ostensibly designed to provide—employment of clients in jobs that can serve as a means for escape from poverty—I think this implication is substantially correct. The manpower programs have, however, served other purposes that have substantial value for the poor community. They have been a vehicle for the politicization of the poor, and in this way they have served to develop skills of considerable value to the community, whatever reward such skills command in the job market. They have also employed large numbers of people from the community in the programs themselves. At the very least, this has made them an important source of jobs and income in poor neighborhoods. It is frequently argued that such jobs have served as critical links in a new career path for the disadvantaged out of the community and into white-collar and professional employment in private industry. This claim has not, as far as I know, been systematically investigated, but it does accord with my own impression of the dispersion of former employees of ABCD in Boston and with the claims of CAP program directors in other cities. It is worth noting, moreover, that the manpower programs about which we have been talking are funded almost entirely by the federal government, so that whatever their net social contribution, they are from the viewpoint of state government essentially free. They are also a symbol in poor neighborhoods of the commitment of the society to the elimination of poverty and are invested with the prestige, however misguided, which the poor accord to education and training. Thus, while the cutting back of many other programs would have a greater impact upon individual lives, it is difficult to find a program whose cutback would have a stronger impact upon the morale of poor neighborhoods.

To the extent that manpower programs make their contributions in these indirect ways, the specific content of the programs becomes of secondary importance. The organizational issues discussed in the next section become of greater interest, particularly the organizational alternatives of the community action format on the one hand and the employment service on the other. Several of the programs' indirect contributions, particularly setting up new career ladders and politicizing poor communities, are realized only in the CAP format.

The indifference to program content that I have suggested should be qualified in several important respects. First, while there is little evidence that very brief crash training is successful for the development either of job skills or of more basic literacy, prolonged educational programs in both these areas seem likely to succeed for at least a portion of the adult poor. The basic objection to this type of program is political: it requires subsidizing able-bodied adult workers for long periods (it is no coincidence that the length of most training programs falls well within the period of eligibility for unemployment compensation). When prolonged adult education becomes feasible, however, it should be encouraged. The WIN program, it will be seen shortly, is one area where movement in this direction seems possible. Second, for workers migrating from non-English-speaking areas—the proportion of such workers was relatively small but in all the urban areas visited appeared to be growing—language constitutes the most important barrier to primary employment. These workers want English courses, language can be taught on a crash basis, and clearly such programs ought to be expanded. Third, many "training" programs can make a significant contribution to the opening of primary jobs if they are coordinated with aggressive antidiscrimination campaigns and their content tailored to such campaigns rather than to the "real" dificiencies of the poor. The implications of this approach should become clearer when problems of discrimination are discussed specifically, but one example may clarify what such a policy implies. The JOBS-NAB program provides large federal subsidies to employers to hire and "train" the disadvantaged. Many employers are participating in this program in order to meet equal employment requirements. The funds are not really being used to "train" the disadvantaged but rather to finance the internal administrative reforms required to effect an equal employment policy. They are nonetheless opening primary jobs to people who would not otherwise have them. Since employers are not supposed to be subsidized for compliance with the law, it may not be feasible to give explicit recognition to this aspect of the program. On the other hand, the equal employment pressure clearly is a critical program component, and the true test of the content of the employer's internal program is the nature of the administrative reforms he is attempting to introduce and the procedures he is following in doing so.

PUBLIC ASSISTANCE

The primary institutional link between the public assistance system and the labor market is the WIN (Work Incentive) program. First tried on an experimental basis in 1964, the program was made a compulsory feature of federal Aid to Families with Dependent Children in the Social Security amendments of 1967, effective in 1968. WIN is designed to provide specialized job counseling, work training, and children's day-care facilities for those who receive public assistance. Job counseling and work training are provided by the public employment service. Welfare clients are referred to the program by their social worker, who is supposed to provide the public employment service with background information that will facilitate the counseling process. The public welfare department is also responsible for ensuring that day-care facilities are available if needed. Participation in the program may be mandatory for certain groups of welfare clients, but the public welfare department maintains that so far most referrals have been voluntary.

Reliable statistics on the WIN program in Massachusetts—or, for that matter, in the nation—are not available, but the consensus among professionals in the manpower field is that the program has been a failure.The immediate cause of this failure can be traced to deficiencies in the program components. Social workers in Massachusetts—again, this also is true in the nation—are overburdened: case loads generally exceed federal standards, and workers do not have time to handle the traditional problems of their clients, let alone undertake the additional responsibilities, imposed by the WIN program, of sifting their case loads for likely candidates and preparing the background material necessary for successful job counseling. Day-care facilities in the state are inadequate, and the day-care provisions arranged by the welfare department, or by the clients, often prove temporary or unreliable. The employment service is unaccustomed to dealing in a remedial way with the job problems of welfare clients, and the training has often proven poor or inadequate.

Concentrating upon the specific program deficiencies, however, gives a misleading picture of what would be required to make the WIN program a viable approach to reducing the burden of public assistance. The deficiencies are symptomatic of a more fundamental problem: the public assistance system, as it is presently structured, operates to discourage the movement of clients into employment. The WIN program is an outgrowth of a generalized public discontent with public assistance and a reassertion of the American work ethic. But the internal structure of the public assistance program, and its relation to the larger economic system, gives rise to no *specific* interest in the day-to-day operation of the program or of any of its components. Neither clients nor social workers nor employers nor day-care center proprietors nor, for that matter, any interest group, public or private, is exerting pressure to make the program work, and several of these groups are openly hostile to the program and its objectives. Under these circumstances, the over-burdened administrators in the agencies involved allocate their time and energy to other responsibilities which they are under specific pressure to fulfill.

The basic features of the public assistance system that work against employment of welfare clients are the high levels of public assistance relative to the local wage level combined with the high rates at which the earnings of welfare clients are taxed. Thus, for example, in Boston, a mother with three children is eligible for a basic allowance of about $3,260 per year. At the minimum wage, a full-time, full-year job could bring in $3,200. This comparison, however, plays down the true disparity between welfare and employment as a source of income. People who receive public assistance are entitled to a variety of special grants, services, supplements, and income in kind that are either not available to nonrecipients or more difficult to obtain. At the same time, most recipients, when they enter the labor market, are confined to the secondary sector, where jobs not only bring low wages but are difficult, unpleasant, and so unstable that they are unlikely to provide full-time, full-year work.

The conflict between work and welfare has been reduced somewhat in recent years by provisions allowing welfare clients to retain a certain portion of their earnings, so that they do not suffer a dollar-for-dollar reduction in their welfare grants. The effect of these provisions has been blunted, however, by a number of factors. First, the maximum standard of living on welfare is maintained by recipient's piecing together a whole out of the many special services and privileges to which she is entitled. The time required for this makes time spent at work more costly than is sometimes recognized. Second, the provisions enabling clients to keep a portion of earned income have varied widely and frequently and, at any given time, are imperfectly understood by social workers, let alone clients. Thirdly, widespread discussion of forcing clients off the rolls and into jobs suggests that a clients' having a job (or having had one) may establish a precedent that will be used to limit eligibility under some future punitive legislation. Finally, welfare clients can avoid having any earnings deducted from their basic grants, as well as possible prejudice to future eligibility, by working surreptitiously at odd jobs on the fringes of the economy in which wages are paid in cash and income is not reported. Such jobs, it may be noted, tend to possess the characteristics of secondary employment in marked degree and thus to foster work habits that prevent the welfare clients who hold them from getting high-wage primary employment at some later date.

The welfare system itself tends to foster habits of behavior and thought characteristic of secondary jobs and antagonistic to success in primary employment. The personalized, dependent relationship between client and social worker is closely akin to the relationship between worker and supervisor in the secondary sector and totally unlike the institutionalized procedures for job allocation and redress of grievance in primary jobs. The many goods and services that supplement the basic public assistance grant are collected through a process involving long periods of waiting in line—a process that destroys the sense of time and respect for time required for successful primary employment.

The Nixon administration's proposed family assistance program will somewhat reduce these conflicts. In some states the proposal would supplant the welfare system completely. In Massachusetts, where present payments are substantially in excess of the proposed floor, the present AFDC program would continue. The major impact of the Nixon reform would be to cover all those low-income families not now eligible for assistance. The new coverage would provide a guarantee for a family of four of $1,500 plus $750 in permissible earnings "tax free", and a 50 percent tax on earnings above $750, so that each dollar earned would result in a 50-cent reduction in government payments. Such a plan would subsidize the working poor, in a family of four, up to an income of $3,750. It would still be advantageous under the Nixon reform for many families to make themselves eligible for AFDC by quitting work or deserting their children, but the incentive to do so would be substantially reduced. On the other hand, if the mandatory work provisions of the Nixon proposals are as harshly administered as the President suggests they will be, fear that any history of employment will prejudice one's claim to assistance may deter clients from working even if the monetary rewards to work are large.

Since nobody knows how many people have made their families eligible for assistance through paper desertions and voluntary unemployment—and it is in the nature of the problem that finding out is impossible—it is really impossible to say how much of the welfare population is even *capable* of responding to work incentives. Probably even the best response will still leave large numbers on an AFDC program very similar to that prevailing today, and the state must decide what to do about them.

Short of lowering the level of public assistance payments—a move that is not compatible with eliminating poverty—or substantially reducing the marginal tax rate upon the earnings of public assistance clients —a reform that is clearly too expensive for the state to introduce without an increase in federal assistance substantially greater than what appears to be forthcoming—what appears to make sense as an alternative to the WIN approach is a restructuring of public assistance upon the assumptions that most clients are unlikely to work while they are receiving assistance and that the program should be designed to maximize their chances of obtaining high-wage, attractive employment when they leave the welfare rolls. Such an approach implies, as a substitute for the crash training for AFDC mothers, a program that takes advantage of the several years they are likely to be on public assistance to equip them with skills that can command high wages in the primary sector of the labor market. Second, it implies the depersonalization of assistance grants and services so that the operational skills and behavioral traits rewarded in the public assistance system more closely resemble those rewarded in the primary sector. Such a depersonalization would imply: (1) the separation of payments and services; (2) the consolidation of special grants and supplements into a single flat grant based on income and family size alone; (3) the formal recognition of elected client representatives in the administration of public assistances and in procedures for handling grievances and complaints; and (4) the provision of social welfare services on a voluntary basis, with the budgets of social service agencies made dependent upon client utilization.

BARRIERS TO MOBILITY

Two sets of state policies have important effects upon structural barriers to labor mobility between the primary and secondary sectors: antidiscrimination policies and occupational licensing policies. The target population for these policies is that group of stable workers trapped in the secondary sector.

Antidiscrimination policy

State antidiscrimination policy is established and administered by the Massachusetts Commission Against Discrimination (MCAD). Under state law, MCAD has investigatory and conciliatory powers and can issue cease-and-desist orders and award back pay. In addition, the state commission has a statutory role in federal antidiscrimination procedures under Title VII of the Civil Rights Act of 1964. The filing of a complaint with MCAD is a necessary first step to obtain relief under federal laws. The action of MCAD, if there is action within a specified time limit, is then reviewed by the federal Equal Employment Opportunity Commission and can be appealed through the federal courts. MCAD thus has not-inconsiderable power to influence employment within the state and could be a factor in the development of a case law nationally. The second role is of some significance because the federal statute is ambiguous and at points contradictory, and national policy in the area will ultimately be defined by the courts.

The potential of MCAD has never, however, been fully exploited. Most of the commissioners have been appointed as a reward for political services remote from the politics of race; they have no expertise in manpower or labor relations and a sometimes dubious commitment to the agency's legislated goals. The agency has been understaffed and tightly budgeted. It has developed a very narrow interpretation of its role and responsibilities. As a result, what real pressure exists in the state against discriminatory employment policy is generated by federal agencies. Employers fear MCAD largely because its proceedings may call them to the attention of federal agencies who, themselves understaffed and overburdened, tend to use such criteria to allocate their time. The first step in making MCAD an effective, viable instrument of manpower policy is appointing knowledgeable, committed commissioners and providing adequate staff and budget. (Ideally, an agency of this kind needs a budget automatically linked to the size of its case load.) Without these changes, MCAD cannot possibly play an effective role even within the narrowest and most confining interpretation of its present mandate.

Specific changes in the governing legislation that warrant consideration are an increase in the penalties which MCAD is empowered to impose and a separation of antidiscrimination policy in employment from other antidiscrimination policies administered by MCAD. Both these changes involve complex political judgments. Employment policy will be more effective the stronger the penalties that can invoked, but political opposition to the appointment of strong commissioners who will exercise their full statutory power is obviously stronger the greater that power is. My feeling is that, given the federal umbrella under which employment policy operates, the need for stronger state commissioners is much greater than the need for stronger state penalties. The separation of employment policy from other MCAD activities requires a consideration of the relative political support of different types of antidiscrimination policy and the relative merits of each. I infer from the relative strength of employment policy on the federal level, and more fundamentally from the constellation of political forces apparently responsible for it, that employment policy will generally be stronger than antidiscrimination policy in, for example, housing. If one were primarily interested in employment, therefore, this would argue for a separate agency concentrating upon employment policy alone. But if one were more interested, or equally interested, in antidiscrimination policy in housing, there is a good case for a single agency in which antidiscrimination policy in other areas can gain strength from the relative "popularity" of the employment segment of the agency's responsibilities.

A final organizational innovation that appears warranted is the establishment of a state office of contract compliance, comparable to the federal Office of Contract Compliance, with power to deny state business to contractors who discriminate in employment. There are, however, three basic understandings about employment discrimination without which the present statutes cannot be interpreted in a manner that will make them effective instruments of manpower policy: (1) No policy will effectively bar discrimination against qualified workers without forcing employers to hire some workers who are unqualified (or whose qualifications are inferior to those of other candidates); any attempt to avoid the second circumstance will permit discrimination against qualified workers to persist. (2) Neither employers administering an antidiscrimination policy internally nor the courts reviewing employment policy across enterprises and industries can operate effectively without imposing racial targets; these targets tend to be treated as quotas by the managers upon whom they are imposed. (3) Instituting and maintaining nondiscriminatory employment policies is a costly process, and the degree of resistance which these costs engender probably cannot be effectively countered under existing legislation unless the government bears at least part of the cost.

The first point about unqualified workers, follows from the statistical nature of employment decisions. Because employment decisions are based upon correlates of job performance, they are subject to two errors, the error of rejecting a qualified candidate and the error of accepting an unqualified one. Any attempt to reduce one error tends to increase the probability of committing the other. The two can be reduced simultaneously only by increasing the resources devoted to the screening process. In the case of hiring blacks in companies with little previous experience with a black labor force in high-quality jobs, obtaining large reductions in the two errors is very difficult—and, it appears, prohibitively expensive. Thus, any set of hiring criteria that employers utilize and the courts accept will either exclude qualified minority workers or admit unqualified ones, and MCAD and the courts must decide in which direction the error will run. Given the goal of eliminating poverty, it is desirable that the errors be on the side of admitting unqualified workers. This is particularly the case where "qualifications" essentially involve stable behavioral traits, for the unqualified will eventually drop out on their own. Title VII does not recognize the underlying problem, and no matter in what direction the courts resolve it, the decision will run counter to one provision or the other of the federal statute.

The importance of targets in administering antidiscrimination policy derives from the decentralized nature of most employment decisions. This, and the fact that employment discrimination tends to be extremely widespread, means that a policy of equal opportunity cannot be efficiently administered save "by exception." The central administration of an organization (or the courts) cannot, in other words, review every hire or promotion, but must confine itself to areas where there has been some previous indication of discriminatory procedures. Targets perform this function of selecting areas for review. The major alternative to targets is an internal complaint procedure, but such mechanisms have not generally been successful; outsiders do not have enough interest to pursue complaints, and insiders fear retaliation. Imposing targets need not necessarily imply a "quota," but it almost always has this effect. Low-level managers, not liking to attract the attention of their superiors, attempt to meet targets even if they are fairly confident that they can excuse their own failure to do so. This is even more true of managers dealing with outside agencies whose entrance into the company's internal affairs can be avoided by meeting prenegotiated targets. Here, again, effective administration conflicts with the provisions of the federal statute, which explicitly outlaws the use of racial quotas; but unless MCAD and the courts recognize the conflict and give priority to equal employment opportunity, the statute will be emasculated.

The problem of statistical errors and the problem of targets feed into a third aspect of the employment discrimination: preventing and eliminating it can give rise to significant organizational and administrative expenses. Public discussions generally fail to recognize this point. Legislative debate usually presumes that discrimination is a matter either of morality or of job monopoly. Economists, unfortunately, have tended to reinforce this view by discussing discrimination as an underutilization of minority workers and emphasizing that increased output should result from their employment in jobs that fully exploit their talents. This view neglects not only the increased costs of screening workers and of developing an administrative mechanism to police employment decisions within the organization, but also the costs imposed by employees' and supervisors' resentment during the early phases of employment integration, by upgrading campaigns for existing employees, or, in the extreme, by generous changes in the wage structure and distribution of work assignments. All these changes, however, are themselves expensive. This raises the question whether a part of these costs ought to be borne by the public at large. One possibility is for these services to be provided by MCAD. Because its present budget is not adequate for the performance of its existing function, however, it seems unwise to significantly expand its role in this direction. As noted, some other existing manpower programs appear to be providing technical assistance and subsidies for the integration of employment, and, for the time being, perhaps the best course is simply to permit this to occur.

Occupational licensing policy

The occupational licensing policies of Massachusetts impose several unnecessary barriers to those seeking access to the primary sector through licensed employment.[4] First, licensing policy is formulated and administered by a multitude of separate boards and agencies operating under several different pieces of legislation. The variety and diversity makes it difficult not only for the poor but for anyone seeking to counsel the poor (or anyone else for that matter) to get information about the range of different occupations.

Second, most of the licensing boards are composed of licensed members of the occupation which the boards govern; hence, they have

[4]For a national survey of state occupational licensing see U.S. Department of Labor, Manpower Administration, *Occupational Licensing and the Supply of Nonprofessional Manpower*, Manpower Research Monograph No. 11 (Washington D.C.: U.S. Government Printing Office, 1969).

strong economic incentives to limit entry. Under present legislation, the boards have a variety of instruments available for this purpose: artificially high licensing requirements, infrequent tests, inaccessible testing centers, inaccessible application forms, insufficient publicity, and so on.

Third, some licensing requirements, reasonable on their face, discriminate against the poor and could be supplemented or replaced by criteria that reduce their discriminatory impact. The requirement of "good moral character," for example, while reasonable for occupations involving house visits, is generally interpreted to exclude applicants with criminal or police records. The adverse effects of such interpretations might be limited, for example, by provisions waiving the criminal record bar if the individual is bonded or can supply personal references.

Finally, present procedures facilitate racial discrimination. Interviews or oral tests are used for this purpose. Most applications for licenses require pictures, and at least one application specifically asks for race.

Most artificial barriers imposed by present licensing procedures could be removed by the creation of a single licensing agency, either as a substitute for the present structure of occupational boards or with the power to review and revise both general regulations and, upon appeal, specific decisions of the individual boards. Such a centralized procedure now exists in a number of states.

DEPRESSED AREAS

Depressed areas in the state (among the cities visited, Lowell and New Bedford, but possible many more) warrant special consideration. The problems of these areas have been conventionally diagnosed as unemployment; the conventional prescription has been to attract new industries. As we noted early in the chapter, these conclusions are called into question by the findings of the study. New industries appearing in these areas have been experiencing labor shortages that have led them to recruit new migrants from the southern United States, Puerto Rico, and Cape Verde. The reported unemployment rates are exaggerated by the tendency of residents who normally work elsewhere to draw unemployment insurance in their place of residence. The high rates of migration to these areas and back to place of origin combine with the instability of many of the new jobs to create high levels of frictional unemployment. But part of the unemployment is quite real and reflects the fact that the older residents of the area are looking for primary employment and not for the secondary jobs which predominate in the new industries. There is some indication that the immigrants too eventually reject the secondary jobs.

The major implications of these findings is that the depressed areas not only may be failing to solve the problem of poverty among those already residing there, but also, in attempting to expand employment, may be attracting a new group of poor people to the state. The present investigation is too limited to support the major revisions in state policy which these findings imply, but it does suggest a major review of policy on depressed areas. Among the alternatives that ought to be considered are taxes that discourage some of the less attractive features of secondary employment: the unemployment insurance tax, for example, penalizes employment instability, and this penalty could be strenghtened. Another alternative policy might formalize the channels of migration between, for example, Massachusetts and San Juan so that secondary employment in Massachusetts becomes a training ground for primary jobs to which workers later return in San Juan. There would appear to be considerable room for innovative manpower programing if existing patterns of labor mobility to and from depressed areas of the state were more fully understood.

The organization of manpower programs

The organization of manpower programs is currently *the* central focus of debates about manpower policy not only in Massachusetts but also in other states and on the national level. Therefore, the subject is treated here as a separate topic, although analytically the distinction between organizational issues (particularly those organizational issues raised in the current debate) and other aspects of manpower policy is somewhat artifical. The concern about organization stems, as has been indicated, from the efforts of the Nixon administration to revise the administrative structure of manpower programs inherited from the Johnson administration, by executive order under existing legislation and ultimately by the passage of a new, comprehensive manpower act. In addition to the administration bill, there are also two other reorganization proposals before Congress: the Stiger bill, which is similar to the administration's bill, and the O'Hara bill, which represents, more or less, the Democratic alternative. At stake in these reforms is control over roughly $2.2 billion nationally for the categorical manpower programs and $284 million for the U.S. employment service. Massachusetts' share of these total amounts is $80 million and $20 million, respectively.

Reorganization at the federal level coincides in Massachusetts with administrative reform of state government. State reform could facilitate efforts of the Governor to gain ascendancy over existing state man-power organizations, particularly the Massachusetts employment service, in the new Office of Manpower Affairs. The Governor has in fact received planning funds from the Secretary of Labor intended to help build in the State House the planning capability required to assert effective control. On the other hand, strong forces oppose reorganization on both the state and the national level and the ultimate outcome of these various reorganizational efforts is by no means certain.

The Nixon proposals are the outgrowth of a fairly broad consensus among manpower experts that existing programs have not been very successful and that their failures can be traced to major organizational and administrative deficiencies. The deficiencies most frequently emphasized are three: (1) Program components are dispersed among a number of federal agencies—chiefly Labor, HEW, and OEO, but also, at times, HUD, Commerce, Agriculture, and Interior. (2) Washington attempts to deal directly with the literally thousands of local administrations and organizations throughout the country. (3) Funds are appropriated in a series of detailed categorical programs.

In all this, I take serious issue with my colleagues in the manpower field. I do not dispute the failures of present manpower programs. I would attribute those failures, however, to the difficulties inherent in the attempt to work against basic social and economic forces, in particular the forces that generate the dual labor market structure. It is not at all clear that any form of organization will be successful under these circumstances. But if these are indeed the circumstances, the prevailing diagnosis seriously mistakes the basic organizational problem. That problem is how to equip the programs to withstand the pressures generated by the conflict between the goal of eliminating poverty and the existing economic structure, which tends to perpetuate it. Those pressures pose two threats: the threat of rejection from the economic system and the threat of capture by its major institutions.

Programs that are administratively clean and neat, that look, smell, and feel well organized and tightly run, clearly tend, from the point of view of the poor, to be a failure. The failure in general results from the fact that neat, clean programs are those that fit easily into the existing institutional and market structure: they are efficiently run because they serve the interests of political and economic powers, and because they serve these interests, the powers have an incentive to ensure that the interests are served well. The administration, in instituting a manpower reorganization based upon narrow concern with administrative efficiency, is thus structuring the programs in such a way as to remove any genuine pressure to serve the poor. In concrete terms, the main effect of the reorganization is the reascendancy of the old-line manpower agencies—the employment service and the public school system—at the expense of the CAP agencies that grew up under OEO. This, it appears, is a far more significant aspect of the reform than any shift in power and control from federal to state government. The nature of the change can be seen by examining the three major manpower agencies—the employment service, the public schools, and the CAP agencies—and their respective positions in the present organization of manpower services which the Nixon administration is in the process of reforming.

THE STATE EMPLOYMENT SERVICE

The employment service was created by the Wagner-Peyser Act of 1933 essentially to act as a placement service. In that role it has traditionally served what I term the secondary labor market—indeed, the best operational definition of a secondary job is one which the employment service has in its files and is able to fill. This situation has several causes, none of them remedied easily and certainly not by the administration's reform bill. The most basic reason is that, because the secondary labor market has such high turnover and relatively undifferentiated jobs and workers, it is the sector which the employment service can most easily serve and which has the most interest in being served by it. In the primary sector, with lower turnover and more stable jobs, employers can afford to make the investment necessary to perform the service themselves, and the services required are more complex and more specialized. This fundamental bias is reinforced by two additional factors. First, the employment service is a large, bureaucratic, but decentralized institution in which levels of management (and government) depend upon performance indicators to monitor and control subordinates. The handiest, most readily assessable performance indicator is *placements.* Reliance upon *placements* as a success indicator biases the service toward the short-run, high-turnover jobs of the secondary sector. This bias has long been recognized, and various attempts have been made to supplement the placement index with other criteria, but the attempts have never been wholly successful. The second factor reinforcing the bias of the employment service toward secondary jobs is the fact that the organization is tied to the state civil-service system, with its low, compressed salary scale and discouraging promotion policy, making it difficult to attract and hold people who are effective in the primary labor market where placement is more than a mechanical referral operation. That the employment service has traditionally concentrated upon the secondary market may not, however, be of central importance in assessing its capacity to serve the poor. Even if the service could be forced, or induced, to operate in the primary sector, it would be under little internal pressure to refer secondary workers to primary jobs and might simply refer primary workers to primary jobs, as it now refers secondary workers to secondary jobs.

THE ALLIANCE OF THE EMPLOYMENT SERVICE AND THE PUBLIC SCHOOLS

The early programs under MDTA (Manpower Development and Training Act), which provided institutional training for skilled and semiskilled jobs, were handled through the state employment service, and these programs broadened the range of its operation from an agency concerned exclusively with placement to one providing training for workers as well. The training it provides is subcontracted, and most of the contract has gone to the public school system. The system has a very strong incentive to obtain these contracts. The training facilities in schools already exist: they represent a sunk cost. In almost all cases, they are idle after regular school hours and during vacations. Hence, they are underutilized. Any money the school system can obtain for the use of these underutilized facilities is thus pure profit. A further advantage of these programs to the school system is that they provide second jobs for its own teachers, most of whom would otherwise have to supplement their incomes in jobs more remote, geographically and in content, from their basic teaching duties and hence presumably less attractive and frequently less remunerative.

The problem with this linkage between the schools and the employment service, from the viewpoint of the poor, is that it builds into the training program all the biases against the poor inherent in the school system. It provides, in other words, training for adults in the same institutions, with the same equipment, by the same teachers, utilizing the same techniques that failed these adults when they were children.

Although perhaps adequate for groups whose failure to obtain high school training is attributable to lack of the motivation later acquired with maturity, such a program is not well designed to help people whose early failure can be attributed to social and class biases among instructors, to the location of schools, to the content of the programs offered, and to the techniques of instruction.

CAP AGENCIES

The basic alliance between the employment service and the public school system in the matter of institutional training has been maintained since the inception of the manpower programs. The War on Poverty, the creation of OEO, and the development of community action agencies as an alternative channel for the funding of manpower programs was, however, viewed by the Division of Employment Security and the school system (and, it should be noted, by the Washington counterparts of these agencies) as a serious threat. And, in fact, the Community Action Program agencies and the series of "community-based" manpower agencies to whom they subcontract have been major competitors with the DES and the school system for manpower funds. The competition, moreover, has not been confined to the "new" manpower activities, but extends as well to the traditional employment service function of counseling and placement. Whether the competitive threat of the CAP agencies produced any substantive changes in the employment service is moot. It could probably be argued that it would take more than four years for the employment service to respond to even as major a change in its external environment as the CAP competition was thought to represent. But what clearly did change was the vocabulary used by employment service officials to describe their mission and the deference, if not the actual power, accorded to those with some genuine interest in the poor.

The CAP agencies, in addition to competing with the employment service, are also very different institutions and respond to different sets of pressures; because they are, they have brought into play an altogether new set of forces. The major difference between the employment service and the CAP agency, as a manpower institution, is that the service is bureaucratic while CAP is political. This distinction has a number of different implications. First, there was, and in some communities there still is, a fight for political control of the CAP agencies. The important division, from this point of view, is the one between the new neighborhood forces which OEO sought to bring into being and the existing "power structure" with which the employment service, the public system, and secondary employers are generally allied. Where the latter group has won the battle, the CAP manpower programs are either operating inefficiently, if at all, outside the economic system, or are either operating inefficiently, if at all, outside the economic system, or else they are not very different from employment service programs catering essentially to the secondary labor market.

There is room for dispute about how best to characterize the CAP agency in which the "community" wins the initial power struggle. My own view is that, in the final analysis, we may fairly say that such a victory does build into the agency's manpower pressures to service the poor and that on the whole the pressures have directed the CAP programs toward efforts to move secondary workers into primary jobs. I would qualify this judgment, however, in two ways. First, that the programs have tried to move secondary workers into primary jobs does not imply that they have succeeded in doing so. Second, in the first year or two of operation, CAP agencies were heavily involved in programs like the Neighborhood Youth Corps and adult work crews that were operated more or less as secondary employment and that, to the extent they prepared people for jobs at all, prepared them for jobs in the secondary sector.

Two major pressures make "community-controlled" agencies responsive to the poor community. First, the budget of the CAP agency depends on its ability to continually justify its existence in Washington in an intensive competition for funds with the employment service in its own city (or state) and with CAP agencies from other parts of the country. The orchestration of this competition is now considered an intolerable administrative burden in Washington and is felt to create the need for decentralization to the state level. The outcome of competition depends upon the various political forces that govern the geographical distribution of all federal largesse. But the only social justification for CAP's role is service to the poor: the need to justify actions in these terms does set limits upon distribution which raw political power can effect, and at the margin it is the deciding factor. The employment service escapes this pressure because the major part of its budget is ensured from year to year. Any training funds it receives are marginal and, except in the long view, not critical to its existence. Further, establishment-controlled CAP agencies, which have no great interest in obtaining the funds, avoid much of this pressure.

The second set of pressures upon "community-controlled" CAP agencies comes from the community itself, for whatever degree of cohesion the community forces manage to achieve in their struggle with the establishment for initial control seldom extends to the exercise of that control once the community has gotten it. The struggle among community groups, like the struggle for funds in Washington, is governed by many factors, among which the kind of "community support" one might expect to derive from providing "quality" manpower services is only one and often, apparently, a minimal one. Nonetheless, it is a good deal more important in struggles for control of a CAP agency than for control of the employment service.

Finally, in addition to the initial struggle for community control, the highly political character of the funding process in Washington, and the competition within the community for power once control has been wrested from the establishment, CAP programs are distinguished from the bureaucratic character of the employment service programs (1)by the distribution of CAP employment as *patronage*, and (2) by *corruption*. The extent of both has probably been exaggerated, but they do exist. The corruption could be reduced, and I gather is to some extent being reduced by more careful controls from Washington (although attempting to do so increases the burdens of centralized funding, and to the extent that such centralization is critical to the CAP structure, a certain amount of corruption is part and parcel of the CAP package). The patronage is very much part of the CAP package and probably could not be eliminated without fundamentally changing the nature of the institution. The availability of patronage sparks competition for control within the community, a competition which, as we have seen, helps determine the agency's responsiveness to community needs. (Opportunities for graft have the same effect.) The patronage jobs within the agency also form the new career ladders out of the secondary sector discussed in the previous section. The experience in non-CAP manpower programs suggests that it is extremely difficult to maintain access to such jobs for the poor under institutionalized systems of job distribution.

Thus, in sum, the CAP agencies funded directly from Washington constitute the key to an organizational structure that will produce manpower programs directed at the movement of secondary workers into primary jobs. The pressures from Washington above and from the community below tend to make these agencies respond to the needs of the poor, even if they do not always succeed. And the competition for funds which these new agencies pose to the employment service-public school alliance constitutes the one real pressure upon the old-line agencies to become responsive.

From this viewpoint, the Nixon administration has been unfortunate. Nixon's election and the gradual unveiling of the administration's manpower policy has resulted in a resurgence of the power of the old employment service-public school alliance relative to the power of the CAP agencies.

Paradoxically, short of reversing national policy, the one hope to save the present organizational structure lies in the administration's own manpower bill, for it gives the Governor power to reassemble at the state level the OEO-CEP structure which is being dismantled in Washington. The clear implication of the preceding analysis is that the Governor ought to attempt to do exactly that.

Summary of policy recommendations

The major thrust of this chapter has been to develop a framework for the analysis of state manpower problems. That framework suggests that the most important decisions in this area are made at the federal level and that the present direction of federal policy is not conducive to effective manpower programs for the poor at the state level. Within the limitations imposed by the federal government, a number of state policies were, however, suggested. These may be summarized:

1. *State manpower planning and coordination.* The control over manpower funds which the federal policy is placing in the statehouse should be used to preserve the Community Action agencies as a competitor to the employment service and the public school system in the manpower area.

2. *Program content.* The content of the manpower programs should be shifted from short-term crash programs toward long-term basic education and occupational training and should concentrate upon the quality of employment opportunities rather than upon quantity.

3. *Public assistance.* A depersonalization of the public assistance system is needed, so that the behavioral traits it fosters are more compatible with those required for primary work. Such a depersonalization would include: (a) separation of payments and services; (b) conversion of special grants into a single flat grant based on family size and income; (c) formal recognition of elected client representatives in policy

formulation and grievance procedures; an (d) provision of social services on a voluntary basis.

In addition, the WINS program for welfare mothers, like other manpower programs, should be shifted from crash training to long-term basic education, occupational training, and language skills.

4. *Antidiscrimination policy:* (a) the MCAD budget should be increased and linked to the size of the agency's case load; (b) there should be increased cordination between MCAD and the various federal manpower programs; (c) precise quantitative targets should be used to evaluate compliance on the part of both business and trade unions.

5. *Occupational licensing:* (a) existing licensing boards should be consolidated under a single state agency; (b) there should be a single standard form for all state-licensed occupations; (c) regular administration of occupational licensing tests should be given regularly at a large number of centers throughout the state in a manner which permits an individual to take the test for any one of the state-licensed occupations at any one of the testing centers.

6. *Depressed area policy.* The state should undertake a major study of economic development in its depressed areas, aiming particularly at understanding the rising in-migration of low-wage workers at the same time that unemployment among longtime residents remains high.

CHARLES I. SCHOTTLAND

public
assistance

Now, when the state is preparing to group public welfare services under a "human services" umbrella[1] along with other state services, and when the federal government is considering new and far-reaching changes that could affect significantly the welfare programs in the state,[2] the time does seem ripe for an analysis and consideration of changes that might improve the cash assistance and social service programs of the commonwealth. Certainly we must either improve the present program of

Charles I. Schottland is professor of social welfare in the Florence Heller School for Advanced Studies in Social Welfare and acting president of Brandeis University. He is pleased to acknowledge the important contributions to this paper of Vincent F. Ciampa who prepared much of the material upon which it is based.

[1]The Modernization Bill, passed by the Massachusetts legislature in July 1969 and effective in April 1971, creates nine cabinet groups. The Human Services cabinet would include the departments of public welfare, public health, mental health, youth services, rehabilitation, and other programs.

[2]For example, President Nixon's proposed Family Assistance Plan now incorporated into H.R. 4173, now before the Congress; his proposed Manpower Bill, H.R. 3472; and a "social services" package now being discussed in Congress and the Administration.

public assistance or replace it with some other form of transfer payment to provide income to those who do not have enough money to buy the necessities of life.

Public assistance in 1970

That government has a responsibility to care for the poor has been recognized since the beginning of organized community life. The colonists brought with them to America the inheritance of the English Poor Laws, which recognized governmental responsibility for relief of distress due to poverty but which limited assistance to residents of the local community[3] and to those who could not be supported by relatives; they also placed such responsibility upon local governments.[4] In 1863 Massachusetts became the first state to establish a welfare department. Today the Massachusetts Department of Public Welfare operates programs of public assistance—Old Age Assistance, Aid to the Blind, Aid to Permanently and Totally Disabled, Aid to Families with Dependent Children, General Assistance, Medicaid (which is closely related to public assistance), child welfare, and related services.[5] It is to these state services that the term "public welfare" refers.

Public assistance in Massachusetts provides money payments to individuals and families whose income is below the standard set by the state. The amount of the payment depends upon a "budget of need."

The major public assistance programs are established by the Social Security Act, and the federal government reimburses the state on a formula established by the act for payments made to individuals and families and for the cost of administering the program. We shall describe briefly the four federal-state programs and the Massachusetts program of General Assistance.

Old-age assistance

Old-Age Assistance (OAA) is the present-day descendant of "old-age pension" plans developed in some states before enactment of the So-

[3]The courts have recently declared unconstitutional a residence requirement for receiving public assistance (*Shapiro v. Thompson*, Supreme Court of the United States, 1969, 89 S. Ct. 1322 [1969]).

[4]More than half the states have transferred the administration of public assistance to state government.

[5]For size of programs see Table −1.

cial Security Act in 1935. Today, it is a federal-state program pursuant to federal law.[6]

In July 1969, 49,600 persons received Old-Age Assistance in Massachusetts at a monthly cost of $4,408,000 (cash payments only). The average cash payment was $88.95, compared with $70.95 for the country as a whole. The figure of $88.95 is the average payment. However, if a person has no income whatsoever, the aged person receives from $112.99 to $160.55, depending upon the person's living arrangements. Unlike AFDC, the Massachusetts average payment is exceeded by those of eight states.[7]

The 49,600 Old-Age Assistance recipients in Massachusetts have characteristics similar to the 2,041,000 (July 1969) recipients in the United States. In the United States, the median age of Old Age Assistance recipients is 76.6 years—4.1 years higher than the median for the total population aged 65 and over. More than two-thirds are women. Because of physical or mental conditions, 17 percent of all recipients are confined to their homes and eight percent are bedfast or chairfast. Of recipients not confined to their homes, one in eight needs help to get around outside the home; about one in six receives some support from children; about two-thirds have income apart from Old-Age Assistance, primarily from Old-Age, Survivors, Disability, and Health Insurance. In Massachusetts about two-thirds of those receiving OAA also receive OASDHI.

The financing of Old-Age Assistance, like that of other categories, has been complicated and changing. The federal government normally pays 50 percent of state and local costs of administration. However, in 1962 an amendment was enacted which provides for a reimbursement of 75 percent of administrative expenses for those portions of a state's expenditures that meet certain minimum requirements for providing services leading to rehabilitation and self-support. The purpose of this increased federal reimbursement is to induce the states to emphasize rehabilitation in the administration of public assistance. The 75 percent provision applies also to Aid to the Blind, Aid to Families with Dependent Children, and Aid to the Permanently and Totally Disabled.

The formula for determining the federal share of the assistance payment to the recipient has undergone several changes since 1935, when

[6]Title I, Social Security Act as amended.
[7]Alaska, $90.70; California, $105.65; Connecticut, $90.35; Hawaii, $96.65; Iowa, $108.60; New Hampshire, $116.95; New York, $93.90; Wisconsin, $90.55.

The formula for determining the federal share of the assistance payment to the recipient has undergone several changes since 1935, when a very simple arrangement provided for federal payment of one-half of the first $30, or a maximum of $15 a month. Changes in the formula have been made every few years. In 1968 the reimbursement formula continued the emphasis on providing more federal matching funds to states with low per capita income. The federal share of OAA payments made in states that have a medical assistance program is 31/37ths of the first $37 of a maximum average monthly payment of $75 per recipient, plus a proportion (varying from 50 to 65 percent, depending on the state's per capita income) of the next $35 of such payment. If, for example, a state pays the OAA recipient $90 in cash, the federal government reimburses the state from $50 to $58.40:

		High-income state such as Massachusetts	Low-income state
31/37ths of the first	$37.00	$31.00	$31.00
50% of the next	38.00	19.00	
65% of the next	38.00		27.40
		$50.00	$58.40

Massachusetts receives the lowest federal reimbursement. Any sums paid out that exceeds $50 a month per recipient must come entirely from state or local funds.

When the Social Security Act was passed, it was anticipated that OAA would be a temporary program and eventually would disappear as OASDHI expanded. However, benefits under OASDHI have remained too low to eliminate all financial needs of the aged. Many people, especially women, have not worked in employment covered by OASDHI, and a variety of other factors have resulted in OAA's remaining a substantial program. The 15 percent increase in Social Security payments voted by the U.S. House and Senate in December 1969 will make some Massachusetts Old-Age Assistance recipients ineligible because their outside income will exceed the Massachusetts standard; many others will receive smaller payments from Old-Age Assistance, thereby saving some funds for Massachusetts. However, Old-Age Assistance will remain at approximately the same level for many years to come unless radical changes occur. The population aged 65 and over has been increasing at a rapid rate. As of January 1, 1969, the U.S. had 19.5 million persons aged 65 and over compared with 16.6 million in 1960, 12.4 million in 1950, and 9.0 million in 1940. This increase will continue sistance should keep OAA recipients at about the same number in Massachusetts for several years.

Aid to the blind (AB)

In July 1969 Massachusetts supported 2,600 blind persons at a monthly cost of $378,000. The average payment was $148.15—the highest of any state.[8] The average for the United States was $95.30. By July 1969 there had been a gradual decrease in the number of recipients in the United States to 80,000, and this decrease is expected to continue as Old-Age, Survivors, Disability, and Health Insurance increases its benefit levels, as vocational rehabilitation and other training programs make more blind people self-supporting, and as medical progress reduces the total number of blind persons. Almost one out of five AB recipients also receives OASDHI in the United States. Recipients are about equally divided between men and women, and more than two-thirds are white. About one out of 12 is employed at least part-time, and more than a third have income other than Old-Age Assistance, mostly from OASDHI.

Financing arrangements with the federal government and federal requirements are the same as for Old-Age Assistance.

Aid to the permanently and totally disabled (APTD)

Aid to the Permanently and Totally Disabled is the most recently established of the federal assistance programs categorized by recipient. It became part of the Social Security Act by means of the amendments of 1950. It was established because of growing recognition that many disabled poor were in desperate need. The Social Security Act makes a person eligible for APTD if he is 18 years of age or older and is "permanently and totally disabled." In July 1969 Massachusetts paid out $1,668,000 to 15,500 APTD recipients, for an average monthly payment of $107.50.[9] The average payment to the 763,000 recipients in the United States was $86.25. About 26 percent of recipients in the U.S. are disabled because of a mental or personality disorder, including 15 percent who are mentally deficient; 21 percent suffer from diseases of the circulatory system, mostly heart disease; and the whole gamut

[8] Nine other states had payments of over $100.00: Alaska, $120.60; California, $145.80; Hawaii, $112.35; Iowa, $123.25; New Hampshire, $115.55; New York, $115.55; Oklahoma, $101.95; Oregon, $111.30; Pennsylvania, $110.45.

[9] Only five states had higher payments: Alaska, $115.55; California, $121.95; Connecticut, $108.75; Hawaii, $131.00; Kansas, $134.15.

of disabling illnesses accounts for more than 53 percent. The number of persons receiving APTD is not expected to increase very much during the next several years because of the impact of disability insurance under OASDHI, increased activities under the federal-state program of vocational rehabilitation, and medical care under Medicare and Medicaid.

The financing of the program follows the same federal reimbursement formula that applies to Old-Age Assistance.

General assistance

"General assistance" is the name applied to public programs of assistance to needy persons that are financed completely by state or local funds and that pay benefits either in cash or in kind to needy persons in their own homes or in institutions. It is a "residual" program, covering cases not cared for under the Social Security Act public assistance categories, and in some instances it may supplement the aid received by the individual or family under the federal public assistance categories.

Fourteen thousand cases representing 26,000 people received general assistance in Massachusetts in July 1969. Payments to recipients during that month were $1,541,000, averaging $109.25 for each case or $59.35 for each recipient. In the United States as a whole 390,000 cases representing 784,000 persons received general assistance at a cost for the month of $37,834,000, averaging $96.90 per case or $48.25 per recipient. However, making comparisons with other states is difficult because eligibility requirements and levels of payment vary widely. In general, the cases on this residual program increase or decrease depending on the level of unemployment.

Aid to families with dependent children (AFDC)

When most persons speak of the "growing crisis in public welfare" or the "welfare mess" or the "welfare problem," they mean Aid to Families with Dependent Children and not the three adult categories discussed previously. AFDC is Massachusetts' most expensive public assistance program. In July 1969 Massachusetts paid out $11,580,-000 in AFDC cash payments to 50,300 needy families that contained 184,000 persons, of whom 135,000 were children. The average payment was $230.10 for each family or $62.95 for each recipient. The national averages were $174.25 and $44.30.

The rapid increase in recipients is due partly to the increase in the child population during the past three decades. In January 1969, the U.S. had 78.1 million children under 18, compared with 49.1 million in 1950 and 42.4 million in 1940. During the next decade, 1970–1980, the number of children under 18 is expected to decrease slightly, if present estimates of birth rates are correct. The rise in the AFDC case load is also affected by the increasing family disorganization in the United States, as is evidenced by separation, desertion, divorce, and birth out of wedlock. An important factor is poor people's growing acceptance of AFDC as a program that does not carry the stigma it once did. More than 233,000 Massachusetts families are "poor," or about 18.1 percent of the state's families (see Chapter 1, Table 1–2). Only 50,300 families are on AFDC, or about 22 percent of Massachusetts' poor families. Without discussing in detail the differences in measuring the "poor" and those eligible for AFDC, we can see that many families are potentially eligible for AFDC and that they provide a reservoir of needy families that will continue to join the AFDC rolls.

AFDC is the modern descendant of the old "mother's pension" programs brought to an end by the AFDC program under the Social Security Act. The Social Security Act recognizes four reasons for dependency of children under AFDC:

1. Physical or mental incapacity of a parent
2. Death of a parent
3. Continued absence of a parent from the home
4. Unemployment of a parent

The financing of AFDC differs from that of the three adult categories. The maximum monthly AFDC payment in which the federal government shares is $32 per month for each recipient ($100 for children in foster care). Federal funds pay five-sixths of the first $18 of the average payment and then 50 to 65 percent of the balance depending on the state's per capita income. Massachusetts receives 50 percent. Reimbursement for administrative expenditures follows the OAA formula.

In Massachusetts some significant facts characterize AFDC:

1. Eight out of ten families consist only of a mother and her children.
2. In 97 percent of families the mother is in the home.
3. The average length of stay on AFDC is one year and 10 months.
4. Eighty percent of AFDC families are white.
5. Families are generally small. Nearly half have only one or two children; 28 percent are two-child families; 20 percent are three-

child families; 23 percent are one-child families; and 17 percent have five or more children.

6. Eighty percent of the children are 12 years old or younger.
7. Only one-fourth of the mothers have finished high school.
8. Of the fathers 82 percent were absent from the home; 32.2 percent were divorced or legally separated; 25.4 percent had deserted or separated without a court decree. Twenty percent of the children had fathers who were not married to the mother.
9. Twelve percent of the mothers were working either full- or part-time. Of the mothers 65 percent were born in Massachusetts.   10.

These characteristics do not bear out some "images" of AFDC. As can be seen, AFDC families are predominantly white and are long-time residents of Massachusetts; the majority do not remain on the AFDC rolls for extended periods, and the mothers have limited education.

Level of assistance

Although many questions have been raised about the low level of assistance in the adult categories, the major controversy and the largest cost to the state of Massachusetts is the AFDC program. The question most frequently debated is, "How high should public assistance grants go in AFDC?" The question reflects the conflicting goals of the state program. The state has sought to provide a reasonable standard to meet the needs of the poorest of the nonworking poor but does not want assistance levels so high that they provide a disincentive to work.

There is little question that the general standards and levels of assistance through AFDC in the United States as a whole are too low to provide poor families with the minimal level of living consistent with health and decency. The President's Advisory Council on Public Welfare, appointed in 1964, made a report that reflected the views of almost 350 individuals and organizations who had studied the question and discussed it in six regional meetings.[10] The report stated the problem clearly and forcefully: "Public assistance payments are so low and so uneven that the Government is, by its own standards and definitions, a major source of poverty on which it has declared unconditional war."[11]

[10]Fedele F. Fauri, "Improving Public Welfare: The Report of the Advisory Council," *Public Welfare*, 25, 1 (January 1967), 3–7.
[11]Advisory Council on Public Welfare, *Having the Power, We Have the Duty*, Report to the Secretary of Health, Education, and Welfare (Washington, D.C.: U.S. Department of Health, Education, and Welfare, Welfare Administration, 1966), p. xii.

Even if the level of AFDC assistance in Massachusetts is among the three or four highest in the country, is this level adequate? Any answer depends upon comparison with some reliable measures of poverty.

Two budgets generally used are those of the Social Security Administration and the Department of Labor. The Social Security Administration budget, sometimes called the "Orshansky economy poverty line," can be compared with Massachusetts AFDC:

	Mass. AFDC yearly grant	Orshansky poverty line (1968)
Three-person family (Mother, 2 children 7–12)	$2,754	$2,600
Four-person family (Mother, 2 children 7–12, one child 13–20)	3,338	3,335
Five-person family (Mother, four children)	3,922	3,930

The Massachusetts AFDC allowance could vary with a large number of such factors as age of children or special allowances for prescribed diets. Nevertheless, on the basis of the Orshansky poverty line, certain families seem to be slightly above and others slightly below such a line. The question is, "Does the Orshansky poverty line permit a family to live in health and decency?" This question was answered *no* by the Massachusetts Department of Public Welfare in the study issued in September 1969. Relying on recent U.S. Department of Labor studies of family needs in terms of 1967 prices, the study set forth a lower budget of $6,251 , a moderate budget of $8,925, and a higher budget of $13,301 (for families of four living in rented quarters).

Without making complicated comparisons of the Massachusetts AFDC budget with the Bureau of Labor Statistics budgets, we can see that the findings and conclusions of the study are significant and serious. The study concluded:

1. The Bureau of Labor Statistics study, "Three Standards of Living," is extremely thorough and detailed, and, together with its related documents, can serve as a valid base from which to derive reasonable assistance standards for the continuing monthly grants to families with dependent children.

2. The existing basic Aid to Families with Dependent Children assistance standards are not sufficient to permit families to acquire the consumption items needed to maintain life at a level of decency.

3. AFDC grants are not large or inclusive enough to permit children receiving them to participate in school, religious or community activities on the same basis as most children.

4. The basic assistance grant to an AFDC family of four provides nearly $1,353 a year less than is needed when the Bureau of Labor Statistics data is used as a basis for comparison. Using the same yardstick, comparable discrepancies exist in the AFDC grants for different size families and different age groupings of children.

5. The greatest deficiencies in AFDC standards result from the fact that essential items of consumption were not included in the basic budget as established in 1947.

6. There are substantial deficits in the amounts allotted for the basic consumption items in the AFDC grant. For these items, even with the application of cost of living increases, the amounts are inadequate.[12]

The basic question is: Can Massachusetts continue to provide a level of assistance that maintains several hundred thousand persons below a standard necessary for a healthy and "normal" existence? As the present system continues, Massachusetts should determine a "reasonable" budget of need and make it available to all public assistance recipients. Such a budget should be updated every year. If we set as a goal "that assistance grants to families with children must have as their purpose to provide an income sufficient to obtain the food, shelter, clothing, and other basic items of consumption needed to maintain family life at a level of decency and dignity,"[13] clearly the level of assistance must be raised substantially, probably in the neighborhood of 30 to 50 percent. This matter must be given the kind of study and analysis that has been undertaken in several states. The Governor of Massachusetts has already taken a step to increase individual grants by announcing, in February 1970, that families of four would receive a "flat grant" of $3,760, which would provide an average increase of about $500 a family and eliminate "special needs" grants except in emergencies.

While we await fundamental long-range changes in the total public assistance picture, we recommend that:

1. The Massachusetts Department of Public Welfare develop machinery for an annual review of levels of assistance.

---

[12]*Study of Standard Family Budget,* p. 8.
[13]*Study of Standard Family Budget,* p. 6.

2. The present levels of assistance be increased by an amount deemed necessary to meet the goals established in the 1969 *Study of Standard Family Budget.*

3. "Special" needs that are in fact universally required by recipients, like winter clothing, should be included in the increased standard budget, and the category of "special needs" should be limited to items that actually are not universally required. Such a policy would reduce administrative work loads and minimize recurring demands for special-need grants.

Level of assistance and work incentives

A basic dilemma faces policy-makers when they try to answer questions about how the level of assistance affects work incentives: When the level of assistance is higher than the minimum wage, will people work? This question will be a major subject for debate as proposals for a guaranteed income made by President Nixon, by the National Commission on Income Maintenance Programs, and by individuals and groups promoting "negative income tax" ideas and family or children's allowances receive consideration in the immediate future.

For the present, however, Massachusetts must conduct its public assistance programs under existing federal-state arrangements. Under the present programs, it must be recognized, very few of the 278,000 persons now receiving some form of cash assistance are employable except under very special conditions. Many believe that work incentives for most of the poor on public assistance are irrelevant. The public assistance recipients are not now in the labor force and, except for a small group, do not have the potential to join the labor force. We must immediately eliminate from the employable category most of the 50,000 receiving OAA (average age 76 and mostly women), the 15,-500 receiving APTD, the 2,600 receiving AB, most of the 26,000 receiving General Assistance (some are too old but not eligible for OAA, others are on assistance for a brief period only, etc.), and also most of the 135,000 children, most of them very young, who are on AFDC. We are left with fewer than 50,000 adults in the AFDC category. Some must stay home and care for very young children. If these women are to work, they must bring a caretaker into the home, for most of these families are fatherless. Or extensive day-care programs must be provided. (Several thousand adults on AFDC are now working, and their grants make up the difference between their earnings and the present budget of need.) Some adult caretakers are not the parents of the children and are not legally responsible for their support; others may be disabled; still other cases may present a variety of factors that make employment highly unlikely or unwise.

Although data are not available, experience in other states suggests that at most 10,000 persons *might* be suitable for employment. But the difficulties must not be overlooked. Lack of education and training, lack of work experience, inability to obtain child care, difficulty of finding jobs for marginal workers—all these factors have greatly limited the effect of such programs as Work Incentive Program or WIN (organized by the federal government in 1967 to place such persons in jobs).

Assuming, then, that every effort is made to place welfare clients in jobs, we must recognize that relatively few will be placed. Nevertheless, there are important values in encouraging those able and desirous of getting work or training to do so. The state must develop adequate plans and programs similar to those that a few other states have developed.

But will a high level of assistance discourage work? We believe that, at reasonable levels of assistance, the disincentive factor has been overstated. The Heineman commission, which studied the disincentive effects of a guaranteed income, felt that they "would not be serious." It recommended an incentive plan that would allow workers to retain a percentage of earnings so that the plan "would always result in significantly higher income for those who work than for those who do not."[14] The Nixon welfare reform proposal likewise has such a provision.

Pending major changes on the national scene, we recommend that Massachusetts develop a scale of "incentive earnings" whereby public assistance recipients who work will be permitted to retain a much larger proportion of their earnings than they now may keep. The formula should include disregarding the first few dollars of earnings, (perhaps the first $100 a month), which would not reduce the public assistance grant, and then reducing the grant by 50 cents for each dollar earned. Assume a budget of $4,800 for a family of four getting public assistance and selected earnings each month:

A maximum income would need to be fixed, and the guidelines for this maximum figure might be those provided by the budgets developed by the U. S. Department of Labor.

---

[14]*Poverty Amidst Plenty: The American Paradox,* The Report of the President's Commission on Income Maintenance Programs (Washington, D.C.: U.S. Government Printing Office, 1969).

Public assistance	Exempt earnings	50% of other earnings	Monthly income
$400	$100	—	$500
400	100	$200	600
400	100	300	650

this maximum figure might be those provided by the budgets developed by the U. S. Department of Labor.

Again, it should be emphasized that even with such incentives, the number of public assistance recipients who will be able to work will be small. However, those who can and should work can be encouraged by the prospect of some economic gain.

GENERAL CONSIDERATIONS FOR PUBLIC ASSISTANCE

Pending long-range changes, certain additional steps should be considered by the state to improve the administration of public assistance. One step is the complete separation of money payments and social services. This has already begun in Massachusetts and is in effect in other states. It is now accepted federal policy.[15] Relieving the public assistance worker of the responsibility for determining eligibility will reduce certain costs of administration and enable many workers to concentrate on more constructive social services.

A second step which has already begun but which should be implemented completely and fully is substituting of an affidavit as evidence of eligibility for the more costly and exhaustive investigation to determine need. Applicants for aid would establish eligibility by a personal statement, just as one files one's income tax; the application would be subject to sample reviews and checks carried out so as not violate the recipient's dignity, privacy, or legal rights.

A third possible step is the combining of all public assistance categories into one overall category based solely on need. Federal regulations now permit the state of Massachusetts to do this if it so desires. Such a step would eliminate much of the administrative work for separate categories. A single set of budgets of need would be applicable to all persons receiving public assistance, and need would be the sole measure of entitlement. Reimbursement from the federal government would become essentially an accounting matter,

[15]It is also the stated position of such professional bodies as the National Association of Social Workers.

the public assistance program should be kept in mind; they provide background for improving the existing state program of public assistance, and for developing the position the Governor and the state administration should take with regard to new appraoches and federal responsibility.

1. Until fundamental changes occur in federal law, public assistance will continue to be the state's basic program to provide a minimum income for the poor of Massachusetts who cannot get income through work, Social Security, or other sources.

2. An adequate level of assistance will be costly, and this fact should influence the state to urge federal assumption of the public assistance burden. However, while the state operates the public assistance program, it must consider the increased costs of more adequate public assistance budgets.

3. The public assistance case load, primarily AFDC, will continue to rise because of several factors:

(*a*) Thousands of poor are eligible for AFDC in Massachusetts but have not applied for it. As they learn they are eligible and overcome their antagonism to welfare programs, more will apply for assistance.

(*b*) Children born out of wedlock, desertion, divorce, and other problems will continue at the present level or even increase, causing a continued increase in the eligible pool of AFDC applicants.

(*c*) Migration into Massachusetts, although not previously a major factor, will continue to bring into the state people who do not have the education, skill, or color to become self-supporting as easily as those without such handicaps.

(*d*) The increasing demand for "skills" and the decreasing demand for unskilled labor will provide an additional pool of possible applicants.

One must look at the increase in recipients as a desirable result, though a costly one. If the recipients are poor and eligible, it means that more of them are finding a minimum income for a minimum existence. It means a better and healthier citizenry.

4. Any work-incentive program will also be costly. The more liberal (and therefore more effective) the incentive, the more marginal workers will be eligible for public assistance.

5. Public assistance itself cannot solve the problems of inadequate wages, and levels of public assistance cannot be established in relation to minimum wages or other criteria not relevant to the minimum cost of maintaining recipients on a level of health and decency.

Public assistance and new proposals for a guaranteed income

Federal assumption of responsibility for public assistance has been endorsed not only by the state governors but large numbers of professional organizations and citizens' groups. These endorsements have been made because of the recognition that the present system is not working. The present federal-state arrangement was established in the depths of the Great Depression, and the idea that each state should be free to support the poor at such level as it saw fit seemed a reasonable objective and, for that period, an adequate one. Today we take a national view of the goal of adequate income for all, and we do not look with approval upon hungry children in Mississippi merely because that state is poor and may not be able to afford an adequate assistance level. Furthermore, the attempt to secure uniform administration under federal regulations has been a failure. Administrative practice under the same federal regulations varies from state to state and even from locality to locality within a state.[16] This fact verifies other studies that indicate widespread evasion of the intent of Federal policies.[17]

President Nixon has proposed a Family Assistance Plan (FAP) that will tackle some of the problems discussed in this chapter. The plan would provide for payment entirely from federal funds, at the rate of $500 a year for each of the first two members and $300 for each additional member, or $1,600 a year for a family of four. The major effect of the FAP would be for the first time to cover the so-called working poor—families headed by a man working full time—by a program of financial assistance established by the federal government. It is estimated that this group of working poor consists of some two to three million families.

[16]See United States Department of Health, Education, and Welfare, Region III, *Report of Findings in the Administrative Review of the Applications Process in the Virginia Department of Welfare and Institutions, October 1959–March 1960.*

[17]See Winifred Bell, *Aid to Dependent Children* (New York: Columbia University Press, 1965); U.S. Department of Health, Education, and Welfare *Study of ADC Application Process in Six Selected Counties in New Jersey,* August 1960.

As a work incentive the first $60 per month ($720 per year) of earned income and 50 percent of additional income would be disregarded in determining the amount of benefit. With specified exceptions adult applicants for assistance would be required to register with the public employment office for training or employment. There are many other specifics in the FAP proposal that need not be detailed here.

The Family Assistance Plan seeks to set a minimum standard of assistance, to encourage work, and to include the poor who are not receiving public assistance. It does present a number of problems:

1. The $1,600 minimum federal payment for a family of four is too low.

2. The plan perpetuates the state-federal partnership; it does not provide for federal operation of public assistance. States would have the option of turning administration over to the federal government, but states are not likely to do that while they are carrying the entire cost. The bill provides newly rationalized standards for state programs, but there is no reason to suppose they will be more readily enforceable. The penalty provided is a variant of the one that has already failed to work —withholding federal funds.

3. Much has been made of the argument that Nixon's program will wipe out a form of discrimination against the working poor, but the FAP will itself discriminate. The working poor will receive the FAP level, while the current AFDC case load and similar persons will receive the higher levels that states will be required to maintain. A lower payment is less discriminatory than no payment at all, but it would not be surprising if the working poor found the new distinction more inflammatory than the old.

4. In at least 40 states in which current assistance levels are higher than FAP's level will be, people will have to apply to two sets of welfare officials instead of one. And possibly—the point is not clear—they will have to satisfy two sets of dissimilar requirements to get the very payment the current program would provide.

Another proposal that is receiving increased attention is embodied in the report of the Presidential Commission on Income Maintenance (called the Heineman commission and previously mentioned).[18]

The central recommendation of the commission is for the creation of

---

[18]*Poverty Amid Plenty: The American Paradox.*

a universal income supplement program financed and administered by the federal government and making payments based on income to everyone who meets the test of need. It is recommended that the program be initiated at a level providing a base income of $2,400 a year for a family of four. This payment would be reduced by fifty cents for each dollar of other income, so that the cutoff point for a family of four would be $4,800. On this basis the program would cost about $7 billion of new federal money, and it would raise the income of 36 million persons, if operative for the full year 1971.

The benefit level of $2,400, which is below the poverty line for a family of four, was chosen because as a practical matter it could be implemented in the near future. To immediately set the program at the poverty line would cost an estimated $27 billion and would provide payments to 24 million households. The commission recommends that the benefit levels be raised as rapidly as is practical and possible after the program is adopted, recognizing that a program of that potential magnitude must move up in steps.

The commission also recommends that federal matching funds be made available on a 50-50 basis for a new, locally administered, non-categorical, temporary assistance program. This would provide for short-term emergency income needs that, because of time lags, could not be met under the basic federal program.

The commission's proposal meets some of the objections to the FAP. Its benefit levels are higher; it acknowledges that the benefit levels should be increased; and it would cover everyone. But it still involves the state, and benefit levels would still be low. It is difficult to justify a program that for years to come settles for a benefit level below the poverty line—particularly when our GNP today makes it possible to establish a higher level.

Massachusetts officials ought to support President Nixon's proposals modified to:

1. Increase the level of assistance to a figure above the poverty line.
2. Eliminate the states as participants and make the program entirely a federal responsibility.
3. Eliminate the compulsory work provisions, making the work decision dependent upon the facts of each case.
4. Broaden coverage to include all the poor.

If these recommendations could be incorporated into the FAP, it would be a proposal that would go far toward eliminating poverty in the United States, enable Massachusetts to divert more than $273 million to other needed purposes, and be a program much more acceptable to the nation's poor.

In summary, Massachusetts should urge immediate federalization of public assistance and enactment of the FAP with certain improvements mentioned above.

The social services

The Massachusetts Department of Public Welfare has developed a variety of social services. A social service program for children has developed through its Division of Child Guardianship. Other "services" have been limited for the most part to the recipients of public assistance. This concentration of services on recipients of public assistance has hindered the development of a comprehensive program of social services for all Massachusetts residents who need them.

With the separation of the money payment from services in public assistance, an inevitable change under present federal policies, the state will have an opportunity to develop a meaningful program of social services such as many envisioned when the state took over the administration of public assistance from the towns. Assuming an adequate program of money payments to public assistance recipients, such recipients, and other people as well, will still require a variety of social services.

BACKGROUND OF SOCIAL SERVICES

The United States has developed over its history thousands of organizations and agencies engaged in social service activities. Settlement houses, family counseling services, child welfare agencies, YMCAs and YWCAs, probation services, adoption agencies—these are representative of thousands of governmental and voluntary organizations rendering social services to Americans. Such a varied group of agencies and programs presents difficulties when we try to encompass them in a single term like "social services."

With the exception of child welfare services, the social services provided by Massachusetts' public welfare program, through the Department of Public Welfare, have grown in connection with the various adult public assistance programs. Such services were promoted by the 1956 and 1962 amendments to the Social Security Act, which set as a goal for such services the decreasing of dependency and the enhancing of self-support, self-care, and personal independence, strengthening of family life, and providing of protection to those who live in hazardous conditions or lack adequate care. The federal law provided that 75 percent of the cost of such services would be borne by the federal government.

Although Massachusetts has received the 75 percent reimbursement, the "social services" provided by the Massachusetts program have been minimal; they have been administered at the client or recipient level by untrained and generally unqualified personnel; and the development of an adequate program will necessitate far-reaching changes if Massachusetts is to have effective social services. It is important that Massachusetts have such a program not only because its residents will increasingly demand it, but also because the Federal government seems likely soon to be launching new moves to have such social services operated by the states. At the present time, the Nixon administration is considering federal grants to assist states in conducting such programs, and the Task Force on the Organization of Social Services recommended that such services be established for "all citizens."

When the state of Massachusetts took over the public welfare program from the towns, it planned to organize the social services through 37 centers throughout the state. State planners are now studying the relation of such centers to alternative ways of making the proposed Human Resources Cabinet an effective mechanism for integrating and coordinating the program. The comments and recommendations that follow are made in the context of such planning under a human services rubric.

Neighborhood information centers

In the welter of services now available, the average citizen finds it difficult to know all the resources available to assist him. The importance of neighborhood information centers and their value in the current urban scene have been studied and evaluated by many persons and groups.[20] Such centers can be established in selected local offices

---

[20]The Ford Foundation supported an extensive study. See *Neighborhood Information Center, A Study and Some Proposals* (New York: Columbia School of Social Work, 1966). See also *Task Force on Organization of Social Services.*

of the Department of Public Welfare, in Model City agency facilities, in neighborhood antipoverty programs centers, and in other agencies. It is recommended that the state Department of Public Welfare should experiment with three or four such centers as a step toward a statewide network.

Universality of services

Unlike present practices, which limit many social services to special groups, Massachusetts should provide social services that in type and quality are good enough for all of its citizens. This universality of services conveys recognition that all citizens may need social services at some time. We do not believe that such services should be organized for the poor alone, as some now are. Generally, services for the poor become poor services. Massachusetts should make its social services a broad, community-based program available to everyone. Certain services should give priority to the poor and disadvantaged but should be organized as a total community service.

Freedom of choice

At present social services are provided mainly by the government and by nonprofit voluntary agencies. Some are of good quality, and some have serious shortcomings. Taken as a whole, services provided by voluntary nonprofit agencies have expanded comparatively little since the end of World War II and hardly more than was necessary to match expansion of the population. Government services have expanded markedly but in an uneven and sporadic manner so that some, such as day care, are woefully inadequate.

One way to secure rapid expansion of needed services is to make it possible for consumers to buy services in the marketplace. At the same time, the quality of government services would be improved by competition with nongovernment agencies. One desirable method which deserves to be tried is an individualized benefit system: the state could make available to eligible people vouchers or identification cards that could be used to purchase service from among competing purveyors. The purveyors would in turn receive payment from the state. A variation of this process could involve cooperatives formed by groups of people entitled to particular services. These cooperatives might then bargain with providers of service over the price, quality, and terms of service offered.

Because the extensive use of this individualized benefit approach would mark a considerable departure from tradition in the social services (the system is widely used in medical care), a series of demonstrations of the system, rather than immediate universal adoption, is recommended.

Manpower

The "manpower problem" in social services has frequently been defined as a shortage of professional social workers. Evidence indicates that the nation does, in fact, need more such professionals. In view of the need to expand the number, kind, and variety of social services, however, the "manpower problem" is viewed here as a problem of preparing workers appropriately for *all* social service tasks. Recent developments have lent increasing urgency to the social services manpower problem.

The Social Security Amendments of 1967 required state departments of welfare, and other public agencies participating in the administration of the Social Security Act, to amend their plans to provide for the training and effective use of paid subprofessional staff members as community service aides and for the use of unpaid or partially paid volunteers in the provision of services. Clearly, subprofessionals and volunteers cannot be recruited, trained, and used as the law requires without having a strong impact on other personnel and on the total service delivery system.

A major roadblock to developing an adequate manpower program is the present Civil Service system in Massachusetts. Absolute preference for veterans; low personnel requirements for highly skilled jobs combined with unreasonable restrictions on recruitment of disadvantaged groups for jobs particularly suited to their backgrounds; low salaries; poor working conditions—these and other factors make recruitment, retention, and upgrading of social service personnel extremely difficult. The state of Massachusetts must include in its overall planning a comprehensive program of manpower to man the expected increase in the social services.

Organizational changes

As social services develop because of federal encouragement, separation of services from public assistance, and increasing demand, Massachusetts can develop its programs only through changes in present practices and administrative organization. The image of social services can be changed when they are not identified with relief or programs for the poor. Consideration needs to be given to:

1. Involving consumers in the administration of the social services.

2. If the Massachusetts Department of Public Welfare is made responsible for the organization and administration of services, developing ways of clearly differentiating social services from public assistance. Perhaps a "Social and Rehabilitation Service" similar to the federal system might be developed as a separate entity to include all the present social services of the department as well as the additional or expanded services discussed in this chapter.

Concentrating on the hard core

A major objective for the social services set up as we propose would be services to hard-core unemployed and public assistance recipients. Although many studies cast doubt on the effectiveness of services to such hard-core people, experienced welfare administrators report considerable success in finding employment, encouraging training, and breaking the cycle of dependency.

The largest number of people who can be identified as needing social services are those now in the AFDC case load, and this case load also contains many hard-core cases. Experience has indicated the importance of an individualized approach to this group. Minimal consideration can be given to some cases while services are concentrated on others.

We must acknowledge that there is no generally agreed upon approach or service that can "rehabilitate" hard-core, long-term AFDC cases. Research on these cases and effective programs are spotty and inconclusive. Some welfare departments report success based on very intensive social services, but the data are insufficient for building a program that will have a good chance of success.

Massachusetts has a challenging opportunity, however, to make a contribution in this area. The Human Resources Cabinet could bring to bear on these cases all the state's programs for health, mental health, social welfare, employment, rehabilitation, and the like, and the universities of the state might be able to conduct the kind of research that can contribute to the base of knowledge about effective ways of dealing with the problem.

Many of our comments and conclusions are intended to indicate issues that need to be considered by the state government of Massachusetts. They have not spelled out details; that is a task for continuous and intensive study by state authorities. We hope that our suggestions will help the state to make progress in its public assistance and social service programs.

BERNARD J. FRIEDEN

housing: creating the supply

What can Massachusetts do to help provide decent homes for the 200,000 families throughout the state still living in inadequate housing? Within the next ten years, the total volume of housing added through private construction, federal assistance, and existing state programs will fall short of what is needed to rehouse slum families. The state can play a decisive role in expanding the supply of good housing; in some respects it can be more effective than the federal government.

To resolve problems of deficient housing in the next decade, Massachusetts must first equip itself

Bernard J. Frieden is professor in the Department of Ur-ban Studies and Planning at Massachusetts Institute of Technology and a member of the policy committee of the Joint Center for Urban Studies of M.I.T. and Harvard University. He wishes to acknowledge the many contributions of Christa Carnegie, who served ably as research assistant for this study. For help with background information and comments on an earlier draft of this paper, he is indebted to Robert McKay and other members of the Citizens' Housing and Planning Association, and to Martin Linsky, David Liederman, Charles Haar, Langley Keyes, John Kain, Harry Durning, Alexander Kovel, Constance Williams, and Jack Plunkett.

to have a housing policy rather than a collection of separate programs, and to adjust this policy to changing conditions. In the short run, the most important things the state can do are to mount subsidy programs that will operate more flexibly and at higher volumes than the present ones, to raise welfare allowances to cover realistic costs of decent housing, and to limit the demolition of existing housing through public land-takings. The state should also work for long-term changes that will promote a higher volume of residential construction, introduction of improved building technology, and equal access for all groups to the private market.

After two decades of steady if gradual improvement of housing conditions, the production of housing in the United States is now falling below the country's basic needs. From the end of World War II through 1965, the housing system and public policies that supported it performed reasonably well. They worked best for middle- and upper-income groups, but they also helped many low-income families improve their housing. Since 1966, with sharply rising mortgage interest rates, the system has failed to produce enough housing even for relatively well-off groups. Many people—but particularly the poor—are feeling the effects of a growing shortage that some observers already describe as the worst housing crisis since World War II.

The states, as well as the federal government, ought to reconsider their housing role in the light of today's changed situation. If the states ever were justified in relying on the private market plus federal programs to deal with the housing problems of the poor, that is no longer the case. Massachusetts has a relatively good record in this field, but its efforts have been scattered and their effects very limited. Now is an appropriate time to ask what the state can do more systematically to help its low-income citizens get decent housing.

How Bad is Massachusetts Housing?

A statistical view of Massachusetts housing conditions can help to define the nature and extent of the problem. First, however, brief descriptions of a few individual cases may convey the characteristics of poor housing more fully than statistical generalizations.

A family of ten has been living in a wood-frame house near downtown Springfield ever since the health department ordered them to leave their last apartment. They are now paying $50 a month in rent plus $700 a year for heating oil. On the ground floor, only one electrical outlet is working and it is overloaded. The kitchen sink has been stopped since they moved in. Wiring is exposed in several parts of the house and makeshift plumbing repairs allow water to leak through the ceiling. Some of the upstairs heating registers are disconnected; there are mice and roaches; the roof has holes in it; the front porch has a broken railing and hazardous steps. Before they moved in, the landlady promised to fix up the place.

In Holyoke, a family of 11 lives in a five-room third-floor apartment with no lighting and no janitor service in the halls. The father has already fallen through the back porch once but now knows which boards to avoid. One night ceiling plaster fell on the sleeping children, leaving one of them with impaired hearing.

A mother and two young daughters lived in a one-room apartment in Boston with broken windowpanes, falling plaster, and undependable heating. More critical was the lack of locks on the outside doors, since alcoholics wandered in and out of the building. During the winter, one of the visitors started a fire in the trash-filled basement, and the building was gutted. This family was not settled permanently again for nine months.

In Easthampton, a family of 11 earns $75 a week and pays $35 a week for a four-room apartment with chipped paint, broken windows, dirty halls, and a variety of insects. The family has all had parasites at one time or another, and a cockroach was imbedded in the baby's ear for a month.[1]

HOW MANY FAMILIES LIVE IN INADEQUATE HOUSING?

Information on Massachusetts housing is far from ideal, but we do nevertheless have the basis for a reasonable approximation of the extent and nature of poor housing. Federal housing censuses taken every ten years report certain housing characteristics that can be translated into judgments of housing adequacy. The conventional definition of substandard housing is based on census reports dealing with structural condition and plumbing equipment. Housing reported as "dilapidated," according to the census definition, "does not provide safe and adequate shelter and in its present condition endangers the health, safety, or well-being of the occupants." To be classified as dilapidated, a house

[1]These are actual cases collected by Christa Carnegie, research assistant in this project, and by the Commonwealth Service Corps, staff members of several antipoverty programs, and the relocation staff of the Boston Redevelopment Authority.

must have one or more "critical defects"—holes over large areas of the foundation, walls, roof, floors, or chimney; substantial sagging of floors, walls, or roof; external damage by storm, fire, or flood—or a combination of lesser defects sufficient to require considerable repair or rebuilding; or it must be of inadequate original construction, such as shacks with makeshift walls or roofs or dirt floors. The absence of a private toilet, bath, or shower, and of hot running water, is reported separately. In the conventional interpretation, a living unit is counted as substandard if it is dilapidated or lacks one or more of these plumbing facilities.

This is a conservative definition because it fails to take into account other deficiencies that can make housing dangerous to health and safety: inadequate or hazardous heating or wiring; lack of an emergency fire exit; poor lighting or ventilation; vermin infestation; or serious violations of local housing codes. Further, the last federal housing census was taken in 1960. (One basic recommendation for state action is to supplement the U.S. census with more frequent and more detailed housing surveys, which can be done on a sampling basis).

According to this limited concept, 139,000 Massachusetts families were living in substandard housing in 1960. This number may represent something like half the 1960 total of Massachusetts families living in housing that is clearly below minimum standards of decency. As a rough approximation of the total, we may add to the 139,000 occupied "substandard" units another 120,000 of marginal quality classified by the 1960 census as "deteriorating." In all, some 260,000 familes—17 percent of all households in the state—were living in seriously deficient housing in 1960.

TRENDS SINCE 1960: MASSACHUSETTS AND THE NATION

In the absence of a statewide housing survey since the 1960 census, recent changes can best be estimated by comparing Massachusetts data with long-term national trends. Comparisons over time can be made by using the limited concept of substandard housing (housing that is dilapidated or lacks plumbing facilities). For the country as a whole, the censuses taken in 1950 and 1960, postcensus surveys designed to test the accuracy of these reports, and a census bureau estimate for 1966 all show a fairly consistent pattern. The number of families in the United States living in substandard housing declined from 15 million in 1950 to 8.5 million in 1960 and to an estimated 5.7 million by 1966.

In Massachusetts, the rate of improvement reported by the 1950 and 1960 censuses was about the same as in the country at large. In 1950, 250,000 families were living in substandard housing; by 1960, this number was reduced to 139,000. From 1960 through 1965, new construction in Massachusetts continued at high levels relative to population growth, so that there is every reason to believe the rate of improvement of the 1950s was maintained or even increased. A projection of the same rate of change shows the number of families in substandard housing reduced to about 100,000 by 1966. To take into account other seriously deficient housing not covered by the definition of "substandard," this figure should probably be doubled. Thus the number of families living in deficient housing as of 1966 can be estimated as 200,000.

In Massachusetts and the country, improvement in housing conditions from 1950 to the mid-1960s resulted mainly from the indirect effects of a high volume of new construction for upper- and middle-income families. Throughout this period, we built a great deal of new housing, primarily in suburbia. At the same time, we demolished relatively little existing housing, and there was a substantial amount of renovation of existing housing in poor condition. As a result of this combination of activities, the supply of good housing grew faster than the increase in the number of households needing a place to live. Families who could afford the new housing moved into it, leaving behind a vacant unit which was then occupied by someone else, and a chain of additional vacancies and moves could then take place. This "turnover process" produced a gradual improvement in living conditions for most American families, including many at low income levels.

Since 1965, however, the turnover process has virtually ground to a halt nationally. From 1950 through 1965, national housing starts exceeded new household formations by a ratio of 1.5 to 1.

After 1965, national housing starts dropped sharply while needs continued to grow. To continue the progress of the recent past would require some two million housing starts a year. At current levels, it is clear that there has been little or no improvement in housing conditions since 1966, and even a substantial tightening of the market in many areas.

Massachusetts has followed the national pattern. From 1960 through 1965, average housing starts of some 27,000 units a year provided a very comfortable surplus over the average household increase of 11,000 a year. But since 1966, households have been increasing at an estimated 18,400 a year, while some 10,000 units a year are being lost, half of them through demolition for public programs. New construction, averaging about 30,000 units a year (including a number of second homes in vacation areas), has done little more than keep up with family increase and housing losses. The number of families living in deficient housing has probably not been reduced much below the 200,000 estimated for 1966.

WHO LIVES IN SLUM HOUSING?

Information from the 1960 census, despite changes since then, is indicative of who in Massachusetts is badly housed. First, inadequate housing is clearly a problem of poverty. Of the 260,000 families in deficient housing in 1960, more than half had incomes below $4,000, and 65 percent earned less than $5,000. Further, many of these families strain their budgets to pay a high proportion of their income for inadequate housing. The usual norm is that a low-income family should not spend more than one-fifth of its earnings for housing. Yet of the 183,000 families who were tenants in deficient housing, some 70,000 were paying more than one-fourth of their income for rent, and of these, 46,000 were paying more than 35 percent in 1960. Still others find housing in reasonable condition but too small for their needs: more than 100,000 Massachusetts families lived in overcrowded housing (with an average of more than one occupant per room) in 1960.

The close connection between low incomes and bad housing means that any effective solution will require some form of subsidy. But it is also true that not all the poor live in bad housing. In fact, even at low income levels, a majority of families do manage to find housing in reasonable condition —although, as I have noted, some do it by spending more than they can afford or by living in crowded quarters. In 1960, 65 percent of families with incomes between $1,000 and $2,000 were living in housing classified as sound, with all plumbing facilities. Among those earning between $2,000 and $3,000, more than 70 percent were in sound housing, and between $3,000 and $4,000 more than 75 percent.

Bad housing is thus very much a problem of a minority of Massachusetts families, even among the poor. This fact can be significant politically in either of two ways. With most people living in good housing, it may be difficult to build political support for helping those who are not well off. On the other hand, the limited size of the problem means that a solution is within the state's capability and resources.

THE STATE AND THE POOR

Most of the people who live in poor housing have low incomes, but in other respects they are a fairly diverse group. Large families, the elderly, and individuals living alone are prominently represented. This diversity means that programs limited to specific kinds of families—such as the now-popular housing for the elderly—will meet only a limited part of the need.

The great majority are tenants rather than owners (71 percent of those in deficient housing in 1960). This fact, too, has consequences for the design of effective programs. First, it means that most residents of poor housing depend upon others for property maintenance and renovation, and that programs designed for tenants must provide realistic rent levels to cover these costs. It may also mean that there is considerable latent demand for home ownership among people who are badly housed, and that programs to help the poor buy houses would be attractive to many.

Black families, surprisingly, are only a small fraction of those in inadequate housing. They are indeed much worse off than white families: in 1960, almost half the nonwhite families in Massachusetts lived in deficient housing. But since they are a small part of the state's population, only seven percent of the deficient units in 1960 were occupied by nonwhites. If political liabilities are attached to mounting programs seen as intended primarily for black people, they ought not to apply to a state housing effort.

One large group of people in poor housing is there because of shortcomings in state public assistance programs. Of the families receiving public assistance, a few own their homes and a larger number live in public housing, but the great majority live in private rental housing. Studies conducted by the state legislature's Special Commission on Housing for Welfare and Low-Income Families indicate that as of 1967 some 50,000 families receiving Old-Age Assistance or Aid to Families with Dependent Children were renting private housing. The commission analyzed the welfare budget of these families and obtained information on current rents for decent housing in many parts of the state. On the assumption that welfare families might be able to spend as much as one-fourth of their income for rent, they concluded that the state's basic subsistence budget is not enough to pay for standard housing and still cover the other necessities of life. The exact number of people on welfare who live in substandard housing is unknown, but the commission judges it is a very large part of these 50,000 families. Changes in the welfare system ought to form an obvious part of a state strategy.

WHERE ARE THE SLUMS?

The residents of deficient housing live primarily in the urban areas of Massachusetts. In the country at large, more substandard housing is located in rural areas than urban areas, but in Massachusetts the opposite is true. In 1960, 84 percent of the families living in deficient housing were within the state's ten metropolitan areas. (Eighty-five percent of the overcrowded families were also in metropolitan areas.)

The urban slums of Massachusetts are scattered across the state. Contrary to popular impression, the Boston metropolitan area does not have a disproportionate share of the state's inadequate housing. Fifteen percent of the families in metropolitan Boston were living in deficient housing in 1960, and about the same proportion of families in the metropolitan areas of Springfield-Chicopee-Holyoke, Worcester, Brockton, and Pittsfield were also housed inadequately. Larger proportions of the occupied housing units were deficient in the metropolitan areas of Lawrence-Haverhill (20 percent), Lowell (20 percent), Fitchburg-Leominster (23 percent), New Bedford (28 percent), and Fall River (30 percent). Slum housing is clearly a statewide problem requiring solutions that can be effective in urban areas across Massachusetts.

Substandard housing is concentrated to a certain extent in particular neighborhoods of the large urban areas. The U.S. Bureau of the Census has delineated urban poverty areas on the basis of a neighborhood index that takes into account such factors as income, educational level, broken families, and substandard housing. Poverty areas in metropolitan Boston, Worcester, and Springfield-Chicopee-Holyoke contain nine percent of the state's housing but had about a third of all the units classified as substandard in 1960. To the extent that concentrations of inadequate housing produce political pressure to find a solution, the poverty neighborhoods of these urban areas ought to be particularly responsive to state programs.

THE COMMUNITY RESPONSE TO HOUSING PROBLEMS

A measure of community interest in improving housing conditions for the poor is the extent to which different local governments have made use of existing federal and state low-income housing programs. Massachusetts communities have built some 50,000 units of housing for the poor and the elderly, under federal and state subsidy programs. The use of these programs does not correspond to the needs across the state, however.

Metropolitan Boston has been more responsive to the housing needs of the poor than any other part of the state. With 43 percent of the state's poverty population (1960 income below $4,000) and 44 percent of its inadequately housed families, metropolitan Boston has built more than 60 percent of all the subsidized housing in the state. No other urban area has built a disproportionately large share of low-income housing. Springfield-Chicopee-Holyoke, Fall River, Lowell, and Lawrence-Haverhill have built roughly in proportion to their share of deficient housing, whereas Worcester, New Bedford, Brockton, Fitchburg-Leominster, and Pittsfield have built relatively less than their share.

Within each metropolitan area, the response has come primarily from the central city. Without exception, the central cities have built a greater share of the subsidized housing in their area than their share of the poverty population. In six of the ten metropolitan areas, the suburbs have built less than 15 percent of the subsidized low-income housing; in another three they have built between 15 and 25 percent; and in metropolitan Boston they have built slightly less than half. If one assumes that each community ought to provide a share of the subsidized housing at least equal to its share of poverty families or of deficient housing, then a major objective of state policy must be to increase the participation of the suburbs. From another point of view, the failure of the suburbs to provide an equitable share of low-income housing is still more significant because they can offer the poor much better access to an expanding industrial job market than can the central cities.

That the central cities have done more than their share does not mean that they have done enough or that they have done much recently. The city of Boston, for example, has had virtually no new construction of low-income public housing for families since 1954—despite long waiting lists and the demolition for urban renewal of a great deal of existing low-income housing.

The role of public policy

Public policies and programs have been concerned with housing for a long time, but many of them have not been concerned primarily with the housing needs of the poor. The policies dealt with in this chapter are those that aim at improving the living conditions of low-income people. The long-term goal of such policies ought to be to create a situation in which nobody will be forced to live in deficient housing for lack of an alternative within his means, and in which no low-income family will be forced to spend an unreasonable share of its income for a place to live. What constitutes "deficient" housing cannot be defined with great precision, but I use the term to mean housing that is unsafe, unhealthy, unsanitary, or below today's standards of decency. (This definition is more inclusive than the concept of "substandard" housing, which refers only to structural condition and plumbing equipment.) Other equally important components of housing, having to do with its location and neighborhood, are not subjects of this chapter: access to work, adequate services, and a decent surrounding environment. These issues need to be dealt with through other urban development policies.

Many housing programs today, particularly in low-income neighborhoods, emphasize still other goals: opening job opportunities for low-income people in construction and management, involving residents in decisions about the design of their housing, increasing the voice of tenants in property management, and building local political strength through involvement in housing activities. These, too, are important goals. They are considered in the next chapter of this book, which is concerned mainly with issues of housing quality.

My policy proposals deal primarily with measures to increase, improve, and diversify the supply of housing available to low-income families—in short, with establishing the basic conditions for meeting the housing needs of the poor. In meeting these needs, however, quality is no less important than quantity. The housing that is provided must give satisfaction to the people who live in it, and satisfaction depends upon more than plumbing equipment and structural condition. Housing programs must be managed in ways that will encourage high standards of design and sensitivity to things that are important to the residents. The best ways of doing this are to involve low-income people in the planning of their housing and to bring them into early contact with developers and designers. Thus the issues covered in the next chapter are significant not only in their own right but also as essential components of programs intended to increase the housing supply.

IMPROVING THE WAY THE MARKET WORKS

One conception of the role of public policy is that it can best help the poor by helping the private housing market operate efficiently and at a high volume, so that the housing supply for the poor will keep expanding through the turnover process. This has in fact been the dominant and traditional concept of housing policy in the United States.

Federal activities illustrate this role in many ways. The federal government has supported the private housing market through FHA mortgage insurance for new suburban housing, banking policies to encourage a flow of investment capital into residential mortgages, federal highway funds to make suburban land accessible to the cities and open it for residential development, and aid for suburban communities to build water and sewer systems needed for community growth. These programs have proven to be effective in generating a high volume of new construction, in part because they have matched the preferences of millions of families who want to live in suburbia. As I have noted, until recently they brought about major improvements in housing conditions for low-income families as well as the middle class.

Consistent with this conception of the role of government, another way of improving the operation of the private market would be to encourage the use of new building methods that might cut construction costs. Several federal study groups have recently recommended policies to promote technological improvements in the building industry, and the federal government has taken limited steps in this direction.

Efficient operation of the private housing market also implies equal access for all consumers to whatever is available. People who are not free to move around to take advantage of vacancies they can afford are not able to benefit much from the turnover process. Racial discrimination has had much to do with the persistence of bad housing conditions for black families, who do not have equal access to either new or older housing. Federal action has included early measures to prohibit discrimination in the sale or rental of federally aided housing and more recent provisions in the Civil Rights Act of 1968 which now cover most private housing as well. Enforcement of these measures has been very weak, however, even in the case of federally aided housing, which has been covered since President Kennedy's executive order in 1962.

WHAT CAN THE STATES DO TO IMPROVE THE HOUSING MARKET?

Although the federal government and the national economy set the basic conditions for the operation of the private housing market, the states can also take significant steps to improve the operation of the market and its ability to serve the poor. In several respects, they are more capable of effective action than is the federal government.

*One obstacle to providing an adequate supply of land for new construction—land that is available at reasonable cost and accessible to jobs and urban services—is the restrictive building regulations set up by local communities that want to discourage growth. Many local zoning laws and subdivision codes impose excessive requirements, such as very large lot sizes or unduly expensive street and utility installations, in order to price moderate-cost housing out of the community. The federal government has no direct way of overcoming these restrictions when they are unreasonable, but the states do have a way. Localities exercise these powers subject to state enabling laws; state legislatures can modify these laws to require that zoning and subdivision powers be exercised so as to provide for a wide range of housing types and prices.

State regulation is not the only way to deal with this problem. To some extent, local resistance to moderate-cost housing is based on a calculation of the cost of servicing new residents compared with the local taxes these residents will pay. New houses with low valuation typically add heavily to local expenses for school children, while they contribute less to the local treasury. States could ease the financial pressure by increasing their support of local educational costs and by adjusting state aid distribution formulas to reduce the penalties communities now pay for permitting inexpensive housing to be built. Reducing the economic cost to the local community would remove some of the motivation behind restrictive local regulations.

Similarly, the states could encourage the use of cost-reducing building technology by adopting uniform statewide codes instead of the current pattern of code variations from one locality to another. Housing has been a discouraging market for new technology because building regulations vary so much from one place to another that components and systems cannot be marketed on a large scale. Further, many building codes specify the use of particular materials instead of setting performance standards and allowing builders to use any product that meets these standards. The federal govenment cannot intervene directly to change local codes, but the states can and should develop uniform statewide codes based on up-to-date performance standards. (New Jersey has recently adopted such a code; California and several other states have begun to move toward statewide code uniformity.)

Eliminating racial discrimination from the housing market ought to be as much a state as a federal concern. Many states have enacted fair-housing laws, but effective enforcement remains a problem for the states as it does for federal civil rights laws. States may be better able to check on real estate practices than the federal government. State agencies are likely to be more familiar with how local markets work, and better able to develop close relations with private fair-housing organizations that can help in monitoring and testing sale and rental procedures.

The states are also in a good position to influence one of the major elements of the turnover process: the rate of demolition of existing housing. A large share of total demolition is accounted for by public land-takings, chiefly for highways, urban renewal, and public buildings. The timing of highway construction is typically a matter for state decision, and the state can influence local government decisions on renewal and other demolition activities. The states ought to use their influence to adjust the amount of housing demolition to suit the nature of the housing market. When new construction is very limited, as it is now, land-takings ought to be postponed for a time. Where housing is to be demolished for state and local programs, the states ought to ensure that fair relocation procedures will be followed and that displaced families will receive enough compensation to pay for decent housing elsewhere.

Massachusetts has made good use of some of the opportunities open to states to improve the operation of the housing market. It has taken the lead nationally in devising a way to overcome locally restrictive zoning where it interferes with the construction of housing for low- or moderate-income families. Legislation enacted in 1969 (chapter 774) provides a special appeal procedure whereby the state can overrule local zoning in certain cases; but it applies only to housing to be built under a state or federal subsidy program.

Massachusetts is also one of the few states that reviews relocation plans in connection with public land-takings. This review enables the state to press local governments and public agencies to develop adequate plans for rehousing displaced people, with state approval required before the project can proceed. Policy in this field could be extended further to include rescheduling of land-takings, as I have suggested above, and state supplements to provide sufficient compensation for displaced people where present programs fall short.

In terms of promoting equal access to housing markets, Massachusetts has had a fair-housing law on the books for many years, but characteristic problems of enforcement have prevented it from being fully effective.

LIMITATIONS OF PRIVATE-MARKET STRATEGIES

Important as these measures are, they will not bring large-scale or immediate help to poor people in need of housing. Private-market strategies depend basically on the turnover process to supply housing for low-income groups, and there are built-in limits on how quickly this process can operate. Turnover depends upon a supply of vacant housing in good condition. Yet whenever a substantial surplus of vacant housing is created, it acts as a brake on further construction. That is, developers will build new housing only when there is an immediate prospect of selling or renting it. Even if housing conditions were to continue to improve at the 1950–1965 rate, it would take until sometime in the 1990s to replace all substandard units.

The turnover process involves still another limitation. During the recent period when housing conditions were improving, the cost of housing was also rising sharply, forcing many families to spend heavily for housing at the expense of other necessities. In both Massachusetts and the nation, the number of families paying more than one-fifth of their income for rent actually increased between 1950 and 1960, and the cost of new housing has continued to soar since then.

Policies to promote cost-reducing technology may hold down the rate of increase in housing costs, but they are not likely to yield significant short-run results. Bringing about major structural changes in the housing industry will take time. Nor are these policies likely to bring down the cost of new housing to levels that low-income families can afford. The President's Committee on Urban Housing (Kaiser committee) estimated that an effective national effort might reduce monthly housing costs by perhaps ten percent.

Even when the turnover process is working well, it works slowly; and just now it is not working well. State efforts alone are unlikely to reverse the present downturn: the states cannot offset the effects of current high interest rates, and the national economy will continue to set the level of investment in new housing. Thus at best these state actions will bring limited and gradual improvements in housing conditions for the poor, unless they are supplemented by more direct measures.

SUBSIDIZING HOUSING COSTS

In contrast to policies that aim at helping the poor through the turnover process, another concept of public policy is that it ought to help them very directly—by building housing for them, helping others build for them, or helping them pay the cost of housing available on the private market. Subsidizing housing costs for low-income groups is clearly a faster and surer way of providing them with good housing than waiting for the turnover process to produce vacancies they can afford. To make much progress under present circumstances in the private market, large-scale subsidy programs are absolutely essential.

The federal government has operated a number of housing subsidy programs for the poor, but their total volume has been small, they have provided little housing in the suburbs, and they have not always produced very good living conditions for their residents. The oldest federal program, low-income public housing, has been the most troubled. Begun in the mid-1930s, it has produced some 700,000 units nationally—a small volume relative to the large number of American families still living in deficient housing in 1970. Further, public housing has been primarily a big-city program, with relatively little built in the suburbs. Thus the location of public housing tends to keep low-income people in locations where employment prospects are declining, while new jobs continue to grow in the suburbs.

Experience with public housing has revealed several issues that are critical for the design of any new subsidy programs. Housing programs tend to set in motion social and political pressures that can undermine their basic purposes. In the case of public housing, the way in which it makes subsidies available tends to create a political forum for opposition to the program. Public housing operates through local governmental authorities that are subject to considerable political pressure. The most serious opposition comes from middle-income areas whose residents do not want low-income housing built near them. As a result, local housing authorities have great difficulty finding sites where they can build. The political problems are less severe in neighborhoods where the poor are already concentrated: thus the tendency to concentrate public housing in large projects on the few sites that are available in poor neighborhoods. Many suburban communities never even take the initial step of setting up a local authority with the power to build public housing. The fact is that the public housing mechanism for making subsidies available also make public housing particularly vulnerable to local opposition, which in turn limits the size of the program, restricts it in terms of location, and in some cases even creates pressure to design the housing to minimal standards.

To meet some of the problems engendered by the local politics of housing, federal subsidy programs have been changed in ways that make them more similar to private housing. The low-income public housing program has become diversified and now offers several alternatives to large projects that are less conspicuous and more like typical private housing. Local authorities can now lease individual units in private buildings and subsidize the rent for low-income tenants; they can buy newly built housing from private developers; and they can renovate existing housing. Although the leasing of existing apartments generates less opposition than other public housing measures, most of these operations still remain subject to considerable political pressure through local government. A more recent federal program offers rent supplements to low-income people who live in specific private developments, where the other residents may be middle-income tenants. The rent supplement program, too, requires a form of local government action that has blocked its use in communities where there is opposition to low-income housing.

Two new subsidy programs (authorized in 1968) operate without requiring any explicit involvement of local government. One provides aid for low-income homeowners (section 235), the other for low-income tenants (section 236). Both work more like typical mortgage assistance programs than like earlier low-income subsidies. A private developer—not a local government agency—is the agent for producing housing. The developer (normally a nonprofit or limited-dividend sponsor) arranges his financing with a lending institution and with the FHA, then builds or renovates housing for low-income buyers or tenants. The federal government then makes subsidy payments to the mortgage lender on behalf of the low-income residents, according to a formula that takes into account the resident's income and the actual cost of his housing. (The present subsidy formula, it should be noted, will tend to limit these programs to families with incomes ranging from about $5,000 to $7,500, while public housing can reach families with lower incomes.) No local government approval is needed, other than the same review given to any new development for compliance with zoning and building regulations. These programs go a long way toward taking subsidized housing out of local politics and treating it instead as part of normal housing market operations.

DO THE STATES NEED THEIR OWN SUBSIDY PROGRAMS?

Recent federal initiatives in diversifying the older subsidy programs and adding several promising new ones may suggest that the states can rely on federal programs to supply most of the subsidies that are needed. Both the history and the current status of federal programs argue convincingly against such a position. Congress has a consistent record of authorizing ambitious housing programs and then funding them for very unambitious levels of operation. In the mid-1960s, all the major federal subsidy programs together—public housing, moderate-income housing, rent supplements, and housing for the elderly—were providing 50,000 to 60,000 units a year.

President Johnson's 1968 message on housing proposed a new target of six million subsidized units in the next ten years, an output sufficient to rehouse all the families then estimated to be living in substandard housing. The Housing and Urban Development Act of 1968 authorizes funding for about 1.5 million assisted units in the next three years. True to form, when Congress actually appropriated funds for the first year following the 1968 act, it provided only a third of what it had authorized for the new home-ownership and rental programs, and less than half of what it had authorized for rent supplements. During 1968, a special effort by the Johnson administration did succeed in raising production to about 120,000 housing starts under the federal subsidy programs. The Nixon administration has maintained this impetus so far, with an increase in federally assisted starts to 165,000 units in 1969 and forecasts of further increases in 1970. There is little evidence that federal programs will reach the level required to build six million subsidized units by 1978, but within the next few years they may produce 400,000–500,000 units each year, which was the level authorized in 1968. Predicting that the federal government will actually live up to its recent authorization is very risky, however, in view of its past record.

Certainly Massachusetts ought to make every effort to get federal housing subsidies. The state can do many things to help its communities and nonprofit sponsors to use the federal programs; but the total size of federal programs does set a limit on how much can be accomplished by this route. Massachusetts has in fact been getting a large share of federal housing aid relative to its population and the needs of other states, and the volume is still small: about 22,000 units in 30 years, constituting about one percent of the state's housing stock. If federal programs continue to expand, however, Massachusetts may be able to increase its annual volume of federally aided housing to something like 5,000 units within the next few years.

Massachusetts has already recognized a need for state subsidy programs, and has gone further than most other states in establishing a variety of housing aids. The principal ones that can supply housing for poor families are: veterans' housing (chapter 200), housing for the elderly (chapter 667), low-rent housing for families (chapter 705), and rental assistance (chapter 707). In addition, the Massachusetts Housing Finance Agency has been established with authorization to make below-market loans for housing based on its own borrowing ability and on a self-sustaining basis; at present interest rates, it cannot reach low-income families without some source of additional subsidies. The newer state programs embody many progressive approaches. The low-rent housing program for families aims at small housing projects on scattered sites, and the rental assistance program provides a flexible assistance formula to help low-income families rent housing in private buildings, with limits on the number of such families that may be concentrated in a single area. All the low-income programs, however, work through local housing authorities.

Despite this impressive array of state programs, very little low-income housing is being produced. The veterans' program has built no new housing since 1954; about a thousand units of housing for the elderly are built each year; and the other programs, enacted in 1966, have not yet broken ground. Why they have not produced much housing ought to be the subject of a careful and detailed inquiry. Whether additional state staffing, managerial improvement, or program simplification would get them into operation is not clear. But in view of national experience, it is likely that their dependence on local housing authorities will limit their ability to build large numbers of houses and may indeed help account for their slow start.

A housing strategy for Massachusetts

The analysis so far suggests several conclusions that can form the basis for a housing strategy in Massachusetts. Two hundred thousand people in Massachusetts are still living in degrading and hazardous conditions that neither they nor the state should tolerate. Inadequate housing is not confined to a few communities, but is a statewide problem, mainly in urban areas. Little relief is in sight from the private housing market, and what the federal government will do is uncertain. Local government agencies have provided some subsidized housing under federal and state programs, but they have not been able to produce anything like the volume of housing that is needed, and they have built housing mainly within the central cities. In some respects, the state is better able to deal with housing problems than the federal government. In other areas of housing policy—particularly in the provision of housing subsidies to the poor—the federal government is better equipped but has consistently lacked the will to commit the resources that are needed. If the states are concerned, therefore, they must act rather than wait for Washington to come to the rescue.

Two general roles for public policy have been described: helping the private housing market to work better, and subsidizing housing directly for poverty families. In the first category, the state can do many useful things to accelerate the turnover of housing in ways that will help low-income groups. The results of efforts in this direction will be slow to emerge, however. Nevertheless, it is important to make a start now, both to take advantage of whatever opportunities the private market does offer in the short run and to set the stage for effects that could be important by the last half of the 1970s.

Providing housing subsidies for the poor is clearly the role that can offer the most immediate and substantial results. It poses problems of overcoming local resistance to low-income housing that has obstructed earlier subsidy programs, and it requires the state to raise revenues to pay for the subsidies. Although the political difficulties are substantial, the real contributions of such a policy toward solving long-neglected problems make it a genuine test of the state's commitment to helping its poor citizens get decent housing.

WHICH INCOME GROUPS TO SERVE?

One major dilemma underlying the design of a state strategy ought to be noted. This has to do with choosing whether to deal with the housing problems of low-income people by a selective approach limited to meeting their needs alone, or whether to undertake activities that will benefit a much broader segment of the state's population, including middle-income groups as well as the poor. (Operating definitions of low- and moderate-income families for housing eligibility depend upon family size and vary from one community to another. For a Massachusetts family of four, the ceiling in a low-income program might be around $6,000, and in a moderate-income program about $9,000.) Dealing with the problems of the poor separately from those of other groups allows one to direct resources in an efficient way toward the areas of greatest need. At the same time, it means providing help for a minority of the state's population that may not be very strong or effective politically. Thus the selective approach may be difficult to sustain or may result in a low level of appropriations.

A broader approach to housing, linking the interests of low-income families with those of middle-income groups, is likely to attract greater political support by drawing on a larger constituency of people who stand to gain from it. The danger with this approach is that the middle-income constituents may shape housing programs to serve their needs more than those of the poor. Thus a broad program could well be deflected away from its initial purposes.

This choice between selective and broad programs must be made at many points in designing and carrying out a state strategy, and must be based on a careful assessment of the political factors at work—an assessment that public officials are better equipped to make than are researchers who offer policy advice. But it is worth pointing out that recent changes in the housing market are hurting middle-income groups as well as the poor. As a result, the potential constituency for broad housing programs is greater now than it has been for some time in the past.

The following ought to be some of the components of a Massachusetts strategy for meeting the housing problems of the poor.

1. *Equip the state government to create and carry out a housing policy.* Many of the state's activities have an impact on the housing of the poor, but the state cannot be said to have a deliberate housing policy. Responsibilities for programs affecting low-income housing are scattered throughout state government, and they cannot reasonably be centralized. They range from welfare assistance to highway land-taking to building regulation and to the operation of housing subsidy programs.

Strong leadership by the governor is essential both to develop a clear housing policy and to align the work of the various state agencies in support of it. Only the Governor is in a position to review the results of different programs, to phase out those that are not working well and to shift funds to those that are. Unless the Governor is personally committed to having a deliberate housing policy, there will be none. If he provides leadership, it will be possible to develop a clear set of targets, try different strategies, and maintain the flexibility to adjust state actions to keep pace with changes in the housing market.

A Governor committed to meeting the state's housing needs should establish a small staff, independent of operating agencies but reporting directly to him, with clear responsibility for evaluating the effectiveness of state activities that concern housing. Such a staff should be responsible for conducting sample surveys of housing conditions from time to time, analyzing the current state of the private market, recommending action to the Governor, and reporting to the public at large how well the state is doing in meeting housing targets. (If there were such a staff now, we might have a better idea of what needs to be done to get the housing programs passed in 1966 into operation.) An advisory panel to the Governor on low-income housing also ought to be established, with the poor themselves prominently represented.

In addition to mechanisms for policy development and evaluation, the state must have adequate staffing of the operating agencies that are concerned with housing. The state's characteristic unwillingness to provide enough staff members was illustrated with unusual clarity in the legislation establishing the Department of Community Affairs (chapter 23B):

> ... the commissioner may appoint ... an executive assistant, a chief counsel, and experts on urban affairs, public information, and intergovernmental relations ... and such other officers, experts, and assistants as he may deem necessary to carry out the work of the department; provided, however, that the total number of appointments to be made by the commissioner under this paragraph shall not exceed two.

Further, adequate staffing is a matter of competence as well as numbers. People with training in housing are very much in demand by federal and local agencies as well as by private firms, and the state must offer competitive salaries to attract them.

2. *Establish and fund new subsidy programs.* New subsidy programs are absolutely essential if Massachusetts is to make substantial and prompt progress toward improving housing conditions for the poor. If we take as a goal providing decent housing within ten years for every Massachusetts family, then it is clear that neither the private market nor existing federal and state programs can come close to the total effort that is needed.

Some 200,000 families now live in deficient housing. To enable these families to move, and also to relieve the pressure on other families who are overcrowded or who pay too great a share of their income for housing, the state should aim at adding at least 200,000 units of new or renovated housing at prices low-income people can afford.

HOW MUCH HOUSING IS NEEDED?

How much of this total can be provided through the private market or existing programs? Predictions are hazardous, but some reasonable assumptions can be made. I assume that the private market for the next few years will add just enough housing to keep up with population growth plus losses through demolition, but that it will not add enough to contribute to the ten-year goal. Within two or three years, falling interest rates should help return new construction to its former high levels in relation to population growth, so that it should once again start replacing deficient housing through the turnover process. If the private market works well through at least the last half of the next decade, it could supply from 50,000 to 80,000 of the needed units.

If federal subsidy programs were to remain at the 1968 level and Massachusetts got a share comparable to its national share of substandard housing, these programs would add another 2,000 low-income units a year. Most likely the federal programs will continue to expand. If they reach the level authorized in 1968—an annual average of 50,000—the Massachusetts share might be 8,000 a year. Over the course of the decade, then, federal programs might add from 20,000 (at present levels) to 50,000 units (assuming a gradual increase to the higher level).

The state program for the elderly now supplies about 1,000 units each year. If the two programs enacted in 1966 are promoted aggressively, they might add another 1,000 to 2,000 units a year. Thus the total from existing state programs might range from 20,000 to 30,000 units in ten years.

Taken together, these sources might account for the following part of the goal of 200,000 units:

From private construction	50,000–80,000
From federal programs	20,000–50,000
From existing state programs	20,000–30,000
Total	90,000–160,000

This output would still fall short of the ten-year target of 200,000 units by anywhere from 40,000 to 110,000 units. New state programs should therefore aim at an average yearly production of at least 4,000 units and perhaps 11,000 units, depending upon the unmet need.

SPONSORS, SUBSIDIES, AND SITES

New programs should be designed to cover three essential elements: finding sponsors who want to build, supplying financial aid for low-income occupants, and making it possible for the sponsors to find suitable sites. The new federal programs for low-income home ownership and rental housing can serve as models. These can operate flexibly through private sponsors, non-profit groups, cooperatives, or public agencies. As with the federal model, opportunities ought to be offered for either home owner-ship or rental housing. Limits on the cost of housing and the incomes of the residents ought to be established by law, with subsidies varying to cover the gap between one-fifth of the occupant's income and the actual total monthly cost of the housing. To keep the actual cost of housing within moderate limits, sponsors should be encouraged to make use of FHA mortgage programs or Massachusetts Housing Finance Agency loans. Subsidy payments on behalf of low-income occupants ought to be available to sponsors who renovate existing housing in poor condition as well as to those who build new housing.

The income and housing cost limits set for these programs will deter-mine how broad a clientele they will serve. If it is considered important to include some middle-income families, these limits can be set some-what higher than they would be for the poor alone. But in any case the annual subsidy per family must be great enough to enable those with low incomes (below $5,000) to use these programs, or their primary purpose will be defeated. Since the income distribution of families who are aided is difficult to predict, as is the mix of new and renovated housing that would be provided, the cost of these programs to the state can be estimated only very roughly. At present cost levels, an average annual subsidy of $2,000 per family might be needed for those with incomes below $5,000. A minimal volume under new programs (4,000 units each year) would involve new commitments of $8 million annu-ally, while the highest estimate (11,000 units) would cost $22 million a year. These annual commitments would be cumulative. They would be reduced only as the incomes of subsidized families increase relative to housing costs.

If these new programs can be used either by private sponsors (profit or nonprofit) or public agencies, then several possibilities will exist for providing a sufficient volume. If private sponsors and local housing authorities together do not apply to build a sizable number of units, a state agency could develop or renovate housing directly. The type of agency recently proposed by Governor Sargent and by several members of the legislature (the Governor's proposal is for a Massachusetts Replacement Housing and New Towns Agency) might be suitable for this purpose. These proposals would establish a new state agency authorized to build housing units equal in number to housing destroyed by public land-takings, which now average some 5,000 units a year; what proportion of this housing could be for low-income families is not yet clear.

If sponsors, private or public, have difficulty in acquiring sites because of unnecessarily restrictive local zoning, they would all have recourse to the state appeal procedure that has recently been established for subsidized housing.

3. *Make the most of existing state housing programs.* While I believe that new subsidy programs are needed, the state should also make greater efforts to encourage the use of existing ones. The two programs authorized in 1966, for low-rent family housing and for rental assistance, provide important opportunities for local authorities to expand the supply of housing available to the poor. So far these programs have been used for no more than a few hundred units, although financing has been available for a much larger volume. The state should find out why local authorities have not applied to use these programs on a larger scale. If there are regulations that discourage the wider use of these programs, they should be modified.

One obvious reason the programs have not been more successful is that they require sponsorship by a local housing authority. More than half the cities and towns in Massachusetts do not have a local housing authority. The state should make it possible for these communities to use the new programs without establishing an authority of their own. Some ways of doing this would be to permit—and encourage—local governments to contract with other housing authorities to build and manage housing for them, to authorize communities to join together in establishing regional authorities, and to authorize a unit of state government to supply such housing upon local request. Further, the state should take the lead in encouraging metropolitan and regional planning councils to formulate housing programs for areas they represent and to secure local commitments to participate in these programs either through existing housing authorities or through the alternatives suggested here.

Whether stronger state leadership will succeed in promoting the use of these programs is not at all clear. The effort should be made. If it turns out that local governments—with or without housing authorities —are simply reluctant to provide much housing for the poor, the state ought to give greater emphasis to programs that do not require local governmental involvement.

Housing that has already been built under the older state programs— for veterans and for the elderly—also needs fresh attention to be sure it is being maintained and managed satisfactorily. The recent report of the Subcommittee on Housing of the Joint Legislative Committee on Urban Affairs has made many important proposals for action needed to allow this older housing to continue providing a decent environment for its residents. The subcommittee found that additional state aid is needed to enable local authorities to cover the cost of maintenance and modernization of the older projects without raising rents to levels that the tenants cannot afford. They also recommend tenant participation in decisions about modernization, improved procedures for handling relations between tenants and management, additional police protection to be paid for by the local authority, and opportunities for tenants to buy their own units. These proposals would go far toward safeguarding the basic objectives of housing assistance for the poor, and they should receive high priority for state action.

4. *Help nonprofit and limited-dividend sponsors to use federal and state housing programs.* Nonprofit and limited-dividend groups that want to sponsor housing are typically long on social commitment and short on real estate experience and know-how. With strong technical assistance, these groups can make important contributions that have been recognized in recent federal programs designed to attract their participation. If Massachusetts is to continue getting a sizable share of federal housing funds, it will be important to encourage formation of nonprofit and limited-dividend groups and to help those that have already started. Particularly in low-income neighborhoods where deficient housing is concentrated, much can be said for encouraging churches, other local institutions, and community development corporations to sponsor housing.

As a further aid, the state should make available interim financing until mortgage commitments are made. According to recent newspaper reports, Boston banks have been unwilling to make mortgage loans at market rates for the new federal home ownership program. If this situation continues, the state should use its considerable leverage with lending institutions (based on regulatory powers as well as the placing of its own deposits) to encourage a flow of investment capital into the federal subsidy programs.

5. *Raise welfare allowances to meet the cost of decent housing.* Studies recently completed by the Special Commission on Housing for Welfare and Low-Income Families indicate that a large proportion of the 50,000 families receiving public assistance who live in private rental housing cannot pay the going rent for decent accommodations. They are forced either to spend too much of their income for adequate housing or else to live in substandard conditions. To adjust their income to realistic rent levels, the commission recommends a monthly increase of $20 in their budgets (a total annual increase of $12 million). This is a minimal adjustment which should be provided; it may still not be enough to enable welfare families to live in decent housing.

In time, it should be possible for many families receiving public assistance to live in housing covered under the subsidy programs described above. But in the interim, welfare budgets ought to be increased to cover the economic cost of decent housing that is now available. If the budget adjustment is realistic, welfare authorities ought to insist that the owners of housing occupied by these families maintain it in sound condition, and they should be authorized to withhold rent when the owner refuses to do so.

These recommendations have dealt mainly with state action to subsidize housing for the poor, as the highest priority elements of a state strategy. Other action should also be taken to help the poor benefit from the operation of the private housing market and the turnover process.

6. *Postpone demolition of existing housing and pay realistic relocation allowances.* To allow low-income people to benefit from the supply of older housing, the state should minimize housing losses, especially during periods of low housing production. The state now reviews relocation plans in connection with all public land-takings and is in a position to influence the timing of housing demolition. Presumably not all projects that involve the demolition of housing are equally urgent. The state ought to review its own projects—particularly urban highways—with a view toward postponing the demolition phases of those that are not urgent until housing production can increase, and it ought to use its review of local relocation plans to urge a more careful timing of demolition.

In addition, the relocation review process ought to be used to check the adequacy of relocation payments that are now made under various public programs. Adjustment payments to homeowners and tenants should reflect the actual cost of available relocation housing. If realistic allowances mean exceeding the limits for which federal aid is available, the state should be prepared to make up the difference.

7. *Enforce fair housing laws effectively.* Black families have been severely disadvantaged in the housing market by their inability to move around freely to take advantage of vacancies. In most parts of the country, at any given income level a higher proportion of white families than non-white families live in good housing, are homeowners, and live in the suburbs. Aggressive enforcement of fair-housing practices is a necessity if black people are to have equal opportunities to live in white or racially mixed neighborhoods or to move to the suburbs. Enforcement should not depend upon the person who wants to move to file a complaint of discrimination. It should include regular testing and monitoring of real estate practices to ensure that they are equitable.

8. *Adopt a uniform building code.* To encourage the development and use of cost-reducing technology in housing, Massachusetts should join the other states that have made a start at replacing local building codes with a uniform state code based on up-to-date performance standards. Attention should be given, as well, to making the interpretation and enforcement of building regulations more consistent across the state.

9. *Authorize rent control as a local option.* The current housing shortage, coupled with intense competition for scarce housing in a few communities of the state, have sometimes led to unwarranted rent increases. Although the long-run solution is to add to the housing supply, rent control may be necessary in the interim to protect poor families who are most vulnerable. Local governments are in a better position to judge the need for rent control than is the state, and they should be authorized to enact rent-control legislation. Rent control could conceivably work against the goal of increasing the housing supply if it discourages new construction. To minimize this possibility, new housing ought to be exempt from rent control, and local housing conditions ought to be reviewed annually to determine whether controls are still needed.

10. *Review state-local fiscal relations.* One of the persistent obstacles to a high level of homebuilding has been the resistance of many suburban communities to moderate-cost housing. In part this resistance is based on the realization that, in short-run financial terms, this housing is often a liability. Both the level and the allocation of state aid to local communities ought to be reviewed to determine what will be needed to offset the cost of providing schools and other services for new, inexpensive homes. On the basis of this review, state-local financial relations ought to be adjusted so that they do not seriously undercut state housing efforts.

Many more elements of a state housing strategy could be suggested, but my purpose here is only to propose the main outlines of such a strategy, and—more important—to indicate criteria for judging the effectiveness of state action. First, the total housing need must be considered and any level of effort measured against it. A less expensive set of proposals than the ones I have suggested may seem more attractive, but less ambitious programs will save money by not providing enough housing. Further, there may be opportunities to shift money from other activities into low-income housing. For example, the $1.5 million that the state now contributes each year to local urban renewal projects actually provides very little help for low-income families. These funds could aid low-income housing more directly if they were redirected to new subsidy programs.

Second, state strategies have to be considered in the light of how the private market and federal programs are operating. When private construction is very limited, as it is now, the need for state action is especially compelling. As conditions change in the private market and in the scope of federal programs, state strategies must retain sufficient flexibility to respond to new opportunities and changing needs.

Third, when the state enters into new subsidy programs, these must deal with the related problems of finding sponsors, finding sites, and providing financial aid. Most current proposals are addressed to only one or two of these elements. In particular, the need for adequate financing is usually overlooked. As far as sponsors are concerned, the state should not continue to depend exclusively upon local authorities. As a guiding principle, local government should not be permitted to exercise a veto over the right of poor people to live in decent housing, whether by failing to serve as sponsor or by preventing other sponsors from finding suitable sites.

In the past, Massachusetts has responded more than most other states to the housing needs of its poor citizens. I believe the state is

The information on which this article is based has been drawn principally from the following studies: Anthony Downs, "Moving Toward Realistic Housing Goals," in Kermit Gordon, ed., *Agenda for the Nation* (1968); Bernard J. Frieden, "Housing and National Urban Goals," in James Q. Wilson, ed., *The Metropolitan Enigma* (1970); Frank S. Kristof, *Urban Housing Needs Through the 1980's* (U. S. National Commission on Urban Problems, 1968); Massachusetts Special Commission on Low-Income Housing, *Final Report* (1965); Lawrence A. Mayer, "The Housing Shortage Goes Critical," *Fortune* (December, 1969); U. S. National Commission on Urban Problems, *Building the American City* (1969); U..S. President's Committee on Urban Housing, *A Decent Home* (1969).

now in a position to move beyond a collection of small programs to a new concept of housing policy. This will involve setting realistic targets and using the state's resources in a number of different ways to meet them. The state has the capacity to deal decisively with the problems of inadequate housing: a sustained effort can make it possible for all citizens of Massachusetts to live in decent homes.

JOHN R. MYER

housing: voicing the demand

It is possible that having appropriate housing can substantially ameliorate the lives of the poor. They have so little that what they do have, such as housing, can mean much to them—for good or bad. Home is the setting of much of creative life; it is where a person fails or succeeds as man-husband-father, woman-wife-mother, provider-receiver, child-sibling, adolescent. It is where we feel so sheltered that we can sleep. It is relief from the exposure of the outside world. It is where we cook and feed, eat and partake, make love. It is individual turf, territory. The physical shell that houses these central life activities and feelings can support them, allow them to succeed, be appropriate. Or it can frustrate them, induce failure—and that is very much another thing.

Yet, historically, the housing industry has been unresponsive to the varying demands of housing

John R. Myer is associate professor of architecture at Massachusetts Institute of Technology and president of Ashley, Myer, Smith, Inc., architects and planners. Much has been contributed by John Perkins as research assistant and critic. The author also wishes to thank the psychiatrist, psychiatric social workers, and readers who contributed to the study.

135

users for appropriate qualities in the housing environment. This lack of response exists in housing for the poor, for those of moderate income, and even for some well-to-do people. Even if the poor were to be made nonpoor, the traditional industry would not produce housing appropriate to the varying demands of its users. The motivations and understandings of those who decide whether and what to build or rehabilitate, and how to manage what is built, tend to be far more sensitive to the profit, security, and time schedule of the venture than to the people who will live there. Decisions about the appropriateness of housing tend to be made on the basis of what has safely sold in similar situations. While this factor is significant, it is not responsive to the changing life-styles of our culture or to the diversity of users of that housing over a period of time. Further, the ways in which public housing (one important source of housing for the poor) gets produced, managed, and occupied tends today toward a crisis level of dissatisfaction on the part of the indwellers.[1] Except for two minor housing events—the recent 221-D-3 submarket housing program and the initial periods of the public housing program in the 1930s— virtually no housing effort has been made that might be described as having any concern with satisfying any need of low-income groups except that they be sheltered, or, to make the point, stalled. In consequence, we have little or no experience in designing for such groups housing environments of a satisfying sort—housing in which the users are thought of and treated as substantial clients, or client groups, whose specific important, needs have a high priority in shaping the housing, and in which the flexibility and adjustability of the design provide for the needs of future users.

Other problems accompany lack of responsiveness. The low-income group of housing users is varied in makeup, age, household size, presence of children, ethnicity, income, and so forth, and requires a variable response to its need. And it is weak in seeking its own interests. Such weakness may be due to lack of supporting institutions in low- and moderate-income areas; for example, information about housing opportunities may be lacking. Or such weakness may come from the inability of many low-income housing users to take advantage of the opportunities that lie about them, either because they are so beset by complex difficulties, or because they are so emotionally disorganized that they cannot make a concerted and positive advance on them, or some combination of these two.

[1]*New York Times*, October 12, 1969, page 1.

In consequence, we may summarize the situation of low-income housing users by pinpointing three attributes:

1. A housing supply that is unresponsive to the varying demands of users; even if the poor person were to be made nonpoor and of moderate income, he would not be able to bring about needed changes in the quality of his housing

2. A group of users who have varying needs that require different responses and who lack ability to elicit that response

3. A typical user for whom housing is especially important because it forms so much of his world.

To act on the problem of housing for low-income people simply as a problem of delivering a certain number of dwelling units each year appears to be inadequate. It is expensive to spend resources in such a way that housing actually encumbers those who live in it, makes them less effective though sheltered. While the adequacy of a person (or a family) presumably does not depend upon any one aspect of his world, for him to be seriously frustrated in an area central to his creativity must be of some significance.

We suggest that strong external forces influence the economy of low-income housing; that many costs and benefits, though not easily quantifiable, have considerable impact on the well-being both of low-income people and of the state; that expenditures which lead to appropriate housing will contribute to the low-income user's ability to cope with life and thereby reduce dependency and spending in many areas of government; that some part of the cost of deteriorating housing stock, both public and private—vandalism, crime, expenditures on welfare, social services, unemployment—may be attributable to an inappropriate housing environment.

We shall recommend that the state seek ways in which to maximize the appropriateness of its housing stock for its users, paying special attention to low- and moderate-income housing in both the public and the private sector.

What is "appropriateness"?

In order to make plain how housing and the housing environment have impact upon the poor, we must understand how they affect the individual, or the family, or the housing locale as a whole. At root it is these units that are failing or succeeding; here lies the power to cope with life or not. We draw on some case studies gathered by psychiatric social workers working directly with the poor, from other housing studies and from newspaper reports. These cases are brief and modest, but they do seem to pinpoint the kinds of difficulties and successes we find the poor having with housing. It is our purpose here, not to establish *the* set of important variables but to make plain the possible relevance of these issues. The case studies were solicited by circulating a memorandum describing what was desired, and in consequence they have a built-in bias in favor of the notion that housing has great impact on the poor. Our expectation, as yet unsubstantiated, is that if further evidence is gathered, it will very much change how we go about producing housing, what housing is produced, and who controls the various portions of the process.

We have used our case studies to focus on several key aspects in maximizing users' satisfaction with the housing environment: (1) *selection* of dwelling units and dwelling users; the key issue here is the appropriateness for the user of the dwelling unit's *position, size,* and *configuration*; (2) *adjustment* of the housing environment to increase such appropriateness; (3) *ownership* and *control* of housing and its locale.

SELECTING A DWELLING OF APPROPRIATE POSITION, SIZE, AND CONFIGURATION

Our brief sample indicates that the position of the dwelling unit is very important to the low-income dweller. The section of the city, the neighborhood, the exact location in that neighborhood, the degree of familiarity to the user, on a high floor, at ground level, near what services such as shops, activity centers, day-care centers, clinics, transportation—all are highly important attributes in the success of a particular dweller in a specific dwelling unit.

Karen, an unmarried mother of 17 (case 4),[2] lives on "the second floor of a dilapidated building. The father of her child is in prison for larceny. ... No one occupies the first or third floor except two dogs. There is no heat except from the oven, and the whole place is falling apart. Her mother, an alcoholic, her father, her sister, and her brother all live here in three rooms and a kitchen. Karen and her baby sleep in

[2]Case studies 1, 3, 5, 7, and 8 appear at the end of this chapter; cases 2, 4, and 6 are quoted in the chapter itself. Case 2 is by Dr. Ruick Rolland, court psychiatrist. Cases 4 and 6 are by Margaret Myer, psychiatric social worker, social service agency.

a big bed with grandmother. .... Karen wants to get out because she doesn't want her child growing up as she did with fights and alcohol." The baby's zealous, religious paternal grandmother, who lives in Brighton, found a cheap apartment for Karen near her. After six weeks of living there Karen and her baby left in the middle of the night, taking everything with them and returning home. Karen was homesick for South Boston, for her friends, family, and familiar surroundings. Brighton seemed strange, hostile, and very lonely; she wants to be on her own—but in South Boston. After attempts at finding other housing in the same building, Karen applied for public housing "right across the street from where she lived. After considerable delay . . . she was admitted. . . . She is delighted because she is on the ground floor and there are other small children about. Being in this locale means everything to her because she sees her friends. She knows no world outside this and to be uprooted, even as far as a mile, is intolerable for her."

The Bradys (case 5) wouldn't consider moving from their neighborhood of Dorchester; Mr. Brady feels that "the only worthwhile thing he has is his extended family and friends."

One key aspect of position, then, is familiarity, nearness to family, friends, and social groups, which are supportive. We may well speculate that in locales which are poor in supporting institutions, proximity to these other, personal resources becomes quite important. Being removed from them brings much loss of support.

A basic means of solving the problems of a difficult housing environment is to move to a different and potentially more appropriate one. Cases 4 and 5 suggest the importance of the familiar context in the individual's dwelling unit; other issues, however, may be even more important to the family, and may take them to a new and entirely different location.

Mrs. G. (case 3) apparently wouldn't hesitate to leave her present neighborhood if better housing were available. She has made a succession of moves trying to find a housing situation that would discourage delinquent behavior in her sons. "During the six years the G. family has been known to the Roxbury court clinic, adequate housing has been a recurring issue. The family has a history of delinquent and criminal behavior. Mrs. G. has been determined that her four sons not repeat this pattern, and her four moves have been motivated by her search for a neighborhood that would discourage delinquent behavior." The G. family solved its problem by returning to the original neighborhood, but to their own home with a yard and adequate room for each family member, and by renewing their interest in social activities provided by the local church. (This case study is particularly worth reading for its account of how the G. Family was frustrated by its environment in its four successive moves, and because a kind of substantial success was achieved at the end of this struggle.)

Schorr[3] points out that "even when their parents are not responding at all" to changes in housing, "children change their feeling about the whole of life—a change particularly noticeable in school. There is evidence that children who are rehoused are considerably more likely to be promoted at a normal pace." Yet a number of aspects in the selection process work against the user's securing a dwelling in the desired locale. The waiting list system of public housing, specifically, is difficult: (1) in federal public housing, the applicant's name is placed at the bottom of the list and waits his turn; when his name arrives at the top, he is offered the first apartment that becomes available; if he rejects it as unsuitable, he goes to the bottom of the list and starts over; (2) in state-supported public housing the applicant gets three chances, instead of one, to find a suitably located unit before his name returns to the bottom of the list. Three is much better than one, but it is still far from producing the best match of dwellers and dwellings. Further, lack of ability to easily look for housing, shortness of time and money to do so, lack of information and institutions to help in securing housing, and short supply of suitable dwellings all work against the applicant's finding a dwelling unit in the neighborhood(s) desired, and one that is economically feasible.

Other issues of position are significant, in addition to those that involve a dwelling unit's location in a specific neighborhood or in a specific type of environment. Child-rearing families have great need for a dwelling unit at or near ground level so that supervision of children can be carried out inside or outside of the unit without the mother's having to be in both places at once. Such an arrangement allows the growing child to range outward from mother in a more or less continuous fashion. Further, easy access to shops and other services becomes a high priority for child-rearing and elderly households alike. And for a number of household types it appears desirable to find a certain local incidence of similar households that will supply social life, mutual support, other children to play with, and so on.

---

[3]Alvin C. Schorr, *Slums and Social Insecurity*, U.S. Dept. of H.E.W., Social Security Division, Division of Research and Statistics, Research Report No. 1, U.S. Gov. Printing Office, Washington, D.C. 1962.

Kelly has four children under the age of four, all still in diapers (case 6). Their building is isolated near the expressway. Her neighbors are single. There are no shopping or laundry facilities nearby. Kelly can't leave the house because she can't get all the children out at the same time. She can't send them down to play because she has no yard. Kelly is from another city and" knows no one to help her. So for days on end she is alone with four babies, unable to move. She has no washing machine and can't get to the laundromat, so she must do all the wash by hand. Once in a while the husband takes the laundry. She is trapped without recourse or friends, having come from another city, and without supervised facilities for the children that would allow her to search for new, more compatible housing or just give her a chance to run errands or relax. Since her husband holds two jobs, his income is too high for public housing and he has no time to search the limited market of available rentals. Kelly was referred for social service by neighbors." The social worker feels that Kelly, herself, and her children even more are in jeopardy.

A way out of such a situation is for the family to relocate to a dwelling unit at ground level, so that children may go outside, in a neighborhood that has other mothers and children, so that work and problems can be shared, where some babysitters may be found, where shops, services, and transportation are near enough to be gotten to regularly. To achieve such a lifesaving move, however, Kelly would need someone like a social worker to intervene and clear the way to achieve the move. Without such help, the difficulty can't be remedied. And cost to the society may be great.

Case 7 reinforces this important need for an intervening agency to act in behalf of and as advocate for families or individuals who are having trouble getting appropriate housing. A family consisting of a mother, a father, and eight children came to this area from New Jersey. "The father is a steady worker but earns only $55 weekly at an unskilled job." Attempts to get the family into public housing at first failed because the family could not meet the minimal three-year residency requirement. The family could not set aside enough money to pay the month's rent in advance demanded by many landlords of private housing. Moreover, no landlord wanted a family with eight children. The family found a small and rundown apartment in Roxbury. It deteriorated even more, and finally "the house was condemned. For more than four months the family lived without electricity or water. The children did their homework by candlelight, and all members of the family brought in water by the pailful from a local gas station. . . . The windows of the third floor (the floor above) were knocked out by vagrants so that rain and snow came in and seeped down into this already cold apartment. The family lived in fear that vagrants who could easily enter the first floor would cause a fire."

The family was refused public housing because, they were told, an apartment with five bedrooms "would be substandard." The parents contemplated separating so that the mother would be eligible for AFDC, a way, perhaps, of opening more doors through increased income. This struggle obviously led to depression, feelings of futility, desperation. Only through the persistent, continuing efforts of two social agencies involved with this family were they finally acepted for housing on the basis of the father's being a veteran. The family was accepted 13 months after its first application.

The size, shape, grouping, and appointment of spaces both inside and outside the dwelling unit can have a significant impact on the success or failure of the individual or the family living there. The *Report of the National Advisory Commission on Civil Disorders* says that "in nearly every disorder city surveyed, grievances related to housing were important factors in the structure of Negro discontent." These grievances fell into two categories: physically inadequate units and overcrowding. Many consequences of overcrowding have been noted: fatigue and too little sleep, inability to study for lack of space and quiet, family activities being pushed outdoors, causing lack of parental control and separation from the family at an early age. An important factor in the solution of Mrs. G.'s problem (case 3) was finding a home where each son had his own room. Kelly (case 6) thinks she could stand "anything if only she had a yard and could live on the ground floor." Her present situation leads to desperation. Karen (case 4) has good impressions of the D Street housing project; she is on the ground floor and there are other small children. Mrs. L . (case 1) emphasizes adequate laundry facilities as an important item when she looks for housing. An architectural design team (case 8), which is designing moderate to low-income housing for families with children, found that despite substantial effort on the part of the architects, the developer, and city and federal agencies, their predictions about which alternative design would be appropriate and which would not turned out to be quite inaccurate. A specific case in point: walled gardens were provided outside living rooms to increase a sense of privacy and private territory. Tenants see these "positive" and not inexpensive arrangements as serious danger points, providing cover for any burglar seeking to get into the house; the garden walls that provide privacy also keep the garden from being observed and policed from the surrounding low-income neighborhood.

Each of these reports indicates the importance of some aspect of the dwelling unit. Case 8 indicates something of the difficulty to be found in predicting what those aspects will be. The delivery side of the market very much needs to be better informed about such aspects of housing. With more study and investigation, issues of size and configuration could be identified and planned for as a function of the life-styles of the users.

Overcrowding, doubling up, and subdividing larger units are functions of short supply, both national and local, and therefore are probably to be treated less by tailoring design than by increasing supply. But it would be unreasonable to neglect the life-styles induced by such shortages. Some important part of our population will get all the raising it will get under such conditions, if the present shortage continues. Further, in our fast-changing, hard-to-predict culture, substantial shortages may very well not be avoided everywhere. Rather, the difficulty seems likely to continue—and to need serious treatment not only in supply but also in issues of appropriateness.

BEING ABLE TO ADJUST THE HOUSING ENVIRONMENT

Apparently, we cannot think of today's low-income population either in terms of the élan of the Latin American squatter who *takes* his land and *houses* his family, however badly, nor in terms of the American student who, with relatively low income, invades such places as Boston's South End and puts those "deteriorating" shells to good use, occupying them, decorating them, and often upgrading them and the surrounding neighborhoods. As we have suggested, an important characteristic of many low-income housing users is, first, that they have serious difficulty in taking advantage of the opportunities that lie about them because they cannot cope with the complex difficulties that stand in the way of getting better housing. Further, control and management of the nation's low-income housing stock cannot be characterized as being in the hands of the users or of persons or agencies motivated to or capable of satisfying its indwellers. Increasing the users' control of the physical environment does not necessarily imply ownership. Apparently, there are many levels of control, from ability to paint, adjust pieces of the physical shell, and grow flowers and vegetables to participation in tenants councils, cooperative ownership, neighborhood renewal groups, and so on.

Two important areas concern us here: the individual's ability to act, which includes both his sense for acting and his skill to do so; and the responsiveness of the environment to such acts, which are determined by the attributes of the physical environment as well as its management. Both of these, to greater or lesser degree, are key aspects of his ability to adjust, achieve a successful fit for himself with his environment.

Kelly (case 6), who lives on the third floor, has to keep her windows shut because there are no screens and she fears her four small children will be in danger of falling.

Schorr refers to report of social workers who "speak of poor sanitation, of doors without locks so that drunks and vagrants wander in." He uses this example to point out the effect of the environment on the individual user.[4]

While we can point such possible remedies as building and health-code enforcement, city-wide rat control, and the like, it is worth noting here that much of the difficulty lies in the users' attitudes toward the physical shells they inhabit and their capabilities in using them. What keeps the indweller from correcting the difficulty himself, from installing the needed lock, putting up a few screens? What keeps him and other tenants from acting together against the landlord, as has been done so successfully, for example, through Roxbury's Fair Housing, Inc.?

We need to pay attention to new institutions that can arm the user with skills, tools, attitudes, and advocates whereby he can operate upon his own housing environment; with new systems of management that are substantially responsive to user need; and with planning and design that increase the flexible use of housing by changing users over time. Alienation from the environment appears to be characterized by weakness with respect to it. With power to operate on the environment meaningfully for one's own ends comes a connectedness or relatedness to it—an adaptation that seems to differ greatly from the one that occurs when a person simply lists his difficulties with the environment. Much would be achieved if the energies of the poor, which are not fully utilized, could be put to use in improving the poor's housing environment. If poor people's sense of power with respect to the environment could increase; if their alienation from it decrease!

[4]Schorr, *Slums and Social Insecurity*, p. 12.

OWNING HOUSING AND CONTROLLING ITS LOCALE

While the process of selecting and adjusting the housing environment may do much to satisfy the user (or to harm him), many people apparently need to own their housing and control its locale to some degree.

The K.'s (case 2) for many years owned their own home on a pleasant street in Roxbury; their own house, a garden, room for pets, and compatible neighbors seemed very important to this southern migrant family, which had owned its own farm in the South.

About seven years ago the K.'s had to leave their home because their street was to be torn down in urban renewal. They were enraged about this because they did not view their block as a deteriorated one. Their financial position compelled the family to move into a low-income housing project. The family was depressed by the move. Loss of space, of their garden and pets, and especially of home ownership was distressing to them, and the behavior of family members deteriorated rapidly. Three of the five younger children soon gained records as juvenile delinquents. These children might have gotten into trouble anyway, but this family presented no problems for the community before its move to public housing, and many afterward. Eventually, the family posed such big problems in housing that it was evicted, moving to a very deteriorated apartment in the community. The family has never regained its former level of functioning.

Mrs. G.'s final and successful solution (case 3) was to return, after many moves, to the original, highly delinquent street which she had left —but to a house of her own. "The house she bought was in a very deteriorated condition, . . . but it stood on a block where people owned their own homes. The boys could play in the backyard and in a field nearby. Each of the boys was able to have his own room. The whole family involved itself in improving the house. The boys worked on the house, played close to home, and became very involved in the activities of the Catholic church a block away—they even became dedicated altar boys! Since they moved nearly a year ago, they have been involved in no delinquent activities and have been doing well in school. the whole family has seemed much happier since the move. Even though they are on the street where they first lived—unimproved since they left it— home ownership, adequate room, outdoor space, and neighborhood projects in which the entire family can get involved seem to have made a great difference to them.

To the degree that such motivation exists and can be made operable, home ownership may be turned to reducing dissatisfaction, stopping the deterioration of the housing stock, and increasing the well-being of the society. We believe that such motivation may be considerable!

MOVING TOWARD A PUBLIC POLICY

Making public policy that will bring about more appropriate housing for the poor is not simple. While there have been many housing programs, few have concerned themselves with the poor and few have sought to satisfy moderate- and low-income groups with housing that is more than shelter. Further, forces in the housing industry lead to unresponsiveness to the various demands of prospective users. In short, we face a set of historical forces that will be hard to counteract, and we have little technical knowledge or experience of how to reverse them. The discussion and recommendations that follow are made in the light of these difficulties.

We have suggested, with limited case history support, that the *qualitative* aspects of housing, the *appropriateness* of various housing characteristics are very important to the user, for good or bad. They include the process of matching users to dwelling units, the process of adjusting housing environments to users and vice versa, the issue of ownership, and so on. Further, we have suggested such aspects have to do with the poor becoming less dependent, becoming nonpoor. Not only is this valuable for the poor; in the long run it reduces dependency upon the state for housing programs, and possibly for other programs, too.

We have attempted to give some sense of the difficulties that inhere in making decisions about the environment's qualitative aspects centrally and at a remove from the people affected. We suggest that this difficulty will probably grow as our world changes and becomes increasingly complex.

We recommend, in consequence that the state as much as possible seek policies that will increase the power of housing users—here, low-income-housing users—to determine which qualities are important to them and which are not. It is not easy to foresee all the important ways in which the low-income person may increase his power over his housing environment. The following recommendations grew from our studies or were suggested to us by others:

Increase the individual's ability to compete for valuable housing opportunities by increasing his ability to spend for housing.

Increase the individual's ability to act upon his environment by making available the institutions necessary for such action at a cost the user can afford. Such institutions are not absent from middle- and upper-income communities: information systems about housing choices —e.g., realtors, newspapers, journals; advocates prepared to act on behalf of the user in order to solve his housing problems—e.g., lawyers, architects, realtors; mortgage loans and insurance policies; agencies capable of judging the reliability of a mortgage-holder and his property in a particular neighborhood—e.g., banks, neighborhood development corporations, insurance agencies.

Increase the individual's ability to act collectively upon his housing environment, whether he is a tenant acting with other tenants to get satisfaction from a landlord or an owner seeking with others to upgrade his dwelling unit and locale, by increasing his understanding that he can act more powerfully in this way, by arming him with necessary institutions (discussed above), by supporting collective efforts with funds for early planning forays and technician-advocates.

One important deterrent to a person's acting to improve his own lot is that his single effort will be lost unless his neighbors also act. If he is a home owner seeking to upgrade the structure, the value of his efforts will not return to him unless home owners in his neighborhood act jointly to upgrade their property. Further, the individual will have difficulty finding mortgage or home improvement loans in that solitary endeavor in a low-income neighborhood. Joining collectively with his neighbors, however, is a feasible course of action if the proper institutions are developed in low-income neighborhoods to do the necessary financing. If the single actor is a dissatisfied tenant, he runs the risk either of bringing about no change or of jeopardizing his tenancy. If he acts collectively, his security and success are much more likely.

Increase the supply of housing available to low-income users in ways that make it as appropriate and valuable as possible to them. Do this by: increasing the motivation of housing suppliers dependent on state support (loans or otherwise) to be responsive to the various demands of users; increasing the information provided housing suppliers about the nature of those demands; increasing users' participation in generating such housing.

Increase the potential for upward social mobility in as many ways as possible. Do this by: subsidizing income to bring it up to the nonpoor level; developing, at low interest rates, a workable scattered-site program with mixed income levels and household types (see the preceding chapter); diversifying unit size and rent, within limits, in existing public-housing projects in low-income areas.

More money and less emotional disorder would appear to increase the housing choices for those of moderate income—but a number of negative aspects that have impact on the poor also influence people of moderate means. In fact, with one exception, the market appears to be substantially continuous between moderate-income people and low-income people, merely growing less appropriate and acceptable as income declines. Moderate-income people suffer from short supply, unresponsiveness to variable demand, shortage of housing institutions, and the phenomenon that the dwelling is of considerable importance to the user, for good or bad, because it represents much of what he has.

Real improvement for the poor in qualitative aspects of their housing can be politically achieved only by providing a real improvement for moderate-income people as well. With respect to questions of appropriateness and users' power over the housing environment, we argue that many moderate-income people may be considered to be not different from the poor. Further, it is not politically reasonable to expect that the poor may become nonpoor through income subsidization, and begin to compete for housing with moderate-income people. Thus, a politically viable program must increase the housing available to moderate-income people. (One advantage of viewing the housing process, politically and economically, as a continuum with no sharp lines between poor and nonpoor is the poor are not required to cross any important lines in becoming unpoor, and the potential for upward social mobility is increased.) Whatever housing measures are considered must be aimed at low- and moderate-income people alike. Certain difficulties will probably require special attention, and therefore measures will need to be more selective in serving some portion of the poor.

What do we recommend?

MAKING STATE HOUSING POLICY

The state should become responsible, in a way that it presently is not, for a serious and evolving housing policy that takes into account quantitative and qualitative aspects of housing, the action of the housing market, and the many actions of state and other governmental agencies which influence the housing supply. Further, it should become informed by means of social accounting which explicitly introduces the many social costs and benefits of the housing environment of the state with respect to the many other state programs, and thus integrate the housing program with these other programs by recommending policy. This substantial task will require staff members and consultants. One of its tasks will be to inform the state about housing people of low-income and recommend policy in regard to them.

SUBSIDIZING INCOME AND INCREASING THE HOUSING SUPPLY

The subsidization of housing in order to increase the user's ability to select appropriate housing for himself has two essential elements. One is the need to subsidize housing income for low-income people so that they can compete for and select from more valuable housing opportunities. This income subsidy should be enough so that not more than one-fifth of the occupant's income is spent on housing. Second is the need to generate enough new housing to satisfy the combined demand of moderate- and low-income groups, so that moderate-income people are not disadvantaged by low-income groups' increasing ability to spend. The several programs used to finance such housing, whether federal programs 235 or 236 or programs of the state, should keep open the diversity of opportunity afforded the user for either renting or owning. It is strongly recommended that in the absence of federal funding the state develope and fund such subsidies. Those developers seeking low-interest state loans should be constrained to meet in every way possible the needs of the potential users and the locale of the housing.

DEVELOPING HOUSING INSTITUTIONS IN LOW-INCOME AREAS

Low-income residential areas are notably bereft of the basic institutions needed for coping with the environment in any normal, nonpoor way. Such areas lack housing information, such technical support as lawyers and planners, financing for local would-be owners, and so forth. The federal government has begun to provide some of these institutions, such as its successful legal aid program; although more of these may be expected, it may be that the state should take on an increasing role in the development of such institutions.

State housing information system

The state should establish and fund an information system that will provide the many policy-makers, housing agencies, housing suppliers, developers, owners, and managers, housing users and housing technicians with more complete information about housing, its current opportunities and constraints for all the people involved in either supply or consumption. Particular attention should be paid to making such information available to low-income people and their advocates and advisers, for this group of users can considerably enlarge its power over its environment through the increase of such information. Through such a state function the experience of professionals serving various low- and moderate-income groups can be collected and made available in new and valuable ways for the next rounds of environmental development. Such a function may be one of the most potent tools for guiding the supply side of the housing market.

Housing advocate system

There is general need for neighborhood agencies that can supply advice or act as advocates for a user, or a group of users with respect to adverse situations in the housing environment: intervening with negligent landlords, putting pressure on unresponsive governmental agencies, and so on. Such service would have to be free or very inexpensive for low- and moderate-income users. Roxbury's Fair Housing, Inc., is an excellent example of such an agency.

The successful federal legal aid programs is another example, except that it is not specifically housing-oriented. The state should take whatever steps are necessary to: (1) reinforce valuable efforts that already exist; (2) bring new local agencies into existence where they do not exist; (3) ensure continued support of both new and existing agencies. Such a program could do much to increase the power of the poor and of moderate-income people over their environment and destinies. Upper-income groups do have such services available and can afford to put them to use. And such services can make useful the information about housing opportunities that would be made centrally available through a state housing information system.

Community development corporations

The state should bring into being and support community development corporations that are familiar with their locales. These corporations could act as intelligent and responsive mortgagers in improving existing housing stock and developing new housing stock; they could aid in securing other such features of development as necessary equity, fire insurance, and so on, where potentially responsible local renewal action exists. Here, as in any banking function, a sensitivity to local life-styles—to which elements in the social group are responsible and which are not—is the only means of making sound judgments. In particular, community development corporations may find local neighborhood improvement groups that, if properly organized, would be suitable recipients of financial support.

SUPPORTING LOCAL COMMUNITY DEVELOPMENT

A dwelling unit must be treated as interdependent with its locale: improvement or deterioration of one dwelling unit, or several, has a significant impact on others in its locale; improvement or deterioration of such local services as schools, playgrounds, and streets can have much to do with the success of the locale. If we are to increase the power of housing users over their housing environment, we must increase this kind of activity. The state should support a course of action that generates and supports local community activities:

Neighborhood development corporations

The state should promote the use of Neighborhood Development Corporations to upgrade the quality of the local housing environment. The state should make available initial planning funds for local groups to form such corporations and employ planners, designers, and advocates to act in their behalf.

Co-ops and condominiums

The state should promote the use of cooperative or condominium forms of ownership of multiunit housing developments to increase the responsiveness of management to the user's needs, to increase value to the low- and moderate-income user, to control rent, and so forth.

INCREASING VALUABLE HOUSING OPPORTUNITIES

To satisfy the present growing demand for housing in the low- and moderate-income range—a demand that will be made more manifest by subsidization of low-income people—we must markedly increase the supply of appropriate housing for people whose incomes are too low to provide them with "market-rate" housing. The preceding chapter recommends a range of approaches to increase the housing supply, including strong support for use of low-interest development loans for both new construction and rehabilitation. In order to ensure that such state programs provide appropriate results, requirements should be placed upon the use of such loans and programs. Such requirements, some of which are discussed below, will produce a somewhat higher initial construction cost and, in some ways, an increase in the complexity of the development process; but it is not at all clear that the net cost of such housing will increase if the owner finds it suitable, relates to it, takes care of it and upgrades it, draws benefit from such activities through ownership or sense of identification or both. The state needs to make careful studies of the costs and benefits of such aspects of housing.

There remains the need to increase the interest of the developing agent's interest in becoming involved with an even more complex process of housing development. (Here it may be necessary to increase the profit allowed on construction.) First, systems, including ownership and cooperative ownership, should be developed in which the planning, design, and management of housing is controlled by the needs of the users, and in which actual, potential, or surrogate users, including those of the local and surrounding housing community, participate. Such housing should take into consideration: (1) the possible benefits to users of a mixture of housing types and rents, and (2) the possibility of making such new housing more attractive to the existing community by ensuring that the housing pays real-estate taxes or their equivalent, by avoiding discontinuity in design between new housing and the surrounding community, and the like. Second, large aggregations of lower-income groups should be minimized, and limited "patches" (as in existing scattered-site housing policy) of socioeconomic homogeneity should be pursued in new housing and in rehabilitation projects. Attention should be paid to diversifying income range and dwelling unit size in existing public housing projects.

INCREASING POTENTIAL FOR UPWARD MOBILITY

In locating and arranging new housing, and in rehabilitating existing housing, the state should take care first, to increase the potential of low-income people to move upward from that income group, and, second, to decrease large-scale aggregations of the poor. The National Commission on Urban Problems, in *More Than Shelter: Social Needs in Low and Moderate Income Housing*, convincingly concludes its discussion of mobility potential—the opportunity for upward mobility in the poor—by saying:

> *To foster individual and family growth and self sufficiency, four elements are required:*
> *1. Sufficient financial assistance or subsidies to underwrite the cost of living in suitable environment*
> *2. Opportunities for advancement, including education, training and employment*
> *3. Community, health, welfare, and counseling services*
> *4. A favorable social environment which provides the models and standards to which persons and families need to conform, if they are to survive in modern society*
> *Unless all four of these elements are present, the prospects for advancement are lessened.*

The commission goes on to say that, while none of these goals is easy to achieve, only the fourth is controversial, in that it requires that unstable, problem-ridden families be given the opportunity to live in an otherwise stable social environment; consequently, it "runs head-on into the aspirations, the values and self-interests of the nonpoor." Implicit in the recommendation is the importance, for anyone but particularly for the poor, of having successful role models to emulate.

Strong forces run counter to the integration of poor with the nonpoor, and at present the Massachusetts program for scattered-site public housing is virtually nonoperative for low-income families with children, its funds sitting idle. Nevertheless, several communities about Boston have a substantial mix of income groups ranging from low to moderate and upper. In the face of this fact, it would be unreasonable to conclude that such integration is unworkable within any town or community. Nor is it reasonable to suppose that these historically evolved patterns of integration can be achieved readily or brought about by simple governmental fiat—that any town will provide a stable social environment or relevant role models for all kinds of low-income people. Rather, it would appear that some degree of economic integration is key to overcoming the condition of poverty, that it is a possible modus vivendi, that the process by which it is to be achieved is subtle, complex, and variable in character from community to community and from one low-income group to another.

Two broad areas of concern appear: the existing extensive aggregations of low- and moderate-income people, and the existing larger aggregations of people of moderate income and higher. Any competent strategy should deal aggressively with both these areas. In both the attempt should be made to diversify the population mix by income, age, and household type, and to diversify in such a way that the resulting coexisting social elements are relevant one to another. In large aggregations of low-income people, success should be permitted to happen, induced by such strategies as: (1) providing sufficient financial assistance; (2) supporting home ownership, community development, increased local control of the schools, and so forth; (3) integrating public housing with that of the housing market in general and, where possible, diversifying the standard dwelling unit plan through rehabilitation; (4) permitting for interconnectedness with other income groups through transportation, institutional location, and the introduction of moderate- and upper-income housing in these areas. Care should be taken not to reduce the number of units available but rather increase that number in these areas, while dealing with other problems as well.

With respect to the second extensive population group, those of moderate income and higher, the strategy should permit for social and physical planning for the state and for each community so that diversification by income and household type, sought by the greater community, the state, can be achieved in the ways most suitable to various regions and local communities. Moreover, the ways in which the state supports housing growth—through low-interest loans, for example—should require local communities to house some important proportion of low-income people.

Policy in these matters should be developed carefully, in order to make diversification as relevant as possible both to the existing community and to the incoming lower-income groups. There are many ways by which such an end may be brought about, some much better than others. To move in counterproductive ways could be costly here. Not to move at all, an all too acceptable course of action, may be more costly yet. The state should move on this problem where local communities cannot do so, with sensitivity both to its variable aspects and to the ultimate power to bring about change.

Case study 1: Mrs. L.

(Case study made by Gail Chang, a hospital social worker.)

Mrs. L. is a 25-year-old Negro mother of four children. She was born in Birmingham, Alabama, and came to Boston five years ago. Her oldest child was born in Birmingham, and joined his mother in Boston when he was almost four years old. The other children were born in Boston. The last, a boy, was delivered two months prematurely while Mrs. L. was hospitalized for pneumonia. Mrs. L. is not married although the last three children are by the same father, who is actively interested in them.

Mrs. L. is a bright, intelligent, attractive young woman who completed the eleventh grade but did not return to finish high school because she had been in a fight with one of the teachers. When she first came to Boston she worked as a stitcher in a factory but had to give up her job after her oldest son joined her and she had had another child; she could not find baby sitters could not afford to pay them. She went on Aid to Families with Dependent Children.

Since Mrs. L.'s arrival in Boston she has lived in about five apartments. Once she lived in an apartment which she describes as "nice," but she did not get along with the landlord and so she left. The other apartments she describes as "lousy"; there was no heat, windows were broken and not replaced, doors fell in.

The social worker started working with Mrs. L. in September 1968 around problems with her oldest son. She was then living in Dorchester on the third floor of a three-family house. The apartment consisted of three and one-half rooms with kitchen and bathroom. It was very run down, with plaster peeling and cracking, and the front and back porches were giving way. Windows were broken and patched up with cardboard, and a closet door had fallen down one day, very narrowly missing the children who were playing in the same room. The door was not fixed, nor were the windows. Plumbing and heating did not work.

Although there was provision for heat, the furnace was in need of repair, and the tenants had to pay for heat themselves. Because Mrs. L. lived on the third floor she came out the worst in that she got no heat or very sporadic heat even though she filled the oil tank every week.

At this time Mrs. L. had three children and was expecting her fourth. The second child, a boy, was three and a half years old and very energetic, and would constantly wander out on to the back porch; Mrs. L. had to watch him all the time. Despite many complaints to the building agent, nothing was done. Mrs. L. had spent one winter in this apartment and was planning to move. However, before she could do so several crises came up: her daughter fractured her arm; one of her sons got pneumonia; and Mrs. L. herself was hospitalized for pneumonia. During this hospitalization she delivered her fourth baby, prematurely, in December 1968.

The baby was kept in the hospital even after he was ready to go home to his mother and the rest of the family. Mrs. L., who was still recovering from pneumonia, went out as often as she could in search of an apartment (this was in January) but was further hampered by not being able to find baby sitters. The Boston Housing Authority was contacted, but it was learned that Mrs. L. had once applied there, had been assigned to East Boston, and had not told the BHA why she refused the project. (She had refused because it meant moving far away from friends and a neighborhood with which she was familiar, and because of what she had heard about racial prejudice in East Boston.) With some urging, Mrs. L. was willing to reactivate her application but did not follow through because she felt she would have no say in where she wanted to live.

The social worker also contacted federal housing to see what they could do about finding another apartment for Mrs. L. She was told that it would take some time since they would first have to send inspectors out to Mrs. L.'s present apartment and serve a notice on the landlord to do something about the heat. Several weeks had gone by; the baby was about six weeks old, and the pediatricians and other hospital personnel were concerned about the maternal deprivation which the infant was experiencing: although Mrs. L. was allowed to give daily feedings to the baby, she was able to come only a few times since she was usually out looking for an apartment or keeping medical appointments for her other children. (She did not keep any medical appointments for herself.) Finally, the doctors decided that the infant would be better off with its mother, and effort had to be made to keep him warm with blankets since space heaters would have overloaded the electricity and Mrs. L. was afraid of faulty wiring.

Coincident with this decision came some action from the landlord to fix the furnace after he had been served a notice by federal housing. Consequently, Mrs. L. brought the baby home from the hospital only to find that there was absolutely no heat because the landlord had stripped the furnace in order to fix it. For two days she was without any heat at all, and after about seven phone calls to federal housing some action was taken, as illustrated by the following phone call from Mrs. L. in which she said, "Miss C., what did you do, there must be about seven men down there fixing that furnace." Although there was much rejoicing, the repair on the furnace lasted only temporarily; moreover, much heat was lost through the missing windowpanes and through cracks in the windows.

Not until spring did federal housing find a place for Mrs. L. This time she moved to a renovated apartment in a building in Roxbury. This apartment is quite nice and has three bedrooms, living room, kitchen, and bath with shower. (The children had never before seen a shower.) It is in a fairly central location, and at first Mrs. L was quite pleased with it. Now she has discovered that there are rats in the building and in her apartment. The tenants in the building have formed an association and have met with federal housing as well as lodged their complaints with the management. So far—in August 1969—nothing has been done. Mrs. L. loses sleep while she investigates every sound coming from the baby's room or from the other children's room. She is even ready to move back to her old apartment with no heat but also no rats, rather than stay in this "nice" apartment and worry about rats. (Her other complaint about this place is that no washing machines are allowed because washing machines are provided in the basement. However, there are only two machines for the whole building, the basement has a dirt floor and puddles of water are always there, and there are no tables for folding.)

Mrs. L. feels that her only resort is to move again; she feels quite helpless to do anything more about the rats. One avenue open to Mrs. L. and the other tenants is to withhold the rent until the management does something, but there is no guarantee that holding back the rent will produce results.

Mrs. L.'s difficulty with housing is not unlike that confronting many families living in this area. Her case points out the energy employed not only by her but by the agencies involved in finding suitable housing—

energy diverted from seeking resolution of her other problems. Although we have no guarantee that manipulation of the external environment necessarily leads to resolution of intrapsychic problems, we know that when housing and other environmental problems are solved, families like Mrs. L.'s become able to concentrate on finding solutions to other problems. One very simple illustration of this that after Mrs. L. moved and before she discovered rats in the new apartment, she spent very little time discussing housing with the social worker, but rather focused on other issues.

Case study 3: The G. Family

(Case study made by Susanne Mosteller, court social worker.)

During the six years the G. family has been known to the Roxbury court clinic, adequate housing has been a recurring issue. The family has a history of delinquent and criminal behavior. Mrs. G. has been determined that her four sons not repeat this pattern, and her four moves have been motivated by her search for a neighborhood which would discourage delinquent behavior.

Mrs G. first moved from an apartment on the street where she had grown up. Her family was one of the few Irish families left on a street which had undergone a rapid transition from Irish to black. She moved her sons, who were becoming involved in delinquent activities, to a largely white project in Charlestown. To her disappointment this dismal project, one with no play space or organized activities for children, was filled with wandering bands of children who amused themselves by throwing rocks at windows, loitering in project hallways until inhabitants called the police to run them out, etc. A few weeks after the move to Charlestown the boys were in trouble with the police, and Mrs. G. was searching for an apartment in a respectable but inexpensive area of Dorchester.

The move to Dorchester improved the family's functioning but did not solve its problems. The family had moved to a neighborhood of older home owners who prided themselves on the order and quiet of their street. Again there was no room for the boys to play outdoors, no nearby playground, and no organized activities. Mrs. G. recognized that the nieghborhood did not meet her boys' needs but could find no housing within her limited means (public assistance) that did. An intelligent, perceptive, and well-organized woman, she searched persistently for a better environment that she could afford. Because she was unable to find it, the family remained in the Dorchester neighborhood for three years. The boys were involved in none of the delinquent activities in which they had previously engaged; however, there was great tension with neighbors who complained of the boys' noise and trespassing on their property. There was tension between Mrs. G. and her sons as she attempted to coerce them into meeting the demands of the neighborhood—very difficult for active boys. After persistent and increasing complaints from neighbors, the landlord insisted that Mrs. G. move her family.

Mrs. G. spoke longingly of her wish to move her family to the suburbs or to lower-middle-class neighborhoods in the city where facilities for children would be available. This, however, was unrealistic. Instead she moved to a busy street in Codman Square where she was able to find a larger apartment which would give her sons more privacy and room to play at home and where there were other children in the neighborhood and neighbors whom she thought would be more tolerant. However, she was able to afford a larger apartment only by moving to a deteriorating neighborhood.

Neighbors in the new neighborhood proved to be tolerant, but they were people with many problems. Most of the children in the new neighborhood had police records. While Mrs. G.'s sons spent more time at home enjoying the larger apartment, they ran into difficulties when they moved outdoors. Again there was no place for the boys to play, and no facilities for organized or informal activities in the neighborhood. The boys played on the grounds of a nearby church and a school, but were run out and on several occasions the police were called. They fought with other children in the neighborhood and became involved with them in delinquent activity—stealing from stores, bullying younger children, truancy. There were many contacts with the police, and the boys' school performance deteriorated badly.

Mrs. G. felt another move was essential. Surveying her limited possibilities, she decided the best alternative was to come back to the same neighborhood in Roxbury she had originally left, but in a home of her own, which she had always wanted. She was able to buy a house for $1,000. (As a welfare recipient, this was not a legitimate alternative for her. She solved the problem by using her brother's name as purchaser.) The house she bought was in very deteriorated condition and on the same highly delinquent street she had originally left, but it stood on a block where people owned their own homes. The boys could play in the backyard and in a field nearby. Each of the boys was able to have his own room. The whole family involved itself in improving the house. The boys worked on the house, played close to home, and became very involved in the activities of the Catholic church a block away—they even became dedicated altar boys! Since they moved nearly a year ago, they have been involved in no delinquent activities and have been doing well in school. The whole family has seemed much happier since the move. Even though they are on the street where they first lived—unimproved since they left it—home ownership, adequate room, outdoor space, and neighborhood projects in which the entire family can get involved seem to have made a great difference to them.

Case study 5: Mrs. B.

(Case study made by M. Myer, social service agency worker.)

Mary S. married her high school football hero, Alby B. He worked for landscape firms but was usually unemployed in the winter. They had three babies, one right after another. The first came while they lived with her family, the second while they lived with his parents, and for the third they had a place of their own, a two-bedroom apartment which was inexpensive and near their friends and family.

When Mrs. Brady became pregnant a fourth time they applied for public housing. They desperately wanted to get in because the cost was within their budget and there were no extras such as heating. They were unable to find an apartment for a reasonable rent in Dorchester, and neither even considered looking elsewhere. After a two-year wait and a final resort to political pull, they were given a three-room apartment. They were thrilled. The project is "very nice." It is well-maintained, there are a few units, all are three stories, it is within walking distance of good stores, and there are play fields.

Three years and another baby later, they are dying to get out. Why? "Because it's a trap—all the people who can't go elsewhere end up here —the kids are bad, the gossip terrible. Everyone here is in trouble and we are all bunched together with no way out because no one will take a big family, especially if there is no father. Being here is like being in jail." It is a very depressing world. This winter Alby B. looked for a place in Dorchester that would take his family. Nothing was available. He will not move out of Dorchester because he says that the only worthwhile thing he has is his extensive family and friends.

Because the neighborhood is vital to this family, their options are reduced. They are trapped: if Alby B. makes "too much" money they will be evicted, and he has been unable to find anyplace that will take four children.

Case study 7

(Case study made by Shirl Fay, social service agency worker.)

This family consists of mother, father, and eight children. The parents are both from Alabama and came to this area from New Jersey. Initially both parents were working but the mother had to give up her job to care for her children. The father is a steady worker, but earns only $55 weekly at an unskilled job. The family found an apartment in Roxbury, the second floor of a deteriorating house. The quarters were obviously inadequate; the family was crowded into three bedrooms, a living room, kitchen, and bath.

Attempts to get the family into public housing initially failed as family could not meet the minimal three-year residency requirement. The family could not set aside enough money to pay the month's rent in advance demanded by many landlords of private housing. Moreover, no landlord wanted a family with eight children.

During the next few months, the apartment deteriorated even more, and finally the house was condemned. For more than four months the family lived without electricity or water. The children did their homework by candlelight, and all members of the family brought in water by the pailful from a local gas station. Mother heated water on the oil stove to do the family's washing in the bathtub and went to neighbors to do her ironing. The windows of the third floor were knocked out by vagrants so that rain and snow came in freely and seeped down into this already cold apartment. The family lived in fear that vagrants who could easily enter the first floor would cause a fire.

At the same time, the family was refused public housing because, they were told, an apartment with five bedrooms would be substandard. The parents contemplated separating so that the mother would be eligible for AFDC, a way, perhaps, of opening more doors through increased income. This struggle obviously led to depression, feelings of utter futility, desperation.

Only through the persistent, continuing efforts of two social agencies involved with this family were they finally accepted for housing, on the basis of the father's being a veteran. The family was accepted 13 months after its first application. It should be noted that the Boston Housing Authority requested a statement from the father, which he supplied: "I have been with my family for 20 years, and I am expecting to continue to live with them."

Case study 8

(Case study made by J. Myer, member of an architectural and planning firm.)

During the mid-1960s, an architectural design team undertook the design of some 200 rental dwelling units on ten acres of land cleared by urban renewal in a black neighborhood of Boston. The financing for the project was carried out under the Federal Housing Authority's sub-market housing program (221-D-3), which produces rents of $100-$150 a month for two-, three-, and four-bedroom apartments for families with moderate income and for low-income families with rent supplements. The Boston Redevelopment Authority chose as a developer for the project a nonprofit corporation organized to undertake new types of housing in Boston. The company might be described as having the best possible intentions with respect to providing desirable housing.

The intentions of both the developer and the Redevelopment Authority were to provide dwelling units for families with children, this being the kind of unit in shortest supply; to provide as good a design as could possibly be achieved; to have the architects be aware of the design and planning of recent housing projects in the same area. From the outset the designers and the developer were concerned that they be informed as much as possible about the characteristics, needs, lifestyles, and aspirations of the people who would eventually live in the project. Two attempts were made to meet with people from the local community. The first, held early in the design process, due to lack of interest on the part of local people or ineptness at arranging for meeting, actually slowed down attempts at gaining good information. The second, part way through, was much more successful and gave clear and definite preferences about how the open space of the project might be used. Neither of these exchanges was felt to be entirely adequate, and the difficulty of gaining such information, the uncertainty at that time of its utility, and the large number of other difficulties attending the project all led to an end to such activities.

The designers, the developer, the Redevelopment Authority, and the FHA, however, gave much thought and discussion to what would be valuable to residents in that part of the city.

At many points they found themselves in disagreement. Some felt that each dwelling unit should have a lawn in front of it; others argued that grass would not survive and that children's play areas near the house were more important. Some wanted to put the kitchen at the back of the house and the living room at the front for reasons of prestige; others argued that control of children playing outside would then not be possible. What is interesting here is that these arguments took place among decision-makers who were all outside the community; they did not turn to potential users for better evidence, and in fact they could not find legitimate and reasonable ways to do so.

These decision-makers, after considerable discussion, shaped the project in the following ways. Because of the need to supervise children at play—and at considerable expense because of bad soil conditions— the dwelling units were all placed on the ground floor and approached mainly by nonthrough streets. For reason of economy and density, a variety of row-house units was employed to take account of varying unit size, ground-level change, and orientation. Kitchens were made large enough for the dining table and placed at the front of the dwelling unit, so that the mother of the household would be in the center of things, able to oversee children's activities outside—in a sense, to police the public world of the street or court as much as possible. The living room was placed at the rear of the unit and had its own outside space or private garden. Bedrooms were placed above the first floor.

In some cases where dwelling units would stand next to a large, noisy street, masonry garden walls were erected to increase the sense of separation and protection. The area outside the front door was given over partly to planting, but in the main was paved for children's play. (Each unit might have two to four children—or 600 children for the whole development.) The combination of paving and substantial new trees to be put in by the city was expected yield an attractive and appropriate place both summer and winter. Cars were parked in small open courts concealed by the dwelling units.

Some aspects of the project, now built and occupied, appear to be successful. But reports indicate that other aspects are inappropriate and even dangerous. Tenants see the walled gardens, provided outside the living rooms to increase a sense of privacy and private territory, as serious danger points that provide cover for any burglar seeking to get into the house; the garden walls that provide privacy also keep the garden from being observed and policed by the eyes of the surrounding neighborhood, which is occasionally dangerous.

The street trees which were to bring shade and nature into the environment, which were essential components in making the large, paved play areas workable and attractive, have not been installed by the city's Department of Public Works. Front yards and public spaces thus appear somewhat bald and hard to relate to. The streets themselves were completed about a year after the first residents moved it. Again, the city's Department of Public Works managed a uniquely slow delivery schedule, leaving a year of muddy approaches to the dwelling units.

The courtyard paving constructed by the private contractor was also slow to arrive. The brick areas were laid after the residents had moved in. In one courtyard, the children tore up all the bricks. This might not have happened if the bricks had been installed before occupancy, and not been seen as small, movable, independent objects by a bunch of bright, aggressive children.

The construction process, a turbulent one, was carried out primarily by white workers in a black quarter. In the main the white workers were afraid to come there because of threats of violence from blacks. The project was understaffed and moved slowly. There was considerable vandalism, breaking of windows, and theft of building materials; two partly built dwelling units were burned. There were persistent demands for changes in the construction and threats of increased vandalism. In addition, because of faulty shoring and high winds, several masonry walls collapsed during construction. While the end product meets the building laws and contemporary standards of safety, residents may have doubts about the security of such shelter because of its turbulent history.

Residents have generally resisted the use of concrete block for the masonry walls between dwelling units; they think of it as being low-cost and second-rate. There are objections to the unrelieved gray paint used on the clapboards and to the use of windows to the floor for reasons of privacy children's safety. During the construction period the black-power group made a series of demands that focused on fear of fire.

Some adjustments were made; for instance, a number of fire escapes were added.

Presently, the condition of the dwelling units appears to be reasonable, but the public areas are in many places unkempt, with paper and bottles lying all about. Management has attempted to keep up with the problem, but finds the costs running higher than the FHA formula allows. Lack of residents' participation in maintenance, most of which occurs in front of each dwelling unit, may be due to lack of identification with the whole project or due to its white origins and turbulent history; it may be because residents do not have a sense of ownership, or because they do not have the traditional front lawn, or because it seems inferior to them to have the front of the dwelling unit occupied by the kitchen. The answer may be one or some combination of these factors, or some other, unidentified issue.

The process, begun by the Redevelopment Authority, of surveying residents' perceptions in other housing projects is a valuable one and may lead to answers to these questions. Such information could be made generally available and used to guide future work and governmental policy. What seems clear to this group of architects is, first, that it is very difficult, from the outside and at a distance, to predict what a group of residents will want of their housing and the environment in which they exist, and, second, that housing and environment seem to be of considerable importance to them.

JOHN G. WOFFORD

transportation

State transportation policy can have a significant but limited impact upon the poor, in terms of the quality of their present lives and, in certain instances, their ability to move up the income ladder. Improvements are needed in transportation services and facilities, in the link between the transportation system and other systems in which the poor operate, and in the process that decides the character of those services and facilities, and surfaces or submerges those links.

Such improvements in service and in process will be no panacea: Transportation problems are subsidiary to other, more basic characteristics of poverty: low-level, deadend jobs; low educational attainment; discrimination by race and age; and inadequate resources, whether from income, welfare, Social Security, or savings, to cope with the

John G. Wofford is research associate in Urban Legal Studies at the Harvard Law School, and director of its Urban Mass Transportation Study. He wishes to acknowledge the contributions of Alan M. Rubin, Douglas Gurin, Matthew A. Coogan, Alan A. Altshuler, and the members of the seminar on "Metropolitan Transportation and the Mobility of the Poor" led jointly with Adam Yarmolinsky at Harvard Law School in the fall of 1969.

physical demands of life itself, from prenatal care to old age. Unlike these more basic structural conditions, transportation deficiencies tend to affect the poor at the margins—restricting but not preventing job-hunting, making recreation areas harder but not impossible to reach, making the trip to the hospital longer but still not out of the question, limiting the scope of comparative shopping but not barring shopping altogether.

Yet the margins can be significant. The costs of transportation deficiencies in time, money, and trips not taken hit the poor in ways that can have an important impact on their ability to cope with the world around them, in both short and long-range terms. The ambiguity of the phrase "mobility of the poor" itself suggests the complex interrelationships among the immediate ability to get around from day to day, the longer-range ability to expand one's options about where one lives, works, and plays, and the still more basic "mobility" of moving up (or down) in socioeconomic status.

This chapter is concerned with mobility problems at the margins— with day-to-day transportation obstacles, the range of their impact on the lives of poor people, and ways in which public policy might deal with some of those obstacles. No new programs of large public expenditures are proposed. Indeed, the present outlines of the road-transit network in Massachusetts are largely accepted; the chapter tries to suggest areas of policy flexibility within those constraints.

The emphasis is upon the particular nature of transportation obstacles facing the poor. As Birch's chapter demonstrates, the poor are not homogeneous. They differ in location, size of family, age, health, and such less obvious characteristics as exact hours of employment. Differences of this kind affect the varying kinds of transportation problems they face.

The chapter will first offer some explanations of the relatively recent concern for transportation problems in government antipoverty programs and the rather stereotyped pattern of that concern. It will then discuss briefly the implications of considering a particular obstacle a "transportation" problem, rather than a manifestation of deeper problems in other systems affecting the poor. The chapter will then look at particular problems facing different categories of poor people and suggest some general dimensions of those problems. It will then suggest public policy objectives and some means for achieving them, with special emphasis at the end upon specific roles for state government.

Concern about transportation and poverty

Transportation is a relative newcomer to the list of services considered significant in helping to solve the problems of poverty. As recently
as 1964, when the Economic Opportunity Act was passed, transportation was not included in the suggested list of services a community
might choose to include in its "community action program." The riots
of that summer, in Harlem, in Rochester, and elsewhere, did not arouse
interest in transportation problems. But the next summer, with the
Watts riots in Los Angeles and the McCone Commission Report that
followed, transportation—or the lack of it—emerged in public attention
as a critical problem for many of the poor. The isolation of Watts—
requiring a two-hour bus ride and several transfers to get to the County
General Hospital, and an hour and forty-five minutes to reach the Youth
Employment Training Center—dramatized for the country a problem
which most metropolitan areas were to find, in varying degrees, in their
own midst.

Several factors help explain why the importance of transportation
was largely forgotten when we considered the problems of poverty in
the first half of the 1960s. First, for the automobile-driving majority,
the chief transportation problems were congestion and safety. To the
extent that drivers thought about it, they could easily conclude that
neither problem distinguished between the affluent and the less-well-off
and that if you waited long enough, and drove carefully enough, you
could get where you wanted to go. If the poor did not have cars, they
could always take transit; it might be a little slower and a lot more
crowded, but in the end it could get you there. After all, Martin Luther
King's 1956 boycott of the buses in Montgomery, Alabama, had pro-
tested not inadequate bus service but segregated seating, relying indeed on Negroes' heavy use of buses to make the boycott effective.

Moreover, by the early 1960s, the Interstate highway system had
begun to improve the traffic situation, especially as a number of industries began to move out to the circumferential routes being constructed
around most metropolitan areas. The implications of those moves for
the nonmotorist were passed off as unimportant, if they were thought
of at all. And so far as the rural poor were concerned, the Interstate
system was considered a means of attracting industry to the rural
areas and of getting the rural poor who lived near the cities to metropolitan job locations. Intercity and commuter rail service may have
been declining, as freight shifted to trucks and net income declined; but

intercity bus service was burgeoning and was used heavily by the rural poor, especially southern Negroes moving north (and then returning periodically to visit family and friends left behind). Thus, things were getting better. If the poor could get all the way from South Carolina to Boston, they could surely figure out how to get to the ball park, the hospital, or the outlying industrial park.

In short, the concern for poverty in the early 1960s came at a time when transportation, for most people, was improving. To the extent that transportation problems of the poor were considered, they were viewed with the kind of blinders the Kerner commission was later to call "racist." Some sensitive analysts, like Kenneth Clark in *Dark Ghetto,* talked about the isolation of the ghetto, but this was mostly described as a psychological isolation that limited the physical horizons of the poor, rather than a physical isolation caused by inadequate transportation facilities. (The film *The Cool World,* made in 1966, featured a daring first-time trip from Harlem to Coney Island—on the readily accessible New York subway.)

Suddenly, the McCone report announced that people were isolated, and angry about it. Policy-makers concerned about high ghetto unemployment began to plot on maps the large number of job vacancies in suburban areas and the number of potential job seekers in the central cities, and suggested that transportation was the essential missing link. Demonstration bus service between the ghetto and employment, health, and other facilities soon followed. Pessimism has now set in, however, as the poor who have gotten jobs have switched to car pools or bought their own cars, and as deeper problems of discrimination and decrease in the number of low-skilled jobs have become more apparent.

The disappointment engendered by these experiences—and the inadequacy of knowledge they reveal about the relationship of transportation to other factors—is not a valid reason for either plunging ahead or doing nothing. Instead, it is a reason for cautious experimentation, based on what knowledge we have and on informed hunches from there.

We should recognize that such an incremental, experimental approach to transportation poses problems. First, some experiments must be sold as permanent innovations, since an essential quality of transportation is its reliability—the notion that one can count on it when making decisions about job, home, and school, and when choosing among various transportation options, including the option not to travel at all. (This point was stressed at the start of the MBTA "Job Express" service from Dudley Station in Roxbury: it was felt that unless the new service was seen as permanent, people from Roxbury would not risk getting a job on the circumferential highway, Route 128.)

Second, special regulatory problems may exist with phasing out an experimental transportation service, especially if it is part of a public transportation system. It is one thing to persuade a state regulatory agency to grant a "certificate of public convenience and necessity" for a new bus line; it is quite another to obtain permission to discontinue such a service—especially after the service has been found to be not only convenient but "necessary."

Third, most transportation, to be effective, must be part of a larger system, and that larger system has serious deficiencies for the poor. To expand the feeder bus service in Boston's outer suburbs (or core ghetto), for example, involves making certain assumptions about the service on the main line-haul operation and the distribution system at the other end.

But such problems are not insurmountable. Innovations can be called permanent without being oversold; regulatory law in this field will become more flexible only in response to demands for such flexibility arising out of particular innovations people want to try; and incremental improvements in transportation can assume the outlines of an existing system without accepting the deficiencies for all time to come.

The functions of transportation

Transportation performs many different functions. A number of these are generally overlooked in discussions of transportation and poverty, but all have significant poverty aspects. An examination of these "transportation" functions reveals instances in which, for the poor, the underlying problem may be deficiencies in another system that show up as a transportation problem.

One function already has been emphasized: *enabling people to get from place to place*. The movement can be from home to work and home again; from home or job to various service, recreational, cultural, or shopping facilities; to see friends, perhaps at their home. The origins and destinations can be in or out of town. The trip can be a five-minute walk to the corner store, a daily commute, a weekend out of town, or a vacation. The trip can assume a stable pattern of life, or it may be one step in changing that pattern (looking for a new job; driving through a town to consider looking for a house there; taking school children on a cultural excursion). Getting people from place to place because there is something at the other end has been the major focus of thinking about transportation as a means of helping to alleviate poverty.

Another function of transportation, of course, is *moving goods from place to place*. Some transportation problems which we think of as involving mainly the movement of people from place to place can better be considered problems of the movement of goods. One problem for welfare recipients, for instance, is to get to the center that distributes surplus food. They often take taxis for this trip. We are inclined to think of this as a problem of facilitating the movement of people, perhaps by making taxi service cheaper or more easily available. If we view the problem as one of moving goods, however, we can focus more directly on questions of how and by whom to move such food. Perhaps moving surplus food all the way to residential doors should be the responsibility of the Department of Agriculture or of the state or local welfare agency, who might hire poor people to do the delivering.

Thinking of the problem as the movement of goods also lets us look more clearly at technological options. Certain substances can be moved in ways that we no longer consider "transportation" at all. In Puritan days, villagers had to go to the village pump for their water; now, in most places, it comes through a pipe directly into our homes, offices, and stores. Electricity and gas are delivered in similar ways. Most garbage disposal is now at least partly a "transportation" problem; if it is incinerated in each house, however, the transportation problem may disappear (except for ash collection, which replaces trash collection), while the air pollution problem increases. Or, if it is ground up and washed down the drain, a transportation problem may become a water pollution problem.

This is not to suggest that other problems always arise when a transportation problem disappears. The point is that technological options and decisions about responsibility for distributing goods or services can change a problem of moving people into a problem of moving goods, or can make the transportation aspects of the problem disappear altogether. And conversely, thinking of some things as transportation problems, particularly involving moving people, may prevent us from appreciating that assumptions about the delivery systems for goods and services should be examined directly for their impact on the poor.

Third, transportation can fulfill the function of *communicating information*. Paul Revere needed his horse because he had no radio or

telephone system. Today, many communication functions are performed without anyone's having to move around. We used to have to
go out to the movies; now we can see them on television. Housewives
can telephone a department store or grocery store shopping service,
and goods she wants can be delivered without her ever having to leave
home. Doctors used to make house calls or require people to come to
their office; particularly for pediatricians, the telephone has made a
good part of this travel unnecessary—even prescriptions for drugs are
telephoned to the pharmacist, who then delivers them to the patient's
home. The implications here for the problem of poverty are obvious. For
instance, the poor often do not have telephones, partly because their
credit is not good enogh, a factor which also makes it hard for them to
get a grocery store or a drug store to deliver. Problems the poor have
in obtaining telephones and credit should not be obscured by thinking
of the problem as one of transportation alone.

The relationships of the poor to professionals like doctors and lawyers, moreover, are usually not so stable that they are able to telephone
the hospital clinic or the neighborhood law office. Legitimate attention
to decentralizing health, legal, and other services (partly so that people
can walk to them), or of developing transportation facilities so that
people can get to large hospitals, should not obscure the fact that these
efforts tend to assume a lack of continuity and stability in relationships
between professionals and the poor. Part of the prescription surely is to
change the character of those relationships.

Fourth, transportation *helps to define the range of options people
have in making long-range locational decisions—especially where to live
and where to work.* The transportation system can serve to widen or to
narrow the range of options. For those with an automobile, the Interstate highway system has widened options, making it possible, for instance, to live in the central city or an inner suburb (Roxbury,
Somerville, Everett), work in the outer suburbs (Needham or Burlington,
for instance), and shop in between. The system also makes it possible
to live in New Bedford (a separate SMSA) and work in an industrial park
on Boston's circumferential Route 128, 50 miles away. Zayre operates
its own bus service for employees who live in central Worcester and
work in the Zayre store in Framingham, about an hour away. Pratt and
Whitney Aircraft Division provides two buses a day to carry employees
between Auburn and its plant in East Hartford, Connecticut, also about
an hour away. Springfield is less than an hour's ride west of Worcester,
and about an hour's ride east of Pittsfield. Residents of Lowell and

Lawrence, and New Bedford and Fall River, all depressed areas in the 1950s because of the decline of textiles and other industries, have many new options for finding adequate employment.

Such an increase in options makes it possible for groups of people to live in homogeneous neighborhoods, either by preference or by constraint, and still work in racially mixed, distant, economically diverse environments. These widening options mean, among other things, that ethnically concentrated areas can become viable residential areas without needing employment viability as well.

For those without an automobile, however, the highway system and the dispersed locational pattern it has facilitated actually have narrowed options. Curtailments of bus and rail service, both commuter and inter-city, are a direct result of the majority's preference for the automobile, and have meant that those without automobiles must either live in the dense core (Boston and the inner suburbs) or be isolated in outer suburbs or rural areas.

Whether positive or negative, the transportation system that has evolved in the 1960s is a major factor in people's locational decisions. To the extent that physical mobility is made easier, other constraints on locational decisions—particularly job and residential discrimination—may become more sharply felt. To the extent that physical mobility becomes more difficult, such other constraints may appear less significant.

Fifth, transportation can serve the function of *providing social status.* This is true for most people regardless of income, but it is particularly important for the poor. An automobile is one of the most apparent and expensive things many of them will ever own. And to be not just a car-owner but a car-driver, with the freedom to go to such places as beaches, is an important part of demonstrating a rise in status.

Sixth, transportation *provides recreation and amusement in and of itself.* People may get in a car, or ride the subway, not to go anywhere in particular, but just to ride around. Driving for pleasure ranks with swimming and picnics as our most popular forms of outdoor recreation.[1] Cruising around a neighborhood, like riding on a rollercoaster, may just be a way of experiencing the sensation of riding—usually fast. We ride on narrow-gauge railroads or on the top of a London double-decker bus to stretch our experiences. Or we may take a walk just to

[1]*Trends in American Living and Outdoor Recreation,* Reports to the Outdoor Recreation Resources Review Commission, 50 (1962).

take a walk—not to see anyone or do anything in particular, but just to move around. In central cities, the streets themselves may become playgrounds. And a car is itself a place—for necking, for serious conversation away from the diversions of a crowded home, for solitude. It is also a thing—a machine, an object to take apart, fix up, rebuild, paint, race, jump on, or steal. Lacking other recreational outlets, the poor may use transportation, more than higher-income groups do, as a source of recreation and amusement.

Finally, transportation itself *provides direct employment.* Adding up all the employees of transit systems in Massachusetts, all the taxi drivers (Boston alone has 7,000 full- and part-time taxi drivers),[2] all intercity bus, railroad, and airport employees, and all employees of car sales and rental agencies, and gas stations and supporting activities, the total would probably come close to 100,000 people. Transportation is an important industry, and few special efforts are made to recruit the poor into the ranks of that industry, particularly at the local level. Indeed, artificial restrictions on taxicab ownership deprive the poor of the chance to use part-time taxi-driving to earn that margin of income that could put them above the poverty line, and to use the taxicab itself to get to a higher-paying job at other times of the day.

The transportation problems of the poor

The transportation problems of the poor in Massachusetts are extremely diverse and particular, varying especially with residential and job location, but also varying with age, health, job hours of the poor person, and the like. The following cases, which are composites of problems and situations often encountered by the poor, demonstrate this diversity and particularity.

INNER-CITY GHETTO, WORKING AGE

> *Mrs. Carson lives in Roxbury. She is 45 and black. She works five nights a week on the clean-up crew for an office building in Boston's financial district. Her shift is from 10 p.m. to 4 a.m. She earns $1.50 an hour and makes a little over $2,000 a year. It takes her six or seven minutes to walk to the bus stop. The bus in the evening*

[2]Frank Morgan, "Death and Taxis," *Boston,* 61, No. 9 (September 1969), 42.

comes by every half hour, pretty close to schedule. She then rides ten minutes on the bus to the rapid-transit station at Dudley Street. The trains come every 15 minutes. She pays 20 cents for the bus and 25 cents for the subway. She makes one change and arrives, 15 minutes later, about a five-minute walk from the building where she works. The whole trip takes about 45 minutes, counting waiting time. When connections are lucky, she can make it in 35 minutes; when they are bad, she may take an hour. Coming home is more difficult. Neither subways nor buses run at that hour. She usually tries to get a taxi home, which costs her $1.65. She can get one to pick her up about two or three nights out of six. The other nights she goes to an all-night coffee shop, gets a cup of coffee, and waits until the subway opens at 5:16 a.m.

Mrs. Carson's nephew, who lives with her, does construction work. He rides to the site out in the far suburbs with a friend who has a 1965 Chevrolet. When the car works, they make it in about 20 minutes. There is no other way for him to get to the job site. He misses three or four days a month because of car trouble or his friend's unreliability. As a result, the foreman doesn't let him move beyond the lowest-skilled of the heavy jobs.

INNER SUBURB, ELDERLY

Miss Ianella lives in the outer part of Somerville. She is 73 and white. She lives on Social Security (about $1,500 a year). She also takes in sewing work (about $300 a year). Her arthritis is getting worse, especially in the knees. She likes to go into the big department stores in downtown Boston once a week, with two of her friends. They live near each other, and usually share a cab to pick up each at her door and then go to the nearest subway stop. The taxi costs $1.10, which they split three ways. They usually get the same driver. The subway stairs are hard for her to handle, but she takes them slowly and with the help of her friends has been able to make it so far. (Her friends are in better health, except that one is deaf—she never hears the taxi when it honks its horn, so she watches for it from the window.) Coming home, they try to beat the rush-hour crowds, but can't always pull themselves away from the stores in time. Most of the rest of her travels are done on foot—

to the corner meat market and the fruit stand down the street, to church, to the public library branch up the street.

RURAL VILLAGE, ELDERLY

Mr. and Mrs. Parker live in a small village about 30 miles northwest of Boston. He had been a veterinarian, but retired several years ago because of cataracts, which have now been removed leaving him with about 60 percent vision. He lives on Social Security ($2,300 a year). He is prohibited from driving, and his wife feels she is too old to learn to drive. To visit their daughter in Worcester is a problem. If they could drive, they could make it in about 30 minutes. Sometimes they can get a ride with the pharmacist. If he isn't going, they take three buses. It takes them over two hours, if connections are lucky. There are three buses a day on Sundays. They are thinking of moving into an apartment in Worcester, but they hate to leave their friends. In the village, they can get pretty much everything they need by walking. If they want to get to the regional shopping center, just off the new Interstate, they can usually get a ride if they plan ahead. It was not so easy when Mr. Parker was in the hospital in Worcester, but Mrs. Parker was able to get a friend to drive her to visit him several times during his stay. The other days they talked by phone.

MIGRANT WORKER, OUTER SUBURBS

Mr. and Mrs. Silvio live in a Puerto Rican neighborhood just outside the circumferential highway. They are in their late twenties and have four children. He gets odd jobs around several nearby factories and works with migrant crews picking beans, peaches, apples, and potatoes in season. He makes about $2,800 a year. He gets to the fields in a truck sent by the farm manager. He can usually get a ride to the factories with a friend. Several friends in the community have cars, all of them used and quite unreliable. Mrs. Silvio stays with the children; sometimes she takes them all along in the truck to work in the fields with her husband. The community has grown significantly in the last several years. There is virtually no public transportation available, although the commuter rail line has a stop about two miles away in one of the upper-income suburbs. A bus line stops about three miles away, inside the circumfer-

*ential highway. Mr. Silvio has been to the office of the State
Employment Service twice. There seemed to be some jobs that he
might be able to get in some factories a few miles away, but they
were not on any public transportation line. He has not been for any
job interviews.*

These rather typical cases should be viewed against a background of the
limited statistical data that we have about the transportation problems of
the poor.

*We do not know whether the poor travel more or less than higher-
income groups.* Many of the "trips" made by the poor are walking trips,
partly because of the dense neighborhoods in which many of them live.
The only available study of trip patterns of the poor in Massachusetts
counted walking trips only when they were walk-to-work trips.[3] We can
certainly conclude that the poor make fewer trips than higher-income
people beyond walking distance from their residences,[4] but we should not
conclude that their lives are necessarily more isolated unless we measure
isolation in physical distance. National statistics on vehicular trips and
miles driven per year support the conclusion that the poor are dramatically less mobile in these senses than higher-income groups.[5]

*For those living in the denser inner suburbs, public transportation is an
essential means of travel, particularly travel to work.* In these suburbs of
Boston, a clear majority (53 percent) of those earning less than $4,000
rely on public-transportation for work trips, and 41 percent rely on it for all
trips. Such reliance is particularly heavy by those who do not own a car.
Usage of public transportation by the non-auto-owning poor living in this
area jumps to about 80 percent for the work trip and 61 percent for all
trips. Bus use is particularly heavy by the poor. Key problems of public
transportation are cost, time and difficulty involved in multiple transfers,
and virtual absence of late-night service.[6]

[3]The data were collected in 1963 by the Eastern Massachusetts Regional Planning Project, Massachusetts Department of Public Works. The data have been examined for
poverty implications by Phillip B. Herr and Aaron Fleisher at the Massachusetts Institute
of Technology. Their results have been reported in "The Mobility of the Poor," paper
prepared for the Transportation and Poverty Conference, American Academy of Arts &
Sciences, (June 7, 1968).

[4]See Herr and Fleisher.

[5]See Lansing and Mueller, *Residential Location and Urban Mobility* (Ann Arbor, Mich.:
University of Michigan Survey Research Center, Institute for Social Research, 1964),
Tables II-1 and II-2.

[6]These statistics were developed by Matthew A. Coogan from the EMRPP data described

For poor people living in the outer suburbs, and for the poor generally, auto-ownership and car-pooling are extremely important. Of those poor people in households that do not own a car, 63 percent of work trips are made as passengers in someone else's car. Looking at the poor in the entire eastern Massachusetts region, 89 percent of all trips are made by private automobile. This is about the same percentage as for higher-income groups. And of all families whose annual income is less than $4,000, 35 percent own cars.[7] This regional average is close to a finding of a recent study of the black ghetto; there, 32 percent of households were found to own cars.[8]

The non-auto-owning poor make a significant number of trips by taxi. Six percent of all trips by non-auto-owning families earning less than $4,000 are made by taxi. This compares with four percent by non-auto-owning families earning between $6,000 and $10,000; and seven percent by such families earning more than $10,000.[9] The poor thus use taxis more than middle-income families, and nearly as often as upper-income families:

To these cases and statistics we need to add some general conclusions about the types of problems encountered:

1. *Statistics about high automobile ownership hide a number of problems.* Saying that a large number of poor people own automobiles is also saying that having an autombile does not get people out of poverty —although their poverty might be worse without the car. Similarly, saying that 54 percent of poor households have at least one person with a driver's license[10] is also saying that 46 percent do not; noting that about one-third of ghetto households own cars is also noting that two-thirds do not. Moreover, many of the cars that are owned by the poor are probably in poor condition. Data gathered in Watts would suggest that 20 percent of them are not in a condition for safe driving on expressways, and 40 percent are uninsured.[11] Insurance in the Boston areas may cost more than the purchase price of many of the used

above.

[7]Herr and Fleisher.

[8]Boston Urban Foundation Study, *Center City* (1969).

[9]Herr and Fleisher.

[10]Herr and Fleisher, *supra,* p. 27.

[11]Thomas H. Floyd, "Using Transportation to Alleviate Poverty: A Progress Report on Experiments Under the Urban Mass Transportation Act," Transportation and Poverty Conference, June 7, 1968.

cars owned by the poor. In addition, car-pooling has obvious disadvantages: unreliability and overdependence on the health of the owner-driver and on the condition of the car, and limitations on the ability of one member of the car pool to work overtime. Overtime pay is an extremely advantageous factor in employment on Route 128, where car-pooling is especially prevalent.

2. *Some poor people will never be able to drive.* A large number of the elderly, the young, and the handicapped do not have easy access to an automobile and cannot drive themselves. For the most part, they must use public transportation. To the extent that they are poor, and are therefore unable to take taxis frequently even if they do sometimes take them, their mobility is defined by their ability to get around on foot, on bicycles, or by public transit. And their ability to get around by public transit is affected, not only by cost and service, but also, and perhaps more important, by the clarity and availability of information about routes, fares, and schedules of the transit system.

3. *For those to whom a car is not accessible, nighttime shifts provide special problems.* Public transportation is still extremely important, especially to the nondriving poor who live in parts of Cambridge, Somerville, and Boston that are close to the central city and who work in the central business district. But the MBTA virtually closes down after midnight, with light service from early evening on. The same is true of Worcester, and undoubtedly of most other cities. Even the "Job Express" to Route 128 assumes a morning commute out and a late afternoon commute in. But night shifts are the ones the poor often must take as their first jobs. To the extent that the poor are part of the secondary labor market, as Piore discusses, they may move from one night shift to another, never escaping from transit deficiencies.

4. *The future is likely to be worse rather than better for the non-auto-driving poor.* Low-skilled jobs are increasingly moving out of the central city—the part generally well-served by radial transit services. These services to the core are generally quite good for the near-in poor, even as they move into the suburbs as Birch's chapter describes. As more such jobs move far out, not only to Route 128 but to Route 495, radial transit, even if extended, will become less and less relevant. The randomness of travel patterns is likely to increase in the next several decades, and the poor who do not have access to a car are likely to suffer most.

5. *Cost of transportation, both by automobile and by public transit, is a real factor for a portion of the poor.* An automobile obviously costs

money (purchase price, maintenance, fuel, insurance, parking, traffic fines), although the costs are not generally associated in the minds of the owner or user with decisions whether to make a particular trip. The turnstile at the subway and the farebox on a bus, however, are much more likely to be deterrents to trip-making, since the cash outlay, even though small, is associated with the particular trip. That amount, of course, is increasing. For some trips through three zones, a one-way fare may be 45 cents, 65 cents, or more. That expense is significant for most people; for the poor it may make the difference between a trip and no trip, while to economically better-off groups, it is more likely to mean a choice between transit and auto. And taxis, used significantly by the poor, are obviously expensive to the individual (although to society as a whole they may well provide a relatively cheap way to meet diverse needs, especially in off-peak hours).

6. *Finding a job and getting to it for the first few days or weeks pose greater transportation problems for the poor than commuting after the job is underway.* Information about the availability of jobs tends to spread informally, either from individuals or from signs in windows. Classified ads may play some role, and for some people official agencies like state Employment Service offices are important. To the extent that the available job is outside the core, transportation may pose a severe problem in the hiring process. The jobseeker may not know anyone who works at the job location or nearby, thus making carpooling difficult. In any event, interviews (and return trips for physical examinations) can mean several trips at odd hours. The time, expense, and uncertainty about routes and timetables seem to pose special difficulties both to the unemployed and to jobseekers who have jobs but want better ones.[12]

7. *Public transportation suffers from service deficiencies, but no institutional mechanism exists to bring these deficiencies to the attention of responsible public officials.* The Silvios, the Parkers, and Mrs. Carson all have specific complaints about public transportation—complaints that might result in new bus routes or new schedules. Yet the citizen-consumer cannot easily make his wishes felt in such matters. He tends to feel at the mercy of a large transportation bureaucracy which makes decisions without getting any input from him but with a large impact on his life.

---

[12]See Carol S. Greenwald and Richard Syron, "Increasing Job Opportunities in Boston's Urban Core," *New England Economic Review,* January–February 1969, pp. 30–40.

8. *Some transportation deficiencies of the poor result directly from public policy which caters to the needs of higher-income consumers; the poor, in fact, are subsidizing higher-income groups.* The well-to-do commuter's interest in fast rail access to the central business district is in many cases directly at odds with the needs of central city residents. The suburban commuter wants fewer stations and higher speeds—once he has gotten aboard. This desire generally results in a cutback in the number of stops in core residential areas, and thus a cutback in service to a significant portion of the poor.[13] Similarly, core residential areas contain few entrances and exits to expressways, thus directly disadvantaging poor communities in the interests of the auto-driving suburbanites.

Furthermore, by way of rebuttal to an argument that the poor are heavily subsidized by the transit system, it is important to note that this is simply not the case. The subsidies run in the other direction. The near-in rapid transit and bus lines, used heavily by the poor, more than pay for themselves; the bus and rail lines to the outer suburbs are deficit operations. And on the highways, it is the peak-hour commuters, composed predominantly of income groups other than the poor, whose fuel and other motoring taxes fail to cover the construction costs of the very expensive urban freeways.[14]

9. *The poor suffer more than higher-income groups from dislocations caused by the construction of transportation facilities, especially highways.* Public works programs "tend to select locations where a high proportion of low-income, minority-group households reside."[15] dislocation causes a loss in jobs, many of them in areas where the poor reside and work; it often leads to increases in rent (for nonhomeowners) and increases in mortgage payments or decreases in percentage of equity (for homeowners); and it reduces absolutely the number of units in the metropolitan housing supply, thus forcing up rents in an already scarce market. Dislocation also divides neighborhoods and disrupts communities—effects which the poor feel more than those who are economically better off.

[13]See Martin Wohl, "The Urban Transportation Problem: A Brief Analysis of Our Objectives and the Prospects for Current Proposals," (Mimeographed October 1969).

[14]See Alan Altshuler, "Transit Subsidies: By Whom, For Whom?" *Journal of the American Institute of Planners,* 84 (March 1969).

[15]Anthony Downs, "Uncompensated Non-Construction Costs Which Urban Highways and Urban Renewal Impose upon Residential Households," Conference on Economics of Public Output, Princeton University, April 1968, p. 42.

The transportation problems of the poor are thus extremely diverse, and many of them are hidden behind aggregate statistics in the complexities of how other systems—like the job system and the credit system—actually work. Simple solutions are not possible. Indeed, for some of the problems it is not clear that any solutions can be developed. On the other hand, the fact that transportation is itself a vast system, linked in many particulars with other systems, is not an excuse for failing to move, even in small steps.

Toward some solutions

In suggesting directions for solving some of the transportation problems of the poor, some general objectives should guide decision-making. First, to the extent possible, technologically and fiscally, public transportation should offer a basic minimum of service.

Second, disparities in service and subsidies to higher-income groups should be eliminated where possible in favor of redistributional welfare objectives. The poor deserve better of the transportation system.

Third, transportation has the key long-range function of widening the range of options people have in regard to where they live and work. It is thus an indispensable part of our freedom.

Fourth, no one can expect that a public transportation system should be available to get him inexpensively from *any* point in the state (or metropolitan area) to *any* other. Even if that were technologically feasible, there are other demands on the public purse which should receive higher priority.

Fifth, transportation deficiencies tend to affect the poor at the margins. Yet it is at the margins that the poor need help.

With these basic objectives in mind, the following suggestions are proposed.

1. *High priority should be given to the job placement function of transportation.* This area of transportation has the most immediate potential for impact on poverty itself, as distinct from mere amelioration of the conditions of poverty. The focus should be on placement and startup, not on providing transportation for the duration of the job. If wages are high enough, people in most cases can solve their home-to-work transportation problems for themselves. Even with its low ridership, the MBTA service to Route 128 should be considered a successful "job placement" bus; the fact that people get jobs and switch to au-

tomobiles is hardly an indication of failure! The service might be expanded at least to cover the night shift, probably on the more successful northern route, with at least one bus each way. Second, industries should continue to experiment with developing their own charter or car-pooling service in small vehicles—sometimes charging a fee which might be given to the driver as a form of compensation for his time (assuming that he also works at the plant or in the area). Third, job-training and job clearing house operations should consider providing vehicles to take applicants to job interviews, and perhaps even try to help the employee for the first week until he can find a car pool. (The Lowell CAP agency has five 11-passenger vehicles which it uses for field trips for job trainees as part of the interview and placement process, among other functions, but it does not provide any transportation to the job once an employee has been placed.) Clear information about existing transportation services can also be significant in job placement.

2. *We should experiment with ways to increase the availability of the automobile to the poor.* Within the confines of existing technology and service, the automobile offers the best means of transportation to get most places in the enlarging metropolitan area except for the central business district and those near-in areas served by rapid transit. Some of the statistics cited above suggest that the poor are already aware of this fact.

There are a number of problems with expanding auto availability. One is the problem of credit. Thought might be given to governmental (federal or state) reinsurance schemes for installment buying of automobiles by the poor, so that banks will not be required to take the risk. Such schemes might be limited, on an experimental basis, to participants in job training programs. Such schemes might also include state financing of insurance costs for the training period and the first six months of employment. Plans have been proposed that would establish car rental arrangements under which the renter could, in effect, buy the car over time if he wished.[16] Such a project might incorporate job-training programs in automotive mechanics, and it might be owned, developed, and run by a community corporation. Or one or more of the large car-rental companies might move into what appears to be a ready market, perhaps renting their used cars at vastly lower rates, like

---

[16]See Sumner Myers, "Personal Transportation for the Poor," prepared for the Transportation and Poverty Conference June 1968.

$1.00 or $2.00 a day. Finally, analysis should be made of the number and quality of driver education courses given in ghetto and other schools for the poor; this staple of suburban life could well be expanded, for adults as well as for youth.

To the argument that facilitating the use of cars by the poor should be rejected, because it will only add to the problems of congestion and pollution, there seems to be a simple answer: the poor have as much right as anyone to contribute to congestion and pollution; they should not be asked to be the vanguard in solving these problems in a piecemeal fashion. And when we do begin to solve them on a general basis —by requiring costly antipollution devices, for instance—we should note that such policies may especially hurt poor people, who rely more heavily on used cars than higher-income people do. Some ameliorative policies (small grants, for instance) may have to be instituted to lessen the impact on the poor of such otherwise worthwhile requirements.

3. *Artificial limitations on the taxi market should be removed.* Five limitations on the taxi market deserve attention: *prohibition of group riding,* which keeps the price high and the demand lower than it would otherwise be; *the "medallion" system,* which under state law limits to 1,525 the number of taxi licenses issued for use in Boston and which means that a person can buy such a license only on the "free" market at a cost, today, of about $30,000; *prohibition of cabs licensed in other cities from picking up fares in Boston* unless "summoned by or at the request of said passenger ... by radio or telephone,"[17] thus making trips from the suburbs to Boston more expensive than they would be if the cab could pick up a return fare; the *metering system,* which seems to give drivers less incentive to be out on the road than does a zone system (like the one in Washington, D.C.), where the owner cannot check on fares collected and thus basically "rents" the cab to the driver for a fixed time period, with the driver keeping all his fares; and finally, the *problem of crime,* which makes it very difficult for a person traveling to the ghetto to find a taxi to take him.

Of these five constraints on effective taxi service, priority attention should be given to legalizing group riding. This could be done by keeping the fare-for-distance as it now is, but adding a surcharge of 50 cents or so per passenger. This would benefit the poor by making total fares lower, particularly in the inner city but also in dispersed areas,

---

[17]City of Boston, Police Department, Rule 65 (a), *Rules and Regulations for Hackney Carriages,* 21 (1968).

where centralized pickup points could be established. It should also benefit the cab owners by increasing business.

The medallion system is more pernicious but harder to crack, assuming that, if the system were eliminated, past capital investment would have to be compensated. (Compensation for 1,525 medallions at current market value of $30,000 would require a public exenditure of close to $46,000,000—hardly worth the investment.) The state legislature could *add* medallions—say, 500 a year for three years—to depress the market and increase the number of cabs. Opening the market in the suburbs, where the medallion system does not operate to the same extent, and where a majority of the poor are now located, might be the most acceptable way to proceed. The number of cabs authorized in any one suburb is established by the suburb's own local government.

For expanded suburban service to be economically viable, however, the third constraint—Boston's rule prohibiting a return fare except in special circumstances—will probably have to be eased. This could be done by having a number of central points—the financial district, shopping districts, major hospitals, government offices, the airport—where a suburban cab would be permitted to pick up passengers destined for his suburb. Similar reciprocity should be established among suburban areas. This would also mean that the cab would return to the suburb it is primarily intended to serve.

Metering seems the least important constraint on change. Simply because it favors owners rather than drivers does not mean that drivers could not be paid higher wages, or that single-vehicle ownership cannot be encouraged. Ideally, for the sake of both service to the poor (and nonpoor) and income to the poor, we should aim at a situation approximating that of Washington, D.C., where 75 percent of the drivers are considered part-time, and over half of the drivers own their own cabs, with the off-duty cab often serving as the family car. Washington, moreover, has 13.3 cabs per thousand population, while Boston has only 2.0 per thousand. But we should be able to move in this direction without having to abandon metering.

Several things might be done about the crime problem, which particularly affects the black poor who live in the ghetto. Increasing the number of black drivers does not seem particularly important, since blacks already constitute 30 percent of Boston's driver force, and they are apparently just as fearful as white drivers. It is hard to say what a proliferation of black owners might do to the crime problem (12 percent of current cab owners are black). More important would seem to be steps toward eliminating cash payments for rides. This system could be begun by letting cabs tie into one or more of the major credit card services, but in order for this to improve rather than aggravate the situation for the poor, steps will have to be taken to make these cards available to them. In addition, technology now makes possible automatic surveillance devices that could be installed in cabs to alert the police in the event of trouble. The deterrent effect of such devices might be very great indeed.[18]

4. *Minibuses for individual and group needs should be tried out.* Minibuses offer some of the best and most feasible solutions for immediate problems. Minibuses are street-operating vehicles with a passenger capacity larger than that of a standard car, but smaller than that of a standard bus or rapid transit vehicle. Minibuses typically carry 11 or 20 passengers. They are now most commonly used as airport limousines, and downtown shopping buses.

The major advantage of these vehicles is their size, which lets them use residential streets and which enables them to carry small groups of people to and from one or several locations. They can also perform line-haul functions on sparsely used bus routes. They are particularly useful in low-density areas. Their capital cost is small (less than $3,000 for a VW microbus), but their operating costs can be large if union rates are applied to drivers.

The flexibility of these vehicles allows special uses which may be of particular benefit to the poor. Among these uses are jitney service—the multiple-stop, group taxi service on a fixed or semifixed route that is quite common in Latin America; "dial-a-bus"—an on-call, computer-controlled, group taxi service that provides door-to-door service to individual riders; limousine service—such as now used for airline passengers, picks up riders at fixed locations for transportation to a specific destination; charter service—picks up specific passengers for delivery to specific destinations; and rental service—in which the individual or group renters control the vehicle's destination. Minibuses can also be used to supplement larger buses during peak hours and to operate in place of these buses at nonpeak hours, such as late at night where there is now no service.

[18]For the general discussion of taxis, with comparative statistics, see Sandra Rosenbloom, "Taxis, Jitneys and Poverty," prepared for the Transportation and Poverty Conference, June 1968, and printed in *Transaction*, 7, No. 4 (February 1970), 47–54. For a discussion of taxi service in Boston, see Morgan, "Death and Taxis," and Morgan, "Getting the (Small) Business in Boston," *Boston*, 72 (November 1969).

5. *Diverse organizations should be encouraged to provide transporta-tion services tailored to the needs of relatively small, but identifiable, groups of people.* There is no reason to assume that innovations in trans-portation service must be initiated by or administered by large public transportation entities (like the MBTA, the Springfield Street Railway Company, or the Worcester Bus Company). The New Bedford model cities agency, we are told, gave the barest consideration to developing a trans-portation component because it considered that "mass transit" was not within its province. "The very words 'mass transportation' have created much of the problem facing the transit industry, for 'mass' implies a homogeneous demand which can be accommodated by a standardized product. Yet we know that in every other aspect of urban life, heterogeneity is the rule."[19] Heterogeneity of need is certainly the case with the poor; the response—and the sources for that response—should be equally diversified.

The fact that the Lowell community action agency has five 11-pass-enger vehicles to use as it sees fit is particularly suggestive. Zayre and Pratt and Whitney, both provide their own transportation services. In Worcester, a volunteer agency provides transportation to the blind. If the agency does not have volunteers available, the blind person can take a taxi and charge the fare to the account of the Association for the Blind.[20]

In Nassau County, New York, the North Shore Hospital operates a "medicar" route to two towns using two nine-seater minibuses. Twelve round trips are made each day on routes carefully selected to reach low-income groups. Average ridership is 280–300 patients per week— or about 40 percent of all the outpatients treated at the hospital. The running costs of this service (driver's salary, depreciation, maintenance, and fuel) are approximately $8,000 a year for each vehicle.[21] This should be tried in Massachusetts, particularly by a hospital in a low-density area.

A proposal to develop a nonprofit public service company for Roxbury is currently being developed by the Urban League. This would provide

---

[19]Lewis Schneider, "Marketing Urban Transit," prepared for delivery at the Informal Con-ference Session on Mass Transportation: Future Research Needs, Highway Research Board 1970 Annual Meeting, January 1970.

[20]*Worcester: Urban Mass Transportation Technical Study* (Second Quarter Report, 1969).

[21]Organization for Social and Technical Innovation, *Poverty in Spread City: A Study of Locational Constraints on the Poor in Nassau County* (Cambridge, Mass., 1969).

minibus service to shopping, medical, and recreational facilities, as well as to jobs. It is proposed that drivers and mechanics from the community be used to keep down costs and provide spin-off benefits to the community in the form of jobs and training.

One public agency in particular might benefit from having a vehicle at its disposal—the State Employment Service offices. Under new federal policy, these agencies are to be given major responsibility for job training and manpower programs. It would seem logical to provide these offices with a vehicle to use in carrying out the agency's job placement function. We are told that some transporting of prospective employees is now done informally by Employment Service staff in their own cars. Formalization of such services should now be tried.

These examples suggest the importance of varied sources for transportation innovation. None of the services can charge a "fare" as such; for that, they would have to qualify as a "common" or "special" carrier, obtain a "certificate of convenience and necessity," and be licensed by the State Department of Public Utilities. They do seem able, however, to offer the service free or to charge a kind of "subscription fee" to "members." And to consider this activity a kind of subscription service is not really far off the mark, since the very notion of the service is to meet the special needs of a particular group of people.

6. *Transportation subsidy and financing arrangements should be imaginative.* The arrangement made by the Worcester Association for the Blind with local taxi companies—letting blind passengers charge their fares to the account of the Association—suggests that we should be far more subtle about the kinds of subsidies and the methods of providing them than we have been in the past. We think of providing transportation subsidies by giving elderly people and school children lower rates on mass transit. The same, of course, could be done for the poor, although the costs in political controversy, especially considering the state of the MBTA "deficit" in the public's eye, are probably not worth the gain. Still, such subsidies for particular categories of the poor —welfare recipients, for instance—make far more sense in terms of public policy than making transit "free" to all, since most people can afford to pay—and indeed to pay more—for public transportation.[22]

Other kinds and forms of subsidy, however, suggest themselves. Perhaps hospitals and surplus-food distribution centers should establish

[22]See Gerald Kraft and Thomas Domencich, "Free Transit," Transportation and Poverty Conference, June 1968.

charge accounts with taxi companies so that people within designated areas could come to the facility without having to pay for the trip. Or, once magnetic credit cards for transit tolls are instituted (this is now technically feasible), rides by welfare recipients could be paid for by the welfare agency. One could look at these arrangements as a way to place the costs of service on those who provide it—a principle that is not unreasonable when the providers are public agencies and the consumers need the service in the first place because they are poor.

7. *Relocation policy should be revised to cover more of the "social costs" of transportation construction, particularly highways.* The Watts riots produced a revolutionary change in federal relocation policy. When the Century freeway was constructed, renters forced to move had to be subsidized for any increase in their rent caused by the move; owners moving to another house were subsidized so that their monthly payments and their equity would remain unchanged; and replacement housing had to be made available before demolition took place. Secretary Volpe adopted the latter part of this as general policy in September 1969. The Secretary has suggested an even more significant step: the Highway Trust Fund, he says, might be used to finance the construction of new, replacement housing on a unit-for-unit basis before demolition.

The implications of such a policy are staggering, especially for the Boston area. The completion of present freeway plans inside of Route 128, it is estimated, would destroy about 4,000 units of housing. At a replacement cost of, say, $25,000 per unit, we are talking about $100,000,000 of capital outlay. (The magnitude of this figure diminishes somewhat when we realize that one mile of eight-lane freeway through an urban area may cost as much as $50,000,000, possibly more.) In any event, without going deeply into relocation policy here, we may say that this seems to be a time to press for change in this area —change which will particularly benefit the poor.

Roles for the state government

A number of roles for the state have been either stated or implied in these seven suggested problem areas. Several points go to the heart of the issues of process and framework that are the state's special responsibility.

1. *Direct services should be initiated.* Expand the "Job Express" to serve the night shift on Route 128; institute an automobile purchase

reinsurance scheme; and provide minibuses for state employment service offices.

2. *Frameworks for innovation should be developed.* The regulatory framework for transportation is not designed to encourage innovation. The inspection staff of the DPU is limited; the assumed burden of proof is on the innovator; and competitors who might be hurt by new service are permitted to argue—and their arguments tend to carry great weight —that they *could* provide the proposed service (without any claim that they *do* provide it or, indeed, *will* provide it). The state can provide a framework for innovation by removing state-created barriers in regulatory policy and procedures.

3. *An "advocate planning" section for the poor should be created within the Executive Office of Transportation and Construction.* A kind of watchdog for the poor, to receive complaints, raise issues, appear at regulatory hearings, examine long-range plans, and propose policy would be extremely useful to balance the power of the "transportation planners" within the new state department of transportation to be established in April 1971. Consideration of such countervailing power is particularly important once the MBTA, the Department of Public Works, the Port Authority, and the Turnpike Authority are all under one administrative roof. A "transportation ombudsman" might be separately identified.

4. *A "technical assistance" office should be devoted particularly to the problems of the poor.* We have discovered no one in any government agency who is keeping up to date on the various transportation and poverty projects and proposals around the country. Such an office should be clearly visible to local agencies and outside groups and should be actively stimulating interest in the problems.

5. *An attitude of trying to make some of the ongoing experiments work should be made more evident than it has been so far.* For 18 months, the "Job Express" took people to jobs on Route 128 and returned to Boston *empty.* The MBTA has recently established a "shopper's special" for the return trip—so that suburban wives can take the express bus to downtown Boston. The same pattern will be repeated in the afternoon, taking the shoppers out and bringing the workers back. It should not have taken 18 months to think of this plan. It may not be the answer, but it is clearly better than running the buses "deadhead" in one direction.

6. *The Governor should press for changes in federal policy, but if they are not forthcoming, he should move at the state level.* Changes in

relocation policy were suggested above, with possible financing from the federal Highway Trust Fund. This kind of change at the federal level should be sought. But we should not overlook the fact that the state also imposes a fuel tax. Presently, the federal tax amounts to four cents a gallon, and the state tax is 6.5 cents a gallon. If the federal government will not provide the funds required to cover more of the social costs of highways, there is no inherent reason why the state itself could not provide them. A one-cent increase in the fuel tax rate would yield roughly $20,000,000 a year. And the impact on the taxpayer would probably not be felt at all.

Conclusion

It is important to add a warning and recognize an opportunity in concluding this discussion of transportation problems of the poor.

The warning: this chapter has not established that transportation problems are a key ingredient in poverty, and it has certainly not claimed that solving the transportation problems that do exist for the poor will eliminate poverty. Indeed, it is not at all clear that many of those problems can be eliminated without changes in other systems at the same time. Nothing would be more injurious to programs to alleviate some of the transportation problems of the poor than to oversell them.

The opportunity: a number of the transportation problems faced by the poor are not different in quality from problems faced by higher-income groups. The increasing irrelevance of radial transit for the cross-commute, the declining service and rising costs (and fares) on far-out bus and rail service, the need for express buses, the need for small vehicles to take care of some travel needs in low-density areas, the problem of providing feeder service to the line-haul function (park-and-ride? minibuses? walk to Dudley Station?), the problem of distribution at the destination, the need for intermodal transportation planning with the opportunity for effective community participation, and the problem of dislocation from construction (through the Lynn reservoir, or the hills of Lincoln, to the four-level interchange of the proposed Inner Belt with the Southwest Expressway at Madison Park), all suggest a convergence rather than a divergence of interests between large portions of the poor and large portions of the nonpoor. Areas of potential conflict exist, to be sure—especially those concerning expressway and rail transit access to the core. But even here concern about pollution, congestion on local streets, and the quality of urban life may lead to more harmony of interest than might be expected. If this is so, the needs of the poor and of the nonpoor may well unite to force the political process to develop an effective and balanced transportation policy.

GERALD ROSENTHAL

health
care

This chapter examines the role of the state in improving medical care services for the poor. Such an objective is integrally bound with the improvement of services for all the people of the state.

The state represents a major influence on those who provide service. Using that influence to stimulate improved access to care and a more equitable distribution of services is an essential first step in achieving adequate medical care for all.

This chapter looks at some of the influences on both consumers and providers of care, identifies aspects of poverty that make such care more necessary or more difficult to obtain, describes some of the health care activities of the state, and suggests ways in which the state's influence might more effectively serve the goals of equal access to and adequacy of health care services for all its citizens.

No estimates are given of the cost of achieving these objectives. Considering the current structure and organization of health care services, such goals may not be achievable *at any cost*. Merely "footing

Gerald Rosenthal is associate professor of economics at Brandeis University and a senior associate in the Organization for Social and Technical Innovation, Cambridge.

the bill" is not enough. It is essential that the influence of the state be directed at ensuring the most effective use of funds to achieve these ends.

The aim of this chapter is to provide some suggestions about how Massachusetts might move in this needed direction.

Influences on the consumer's views

The availability and utilization of health care services have become central to the interests of a large part of the American population. Not a day passes without reference either to the tremendous technical advances in medical care or to the "crisis in health in the United States." To some extent these two circumstances are reinforcing, and some attempt must be made to place them in perspective. For most Americans it is a safe generalization to say that they are healthier than ever before; life expectancies are up; infant and maternal mortality rates, while not the lowest in the world, are still low; infectious diseases have been considerably reduced in both ubiquity and severity; and the diseases that threaten existence are diseases that only a few short decades ago were of little signifiance because many Americans did not live long enough to develop cancer, heart disease, stroke, and the other chronic, debilitating diseases that occupy much of contemporary medical attention. Given this environment, then, why is it that today large numbers of people feel that their health care services are inadequate, difficult to obtain, too costly, and generally not what they ought to be?

IMPACT OF TECHNICAL CHANGE

Expectations with respect to health and medical care services have been increasing, and new technical developments are quickly incorporated into that set of services which people feel ought to be available. Most important is that almost all the technical change has been directed at improving the quality of medical capability rather than reducing the cost of existing activities.

The country has probably paid a considerable price for the emphasis on outreach and improving technical capability. Considerably less attention has been given to the floor of health care services than has been given to the peak. *In our effort to devote resources to extending the frontiers of medical care, we have given little systematic attention to the problem of establishing a minimum level of medical care for the population at large.* If adequacy is defined by the kind of technically sophisticated and resource-intensive technology of which much of the population is aware, then *most* people in this country do not have easy access to adequate medical care services.

This point must be emphasized. Clearly, the discomfiture with respect to medical care services is not limited to the poor or any small and relatively restricted part of the population. Rather, it is a pervasive sense that is shared generally by the vast majority of Americans. It represents to some extent the discrepancy between reality and expectations (or the promise and the delivery) which has been supported by the emphasis on technical improvement and sophistication in the country as a whole.

IMPACT OF ORGANIZATIONAL CHANGE

Technical changes have contributed to, and even required, equally significant changes in the organization of services. In earlier years medical care was primarily the responsibility of an individual physician. Each family, in establishing a relationship with a physician, was essentially establishing its right of accessibility to care.

As the technology of health care developed, however, less that was potentially medically appropriate and useful was to be found at the first level of the family physician. More and more, medical care requires utilization of laboratories, hospital facilities, and other capital-intensive settings. The response to this need was the development of a highly institutionalized set of activities, usually centered around the hospital, to which the physician had access by virtue of his staff privileges. In addition, the physicians themselves began to specialize and concentrate on one area of medical care services which required all their competency and occupied all their interest. As a result, fewer and fewer physicians were concerning themselves with first-line health care services. At the same time, those who utilized health services were obtaining them, not from the physician first encountered, but from a whole group of other physicians, health personnel, and institutions, to which their family physician was, in principle, providing access. While the number of physicians in Massachusetts has risen, the number of physicians providing first-line health care services, primarily those in general practice, internal medicine, or pediatrics, has decreased considerably relative to the population. This means that the form of accessibility to health care services (that is, a family physician) which has been considered by the consumer to be the norm, has been less and less available for more and more of the people.

While availability of first-line health care services has become more restricted, the redistributive functions served by the physician in the community have also ceased to be effective. When communities were smaller geographically and more heterogeneous, a physician in an area would provide health care services to the rich and the poor alike. He would adjust the compensation he received for these services according to an ability-to-pay scale that was designed to ensure that access to health care services would not depend on a person's income. As the population increased and communities with a greater degree of homogeneity began to develop, the locational restraint of access to individual physicians has meant that each primary-care physician is likely to encounter a much more homogeneous set of patients. Since the decision where to locate the practice is based to some degree on the potential rewards from practice, poor communities are less likely to attract first-line physicians than are higher-income communities.

The physician in individual practice has previously borne the brunt of responsibility for allocating and distributing health care services among the population, thereby compensating for the inability of the market to ensure that medical, and not economic, attributes would be the basis for such distribution. In the current development of medical care, such a decision-making device has proved to be inadequate, and more and more people are demanding of the *system*, rather than of their physician, the development of mechanisms that will ensure access to needed health care services.

IMPACT OF FISCAL ARRANGEMENTS

As developing technical capabilities are manifested in greater and greater use of resources being devoted to health and medical care activities, the development of a shared burden of payment for these services has made the costs of care highly relevant to individuals *many of whom will not, in a particular period of time, avail themselves of any of these services.*

At the same time, the existence of a widespread burden of payment serves to increase the expectations of all the individuals participating in that payment of having services available under satisfactory circumstances whenever they feel those services might be needed. The financing mechanisms themselves, while directed at reducing the degree of financial risk associated with ill health in the population, have nevertheless served to directly involve the vast majority of the people with the cost side of the health and medical care system.

The changing technology, organization of services, and financing of costs have all contributed to a situation where dissatisfaction with the current state of medical care is widely felt by the consumers. The poor, who share the same expectations, are supported by the traditional arguments that "medical care is a right" and that "all who need care should get it." Part three of this chapter will discuss the special circumstances of the poor; but it must be emphasized that many of the differences between the poor and the nonpoor in their views as consumers of medical care are differences more of degree than of kind. This creates a special setting for any public policy directed at reducing medical care inadequacies for the poor, for many of the problems are inherent in the organization and structure of medical care and not in the poverty of the consumers.

Influences on providers

While the changing technology, organization, and financing of medical care have served both to raise the expectations of consumers generally and to make relevant to a wider proportion of the population the implications of these changes for increases in costs, they have equally significant implications for the behavior of the providers.

IMPACT OF TECHNOLOGY

For the providers, the institutional and the technical changes have been highly interrelated. As the quest for technical capability developed in American medicine, more and more of such medical care required the use of large amounts of capital equipment in the form of hospitals, operating rooms, and such associated services, in those capital-intensive environments, as nursing care, X-ray technicians, and the like. Since each physician's practice became more dependent on access to capital which his own individual practice could not afford, the institutions themselves began to grow and develop.

In many cases the acquisition and development of the capital equipment and auxiliary services required to support the activities of the physician was undertaken as a community responsibility. In principle, the community, through philanthropic support, and often through direct public support, would seek to make hospital facilities available to the physicians. The physicians, in turn, would provide services without charge for those who were responsibilities of the community at large, primarily the poor. This represented, in a real sense, payment for the use of the community's facilities. In fact, however, the community at large rarely owned the facilities. Rather, they tended to be voluntary, nonprofit organizations under the direction and control of boards of trustees ostensibly representing the community. They are, in fact, technically operated by the physicians who make up the staffs and who are, for the most part, not employees of, nor formally at the direction of, the institution itself.

With increases in the complexity and diversity of services required to support the medical care needs likely to be encountered by each physician, the medical staff of each institution seeks to incorporate within that institution the widest possible diversity of technical medical capability. Their own dependence on laboratory facilities, on intensive care, X-ray, and surgical facilities requires that they have access, either directly or through referring their patients to other physicians, to the widest range of services. *To the extent that their staff privileges and referral networks are constrained in the services to which they have access, those patients for whom they are responsible are also constrained in their access.*

Talking about the degree to which the community has adequate supplies of hospital facilities, nursing home beds, X-ray equipment is often fashionable—but such a focus is hardly consistent with the orientation of the individual institutions. Regardless of the geographic location of a facility, access to it is determined by the patient population served by the physicians on its staff. For these physicians, the only capital and facilities relevant to their own practices are those to which they personally have access—usually in those institutions in which they hold their staff privileges.

Each institution in its own growth and development seeks to acquire *within itself* the maximum degree of technical breadth and competency regardless of the existence of nonexistence of similar capabilities in other institutions within the same geographic area. While the geographic areas covered are likely to overlap, the population served and the the physician for whom those services are relevant may be considerably different.

This pressure to contain within each referral net and within the locus of each physician's staff privileges the widest variety of services also gives rise to some interinstitutional competitiveness. The mythology of medical care has always attempted to perpetuate the notion that each physician ought to be competent to provide all medical care services, and, similarly, that each institution that calls itself a hospital ought to be able to deal with the full range of activities for which hospital services are likely to be technically appropriate.

If medical care were not in its unique position as an item of consumption, then competition would occur within a marketplace where some providers would not be able to compete with others in the provision of certain kinds of services. Because of the significant nonoverlapping of staff privileges and the high degree of aspiration on the part of the consumer to have a single physician centrally responsible for his medical care, no real competition exists among these institutions in the provision of services. From the viewpoint of the consumer, the existence or nonexistence of various kinds of facilities in the area is less relevant than the degree to which the physician who is responsible for providing medical care has access to those services. The institutional barriers to rationalizing the *total* supply of services, coupled with the technical pressure for each individual institution to grow, develop, and expand its own capability, are responsible in large measure for the rapidly rising upward pressure on costs. It has been estimated that "the saving across the nation of consolidation in metropolitan areas of obstetric units alone would reach into the hundreds of millions of dollars in capital and annual operating costs."[1]

Such a consolidation would require considerable adaptation of existing patterns of staff privileges and influences on the motivations and organizational structure of existing providers of such services. When the services are less rewarding for the provider, as is the case in maintenance of emergency service, attempts to share responsibility are more likely to occur. For services more directly relevant to the existing patient mix and practice structure of the providers, such consolidation is often inconsistent with existing objectives and therefore more difficult to achieve.

[1]Sidney S. Lee, M.D., *New England Journal of Medicine,* Vol. 281, No. 15.

IMPACT OF ORGANIZATIONAL CHANGE

While the impact of technology has been to increase the capital requirements associated with the provision of health care services, and,
indeed, to increase the centrality of hospital and associated medical
facilities in the menu of available health services, organizational
changes have not kept direct pace with these changes. While many of
the services in a typical illness episode are provided within an institution
such as a hospital, the primary physician still is responsible for the
activities carried on there and still decides what activities will be carried
on and to whom they will be provided. The argument is that these
decisions should be medical rather than operational or economic, and
that only the physician is competent to decide what is an appropriate
mix of services for each illness episode for which he has responsibility.
However, each of the physicians' decisions has great implications for
the direction, growth, and utilization of the health facilities themselves.

What must be emphasized in this observation is that the criterion for an
appropriate mix of services is not the public interest or even the general
interest, but rather the physician's perception of the interest of that set of
potential consumers for whom he has direct responsibility. For the institution as a whole, it is that set of actual users of services for whom the
physicians on their staff have responsibility. The pressure is always to
improve, increase the services relevant to the patients of the institution's
staff. *This system contains no direct dynamic to expand services in an
effort to make more accessible, to those who do not currently have access
to them, the same kinds of services that currently exist.*

There is, however, one major exception. More and more the institutions
themselves, primarily through their emergency departments and often
through their out-patient departments, begin to perform the role of first-
line physician. In many out-patient departments, however, a referral is
required either from the welfare department, if the patient is poor, or from
a physician on the staff. The emergency departments, on the other hand,
tend to deal with immediate needs on a walk-in basis. In those cases where
the public, primarily through the cities and towns, has attempted to provide services to the poor, this has been the form that provision has traditionally taken: that is, "clinic medicine" centered in an institution rather
than an individual physician with whom responsibility to the patient re-
sides. To some extent, this difference in the organization of medical care
for the poor relative to the rest of the population has been changing.

INFLUENCES OF FINANCING MECHANISMS

Traditionally, medical care services have been paid for by those who use them. The assumption has been that the providers have a general responsibility to make such services available without regard to economic circumstances of the individual. The traditional mechanisms for implementing this objective have been price scales based on the ability of the person to pay. For physicians' services, the price charged by the physician would vary from the fee paid by his well-off patient to little or nothing at all when the services were provided to an indigent patient. Within the institutions, because of their community-based status, the prices charged for private and semiprivate accommodations were high enough to offset the costs incurred by the hospital for patients in the ward, who were generally charity patients.

Physicians' services were provided to these patients by the physicians on the institution's staff and represented the physician's contribution to the community. This system of financing led to a significant distinction, in the organization and structure, between services provided to the poor and those provided to the nonpoor.

With the development of widespread insurance, the whole concept of "ability to pay" ceased to have operational relevance. Surely a third party, such as Blue Cross, could not be expected to pay more (or charge more) for well-to-do subscribers than for all others. The movement away from individual payers was also a move toward price standardization. However, the price has tended increasingly to take the form of cost reimbursement, which leaves little room for the subsidizing care for the poor from the payments of the wealthy.

Basically, cost reimbursement provides a payment mechanism to the institution which does not directly affect its own decisions about what constitutes appropriate behavior or the appropriate services to be embodied within each medical experience and within each institution. Even though the community is the basis for premium determination, more expensive institutions receive greater reimbursements for services identical to those of less expensive institutions without any independent estimate being made of qualitative differences or the necessity of the differences in the experience of the patients.

The definition of reimbursable costs means that an institution with a greater complexity and diversity of *capability* will have higher costs even for those activities which may not utilize that capability. For example, an institution that maintains an operating room equipped for complex surgical procedures, intensive care units, and high-level special nursing personnel will operate at higher cost than an institution which does not. Much of this increased cost will show up in the reimbursement rate for hospital care for tonsillectomies, diagnostic procedures, and other activities that may or may not use the high-cost facilities. Since the reimbursement structure provides no specific stimulus to efficiency in an economic sense, the objectives of the institution itself will be determinant in developing the complexity of services and the nature of the services provided within it. Since, as we argued in an earlier section, each institution operates within a limited environment rather than a community-wide context, each institution will select for itself that part of the community toward which it will direct its activities and whose interest it will regard to be paramount in defining its activities.

While the Blue Cross mechanism was developed and expanded, it was not used for providing medical care to those who could not afford to pay the community-wide premium. In those cases, as we noted earlier, the institutions and the physicians used to provide free care. Through the mechanism of payments to vendors through public assistance, more and more such services were paid for out of public monies. The rate of such payments was usually considerably lower than the rate at which other patients were charged for the same services, thereby representing a public and an institutional subsidy.

The Medicaid program, following a process begun with Medicare, represents a movement away from differentiated reimbursement. Both Medicare and Medicaid are cost reimbursement mechanisms designed to be "neutral" about decisions of the institutions on the mix of services, but not, however, about their willingness to provide services to people in the population who previously did not have them or were not able to obtain them.

Although all the three major sources of reimbursement for institutions are cost reimbursers, the costs that are reimbursed are not identical for each program. In many cases the reimbursement rate for Blue Cross does not include costs that may be included under the Medicare and Medicaid reimbursements. This means that an institution may receive a greater reimbursement for services provided to the poor or the aged than for persons covered under a standard Blue Cross contract.

So far we have commented specifically on hospital and institutional services. Similar changes have occurred with respect to physicians' services, particularly for the poor. As more and more services are covered under insurance, the ability to pay has become a function of insurance coverage rather than of the patient's income. In the implementation of Part B of the Medicare program, and under Medicaid, "usual and customary fees" were to be paid for physicians' services. This means that those who used to be at the low end of the physicians' price scale are now moved up at least to the median. It is no surprise, then, that the average price of physician services rose considerably, since, at the very least, the bottom half was compressed to the median without any reductions necessarily taking place for those who paid more.

The whole dynamic has been directed at reducing the distinction between the poor and the nonpoor in terms of prices charged and therefore, one hopes, in terms of the forms in which services are rendered. *A major public policy objective is to make the service activity indifferent to the economic circumstance of the individual,* since previous experience has demonstrated that this will not automatically occur within the existing medical care structure and its activities. These programs have been directed not at providing services but at making it possible for consumers to pay for such services through some third-party mechanism which, in the case of the poor, is a public financing vehicle. However, the form in which the institutions and the providers themselves are reimbursed has been directed not at affecting their behavior but at responding to and paying for those changes and adaptations that the providers themselves consider to to be desirable. While Medicaid pays for physicians' services for the poor, it does not attempt to affect either the scope, scale, and nature of such services that institutions provide or the accessibility of such institutions, either through expansion of their staff privileges or by relocation and development.

The fact that Medicaid often pays a higher reimbursement rate than Blue Cross has accounted for a significant increase in the utilization of hospital services by the poor, just as Medicare represented an opportunity for a significant increase in the utilization of hospital services by the aged, many of whom are also poor. This turns out to be an attempt to use the natural market influences on the operation of the entire medical care structure in a way that serves the public objective of providing health care services to the poor.

Without a direct impact on supply, however, that influence coupled with a cost reimbursement structure providing no real economic restraint has also tended to stimulate considerable expansion within each institution and has not increased the degree to which coordination and community-wide orientation of the organization of health care services has taken place.

The nature of the competition among institutions provides a stimulus for bidding up the price of already scarce resources in the face of an increasing demand. No profitability criterion constrains the degree to which an institution can expand. Rather, as a significant proportion of all of its patients are paid for through some cost reimbursement mechanism, the institution has a blank check for any growth and development pattern which it feels serves its interests and those of the people, both patients and physicians, that it serves.

These comments, we emphasize, do not imply that services are provided which are not appropriate in the sense of being technically relevant or that the institutions and physicians are not serving their patients' interests. Rather, given scarce resources and the public objective of getting care to those who get little or none, the interests appropriately served *under the current organization of medical care* may not yield the desired results defined by the public interest. Since the current behavior reflects the influence of existing public policy, the forms that such policies have taken merit reevaluation.

Health care and the poor

The first two sections of this paper attempted to spell out some of the changes that have taken place in the organization and distribution of health services and their implications for both providers of services and consumers. Basically, the argument focuses on the dimension of accessibility to care as being crucial. As in any system for providing service, the point of entry into the system is strategic in determining the distribution and utilization of those services. In the case of the poor the difficulty of access and the uniqueness of the forms of access are well understood. This section will attempt to deal with two aspects of health care for the poor: first, the degree to which poverty itself affects the medical requirements of a population; and second, the degree to which poverty and the living conditions of the poor affect their access to the services they need.

A few comments may be in order about the relationship between poverty and medical care. It seems reasonable to suggest that the health of the poor is affected more adversely by poor housing, locational constraints, low incomes, and the generally bad environmental conditions associated with poverty than by the absence of medical care. The difference in the health of the poor compared to the health of the rest of the population does not necessarily reflect the absence or presence of medical care services. However, it is appropriate to ask to what extent improvement in medical care services would contribute to a reduction of poverty.

While it is not possible to answer this question directly, other chapters in this book do suggest that health care services and the manner of using such services may have some implication for the employability of the poor, many of whom do hold jobs. For the poor illness may exact a higher penalty in terms of income reduction than would be the case for those employed in the primary labor market. Since the characteristics of the secondary labor market, described in the chapter on jobs and training, include highly casual labor, day-to-day employment, and lack of certain fringe benefits, such as sick leave and health insurance, then lost work time due to ill health will result in a direct reduction in the incomes earned by the working poor, Evidence suggests that the higher rate of illness among the poor, which we will discuss below, contributes to the nonstability of the employment they can obtain. In addition, the access to care often means that the poor must spend more time to obtain a given type of health care service, if such service is available. This also suggests that the income loss associated with using health care services may be higher for the poor than for the nonpoor.

Ill health, it can be argued, certainly contributes to poverty. However, it cannot be argued conversely that an improvement in medical care services would significantly improve the economic circumstances of the poor. To the extent that the ill health of the poor reflects more than just the absence of medical care, merely providing readier access or more thorough medical care services alone will not necessarily deal with the ill health of the poor. Certainly factors such as nutrition, environment, and housing play a significant role in the health of any population. For the poor many of these attributes of existence contribute to high mortality and morbidity. If nothing is done to deal with these issues, medical care may turn out to be more palliative than curative.

THE POOR ARE SICKER

There is little doubt that the poor are sicker and that illness rates are higher in low-income areas than in high-income areas.

In 1960 in the city of Boston, the infant mortality rates in three listricts with high poverty populations were between 38 and 39.5 infant deaths per thousand live births; the rate for the entire city of Boston was 24.1 deaths per thousand live births. In another study of perinatal mortality in the Boston Standard Metropolitan Statistical Area, members of the highest socioeconomic group had a perinatal mortality of 24.7 per one thousand as opposed to 46.0 in the poorest group. That particular study also found that the incidence of unsatisfactory prenatal care was eight to nine times higher in the poorest group. More recent studies of obstetrical care in the city of Boston again point out that women with the highest-risk pregnancies, particularly unmarried women and nonwhites, were the ones least likely to receive their care from a board-certified obstetrician. It is not clear that the absence of medical care is the circumstance that accounts for high infant and mortality rates among the poor. Certainly the significance of nutrition during pregnancy is difficult to overemphasize. However, inadequate levels of nutrition among the poor may make better prenatal care more important than might be the case among better-nourished women.

A study of deaths from cancer in Massachusetts showed that death rates from cancer were higher in the poorest groups than in higher-income groups, and that poor people got medical treatment for cancer later than more affluent people. Ample evidence indicates that tuberculosis rates are higher in poor neighborhoods and that the incidence of communicable diseases is also higher. The incidence of tuberculosis per 100,000 people provides some indication. For the state as a whole, the rate reported in 1968 was 16.7. For whites the rate was 14.4; for nonwhites it was 89.2, a rate not found among whites since the 1920s. While these rates may reflect more the quality of housing and population density, they nevertheless provide a basis for requiring more health care services for the poor than for the nonpoor population.

The higher medical care requirements of the poor also relfect the fact that a greater proportion of the poor are aged than is true of the population in general. While only 15.4 percent of all families in Massachusetts were headed by a person 65 or over in 1961, almost 41 percent of poor families fell into that category. Almost a third of all families in the state headed by a person 65 or over are poor families. The higher rate of illness and the higher requirements for medical care are well documented for the older population. Since they represent a larger percentage of the population of the poor, it is reasonable to infer that this higher incidence should be reflected in a higher requirement for and emphasis on greater access to health care services for the poor than for the nonpoor.

MORE SERVICES FOR EACH ILLNESS

More services for each illness may be required by the poor than by the population in general. The inadequacy of housing and the high proportion of aged poor not living with a family require that a greater proportion of medical care be institutional and residential. This circumstance points to a heavier investment of resources and a greater intensity of service than the identical patterns of illness require in a different environment. The difficulty of follow-up, the lack of home-care services, and the necessity to ensuring that the patient follows the therapeutic regimen may also provide strong motivation for a longer stay in the hospital and a more intensive application of services for particular illness patterns for the poor.

Thus, both increased rates of illness among the poor and need for a higher level of services for each illness provide the basis for arguing that, other things being equal, the poor have a higher requirement for medical care services, and that even a policy designed to make given services equally accessible to the poor and the nonpoor might not, in terms of relative needs, yield an equitable distribution of care.

HOW DOES POVERTY AFFECT ACCESS TO SERVICES?

In an earlier section of this chapter, we argued that access to first-line physicians' care is a significant entry mechanism in obtaining health services and is perceived as such by both the poor and the nonpoor. To the extent that health care services are to be provided in the mode considered to be the norm by most of the population, then access to such physicians' services is essential. The supply of such services, while dropping generally, has diminished much more greatly in the poorer areas of Massachusetts than in the less poor areas. For example, between 1940 and 1961 in the cities of Boston and Brookline, the ratio of general practitioners per 100,000 population fell from 132.3 to 67.0, a drop of 50 percent.[2] The ratio of intermediary practitioners—pediatricians and internists—who perform the same access function, rose only from 34.6 to 50.8. The total physician-to-population ratios for community-based physicians, primarily or potentially available for primary health care, were 166.9 per 100,000 in 1940 and 117.8 in 1961.

[2]Joseph Dorsey, M.D., *The Distribution of Physicians by Census Tract, Boston and Brookline, 1940 and 1961* (unpublished master's thesis, Yale University School of Public Health, 1968).

This decline has not been uniform by the socioeconomic class of the population surrounding the location of these physicians. Dorsey's study showed that the relative decrease in general practitioners per 100,000 population, by social class of the district in which the practice was located, was greater in the higher social class areas between 1940 and 1961 than in the lower; but the actual numbers of such physicians relative to population continued to be lower in poorer neighborhoods. In the highest social class neighborhoods, 104.7 general practitioners served 100,000 population, while the lowest had exactly half the ratio, 52.3 per 100,000. For intermediary physicians, who with general practitioners make up the primary medical care providers, the number in the highest socioeconomic class areas rose from 117.8 per 100,000 to 159.4, while in the lowest income class areas the numbers shrank from 1.4 per 100,000 to 1.3.

While the number of general practitioners and intermediate practitioners, who represent the traditionally desired forms of physicians' services, is considerably lower relative to the population in poorer areas than in higher income areas, that observation obliterates the major change in the location and nature of a physician's practice that has taken place. Over this period of time a substantial increase in the supply of hospital-based physicians has occurred, and the proportion of the total physician pool that is hospital-based has also increased. The ratio of hospital-based physicians per 100,000 population increased from 119.4 to 289.4 between 1940 and 1961. In 1940, 65.4 percent of all physicians had their offices located in the community rather than the hospital; in 1961, close to 60 percent of physicians had their offices based in hospitals.

Much of this change reflects the influence of the increasing institutionalization of medical care that was described earlier. Nevertheless, it does suggest that for the poor, and indeed to some extent for all, access to physicians' services may more and more become an institutional access, which has traditionally been gained through access to physicians. If the trends observed here continue—and we have every reason to believe that they will—changes in the organizational form of access will have to occur, not only for the poor, but for all consumers of health care services.

Not only does the relatively restricted access to physicians' services make it more difficult for the poor to obtain health care; other aspects of the living circumstances of poverty also tend to make the acquisition of care more difficult. Certainly the poor, depending heavily on public transportation in urban areas, and having a high proportion of aged with all the concommitant constraints on mobility, are much more susceptible to the cost and time implications of travel to required health services. The increasing dependence on the mobility of patients rather than physicians makes this particular constraint more acute. Increasing dependence on centrally located health services and operating on a larger scale requires that the patients who use those services must be more widely distributed. The issue is not distance, but rather the time and cost of traveling to the locus of care. People with automotive transportation may have very rapid access to services located many miles away, while people who are 15 to 20 blocks from an institution which can serve them may be three times farther away in terms of the time it takes to get to the services.

A third factor affects the difficulty of access to medical care for the poor. The need to get medical care services during the working day exacts a more immediate cost in terms of lost income and, potentially, loss of job for the working poor than for the nonpoor. This means that the costs of obtaining a given service may be higher for the poor than for the nonpoor. In 1960 almost 60 percent of all poor families had at least one earner; thus, loss of working time represents a significant cost constraint on the utilization of medical care services.

A few last comments seem in order. As the demands of the poor for increased access to medical care increase, and the absolute and relative supply of first-line physicians declines, any increase in the volume of services provided in the short run has to yield a decrease in the intensity of existing physicians' services. This may emphasize the tendency to move patient responsibility to the instituions, thereby reducing the degree to which encountering an independent physician outside an institutional setting is the basis for access to medical care services.

While institutionally based ambulatory care (clinic medicine) has been associated with second-class care for the poor, such organizational structures must inevitably increase in importance rather than decrease. Such changes cannot and will not be limited to services for the poor. However, the areas having the most poor people also are the areas having greatest need for expanding services, and the expansion of services generally is likely to take a more institutional form. If the needs of the poor for medical care are to be met, the expanded services must be accepted and utilized by the poor who have a right to, and expect to receive, services they perceive as "first class." To overcome the stigma attached to "clinics," new organizational and institutional forms, such as neighborhood health centers, satellite outpatient departments, and the like, are being developed. More attention must be given to the quality of the medical care experience in the form of environment, relationships with patients, personalizing of service, and consumer involvement with the provider.

The development of Medicare and Medicaid provides a basis for consumer choice that the poor have rarely been able to exercise. This, coupled with growing expectations about the form of care, makes it essential to avoid limiting the choice to a form of care which looks and feels like "the same old thing." The poor are in the forefront of the inevitable and necessary changes in providing medical care in Massachusetts and in the country as a whole.

Health services and the state of Massachusetts

The Massachusetts Health Department, founded in 1869, is the oldest in the United States, and ever since that time the state has had some formal responsibility for certain aspects of health and medical care services. However, with the exception of mental health and certain chronic diseases, the state has not had significant direct, primary responsibility for actually providing services.[3]

The state's responsibility for the wide diversity of health care services with which it is concerned and involved does not stop with the Massachusetts Department of Public Health. The welfare department and the Commission on Rehabilitation, for example, represent other loci within the state that have some operational health service responsibility. Indeed, the major identified planning function exists within the governor's office directly and does not come under the aegis of any of the operating departments of the state.

Basically, the state's role in the scale, distribution, and delivery of health services takes four general forms: providing services; supervising and controlling quality; financing services, and planning.

---

[3]The development of mental health services has been quite different from the development of services to deal with other forms of illness and is ommitted from direct discussion in this chapter.

PROVIDER ACTIVITIES

Perhaps the most significant among services under the direction of the state are the seven chronic disease hospitals, which represented expenditures of about $24.5 million in 1968–1969, almost 50 percent of the budget of the Massachusetts Department of Public Health. These institutions provide services for a wide variety of illnesses, including cancer and allied diseases, tuberculosis, and kidney disease. In many ways these institutions function like other hospital providers in the system. Of the $24.5 million, 70 to 80 percent is reimbursed to the institutions through Medicare and Medicaid. Since the funds for this reimbursement go back into general revenues, it is not possible to ascertain exactly the net cost to the state of operating these institutions directly. Nevertheless, they represent a significant part of the state effort in the direct provision of health services.

The state also operates centers for the treatment of drug addiction, which provide direct medical services. For tuberculosis, the state's effort is significantly large. In 1968–1969, 143,000 days of in-patient care were provided. State-supported clinics had more than 130,000 visits. In addition, the state supported large numbers of out-patient diagnostic screening and follow-up clinics, as well as laboratory services. These activities in the area of treatment of disease represent a significant direct fiscal effort.

In addition, both the Health Department, mainly through Lakeville Hospital, and the Commission on Rehabilitation have responsibility for developing rehabilitation services. Several of the renal dialysis programs in the state are undertaken by these offices. During the past year, more than 20,000 handicapped individuals received some kind of services, not all of which were direct health services. The Commission on Rehabilitation spent in 1968–1969 close to a million dollars of state funds in conjunction with almost five million dollars of federal funds. A movement is now underway to incorporate the functions of the commission into the Department of Public Health, on the grounds that the overlapping of responsibility would provide opportunities for more coordinated efforts.

Another major area of service provision in the state is that of prevention. Tuberculosis screening by the state includes over 400,000 screening tests distributed to local communities for use by local health departments. In addition, the state has taken as a major objective the elimination of certain diseases for which inoculations are likely to be useful. The measles immunization program has accounted for a decrease of better than 98 percent in cases of measles in Massachusetts in the past three years. A similar program is being undertaken for mumps and rubella, and it is anticipated that within two or three years both these diseases will cease to be of any significance in the state. In the spring of 1969 legislation gave a secondary prevention responsibility, monitoring the rabies immunization requirement for dogs, to the Division of Communicable Disease. Such prevention activities are traditionally a role of health departments.

Another major area of service provision comprises the activities of the Maternal and Child Health Department. This division of the State Health Department runs a number of child development clinics and preschool vision screening programs, and monitors the school health programs. The activities of the Maternal and Child Health division also include direct provision of services through a number of state-supported health centers not restricted to the "well-baby" care traditional in departments of public health. The Maternal and Infant Project and the Child and Youth projects of the Department of Public Health maintain units in a number of hospitals in the greater Boston area designed to provide services primarily to the poor. Currently, such programs are supported under Title V and provide over half of all maternal and infant care services to indigent patients in the city of Boston. It should be recognized that Title V funds are meant to stimulate the development of high-quality programs and to attract providers. Ongoing fiscal responsibility for these programs must shift to Title XIX, with the quality control and standards extended to all Title XIX providers. The activities of the maternal and infant health programs of the state play a significant role in demonstrating the feasibility and effectiveness of implementing such standards.

SUPERVISORY ACTIVITIES

The state is responsible for licensing many health service activities and institutions. Licensing of hospitals and nursing homes is a responsibility of the Division of Medical Care of the Department of Public Health. This division, in conjunction with the Department of Public Welfare, also is responsible for establishing standards for services provided under the Medicaid program, although it has no direct operating responsibility for that program at the moment. In addition, the division of Maternal and

Child Health is responsible for licensing day-care centers. In this supervision and quality-control activity, the state also maintains a laboratory which both serves as a reference lab and provides technical assistance and quality control for existing laboratory services in the state.

The licensing responsibility represents a significant potential vehicle for influencing the structure of activities and institutions within the state. Not only does the absence of a license preclude the development of a service, but the requirements for getting a license may have significant influence on the form that such institutions and activities take. This assumption has been incorporated in recent activities of the Division of Medical Care, primarily in the nursing home area, in which for the first time an effort has been made to distinguish among classes of nursing homes for licensing purposes and ultimately for reimbursement and payment purposes. A single set of criteria for licensing a service that encompasses a broad range of required intensity of care suggests that for some the licensing requirements require too complex or too costly a set of services. For others, the licensing norms will be too low since the most complex services are unlikely to be achievable by a sufficient number of institutions to ensure an adequate supply of services.

The use of the licensing mechanism to differentiate, by intensity of service that an institution provides, gives an opportunity to rationalize the system without directly controlling the provision of the services themselves. The effectiveness of this approach depends entirely on the degree to which it incorporates inspection and review and is coordinated with and able to affect the financing and reimbursement activities that relate to these same institutions. This initial experience with the Division of Medical Care and its nursing home licensing activities is in many ways prototypical of the directions in which statewide planning for health services will be required to move, if any effective impact is to be achieved.

FINANCING ACTIVITIES

The third major activity of the state is financing direct medical care services, primarily through the Medicaid program operated by the Department of Public Welfare, which provides direct payments, from both federal and state funds, to vendors for services rendered to eligible people. The magnitude of these expenditures and the impact of their form on the health care system has been significant, and indeed the commitment to provide services under the cost reimbursement structure currently in effect has presented the state with a rapidly escalating level of cost for the program. In fiscal 1969, Medicaid reimbursment to providers was $228 million. This amount paid for services to an average of 231,523 individuals. More than 60 percent of these funds were for services to people over 65 years of age. These expenditures through the state include federal funds and represent a major commitment to health care for the poor.

For the most part, the Department of Public Health has been only slightly involved in the organization, structure, and operation of the Medicaid program in Massachusetts. Because this program was directed specifically at the poor and (at least in the intent of the federal legislation) the near poor, the issues of eligibility and payment became central to the program. Those functions were already the responsibility of the state welfare department, particularly since the recent welfare reorganization bill moved the responsibility for local welfare services from the individual towns and communities to the state. Inevitably, the operation of the program fell to that department. That has made a significant impact on the degree to which the Medicaid program has been seen or used as an adaptive influence on the organization, structure, and services rendered by the providers.

The Medicaid program has no doubt had a significant influence on increasing the amount of services provided to poor people in Massachusetts. While the program has served to pay for many services that would not otherwise have been provided, it has not utilized its tremendous fiscal impact on the providers to affect directly the deficiencies in the organization, structure, and coordination of services within the health care system which preclude the ultimate implementation of the objective of equal access for all. The use of a cost reimbursement structure without a vigorous program of cost, quality, and utilization review (and control) leaves providers still free to pursue individual and institutional objectives inconsistent with the effective use of scarce resources in the public interest. The emphasis on issues of eligibility and payment has resulted in a response to rising cost in the form of limiting eligibility. Such a response is inconsistent with the espoused public objectives of the Medicaid program. However, without adequate systems of medical and economic review, no alternative basis for cost controls exists.

PLANNING

The other major area where the state exerts a direct influence on health care is through mechanisms for planning. Health care planning has developed primarily as planning for institutions rather than services. The major impetus for health care planning and the regionalization of institutional activities was through the Hill-Burton (now Hill-Harris) Act, which provided grants-in-aid for the construction of hospitals and other medical care facilities; it also established area-wide planning councils and state Hill-Burton agencies that were to approve applications according to some kind of plan for reasonable distribution of services. Since the act was originally developed to deal with inadequacies in geographic distribution—primarily, absence of facilities in rural areas—the emphasis was on location of facilities rather than on services and the form in which services were provided.

As experience is accumulated, it is increasingly evident that location and access are not synonomous, particularly with regard to health services for the poor. Emphasis on access means emphasis on services and the forms of obtaining services, perhaps even more than emphasis on the institutional settings themselves.

The planning under the Hill-Harris program has been primarily "defensive" in that it is responsive to requests by institutions for funds to increase capacity and, in some cases, to construct new facilities. The authority of the planner is merely to approve or disapprove the grants. This kind of planning is peculiar in that it influences only those institutions that most depend on the Hill-Burton money for capital funds and provides no direct influence on those institutions that have alternative sources of capital. Since one emphasis of planning has been to coordinate the services existing in a particular area, the ability to influence only some of the participants in the system, usually those with the least economic resources and perhaps of the smallest scale of operation, has been less than ideal in terms of generating real and significant change.

The planning agency in Massachusetts, as in many other states, has had no direct influence on expenditure of other state and federal monies on those institutions, even those that were constructed without approval. This means that the costs exacted from an institution for ignoring the plan are merely the opportunity costs of going elsewhere for some of the capital funds required for construction.

A second major deficiency is that little or no attempt has been made through the planning mechanism to generate new services where an existing institution has not had the desire to expand those services. In this sense, there has been no creative planning. The "defensive" approach of responding to stimuli means that the planning agency itself is limited to a narrow range of choices with respect to its overall objectives in the distribution of services, and that the stimulus for developing those choices comes from the providers, who, as we have noted, may not share the objectives that are to be served by the planning process.

More recently, with the passage of the "Partnership-for-Health" Act of 1966, federal money has come to the state for the operation of a state Comprehensive Health Planning Office under the Commissioner of Administration and Finance. The mandate for this planning has been to concentrate, not just on facilities, but on the total distribution and accessibility of health services in general. The vehicle for implementing the plan has been widespread involvement of both consumers and providers in the hope that somehow, by indicating more desirable considerations, the system could be influenced for change. No direct money is provided for developing and operating services, nor are there direct responsibilities for overseeing existing services within that office.

In addition, the state has been divided into a number of regions for which funds are available for developing comprehensive health planning councils to operate at the regional level. In Massachusetts, only four of these area-wide comprehensive health planning agencies have received planning grants, and in Massachusetts (as elsewhere) they are likely to be much the same organizations that previously has been the hospital planning councils. This means that once again, regardless of the participation of consumers on the board, providers will be the major influence on planning through Regional B agencies.

Perhaps most important, however, is that the major influence of all the planning activities has been on approval or disapproval of proposed changes by the providers of services and its effect on obtaining capital funds. To the extent that the capital acquisition process does not depend on funds controlled by the state, such influences are not likely to be overpersuasive.

If the major objective of planning is to deal directly with the supply of services and their accessibility to the relevant populations in the state,—not only the poor, but certainly including them—then equality of access is the key. Planning must include the ability to influence directly the nature of the services provided by the institutions for which planning is being undertaken. A major source of operating revenue for these institutions is either direct state or federal money through Medicare and

Medicaid or is under the rate-setting responsibilities of the Commissioner of Administration and Finance, as in the case of Blue Cross. The ability to utilize those funds in a manner consistent with the objectives of the planning process is essential for effective achievement of planning objectives. This observation follows directly from the earlier argument that the individual focus of providers, while appropriate for the providers, nevertheless may run counter in behavioral terms and in service accessibility terms to what would be considered appropriate behavior from the focus of the state as a whole. That basic difference generates the need for planning in the first place, and a direct acknowledgment of that difference, and the development of the tools to change providers' behavior, are essential to the success of any planning process.

OTHER AREAS OF STATE INFLUENCE

While these areas are the major ones for the state involvement in health care, they do not exhaust that involvement. The state also carries on and supports the activities of the training center for comprehensive care, which is directed specifically at improving manpower in the health field by training the poor for jobs in health and by attempting to influence the system to enable persons trained in these jobs to obtain some degree of upward mobility. So far, over 65 percent of those initiating the training have completed it and obtained employment—a highly significant batting average. In addition, the Division of Research Development and Professional Training is also directed at upgrading both the techniques and the manpower.

Toward a more active state role in improving medical care services for the poor

This chapter has presented eight basic points about the organization and provision of medical care services in Massachusetts:

1. *The expectations of consumers, rich and poor, for traditional modes of access to physicians' services are being modified considerably by increasing demands for services, changes in technology of medical care and nature of physicians' training and practice, and the*

obvious inability to meet the current requirements for the system in the old organizational modes.

2. *Each provider responds to and serves a certain segment of the population represented by its own sphere of practice and influence.* Access to service for the physician is limited to his referral links and his hospital privilege for the institution, access to various kinds of technology means that which is contained within the institution. These factors determine providers' views of adequacy of services regardless of community-wide accessibility criteria from the consumers' standpoint.

3. *The lack of coordination among individual providers inherent in the system is inconsistent with the objective of increasing the accessibility of services and even more inconsistent with maintaining a constraining influence on the costs of those services at a time of high and rising demand.*

4. *For the poor, conditions of access are even worse.* Since the individual providers are most responsive to the operating requirements of those for whom access is already a reality (i.e., their patients), the poor are less likely to be considered in the planning of individual institutions.

5. *If an objective is equity in the distribution of health care services with respect to need, then greater resources must be applied to the poor than to the nonpoor*, for their conditions of existence contribute to higher incidences of medical disability, their older age contributes to an even greater proportion of chronic disease, and their environmental circumstances and housing circumstances may require greater services even if their medical circumstances were identical to the nonpoor.

6. While not providing directly a significant share of the health care services, *the state has sufficient direct services under its control to play a significant role in demonstrating new modes of care and new opportunities for making more effective use of existing resources.*

7. *The state pays for, or influences the payment for, a large proportion of care for the poor.* In addition, it influences the rates paid by the nonpoor for care covered under the Blue Cross prepayment mechanism.

8. *Generating behavior on the part of the providers consistent with the public interest, and therefore somewhat inconsistent with the individual provider's desires, is not likely to be effectively achieved through planning mechanisms without "teeth."* The potential for influencing the providers of health care services is highly dependent on the willingness to utilize the payment mechanism to stimulate the kinds of changes that the planning process indicates are desirable and appro-

priate. As long as one is willing to pay for performance, inconsistent with the public objectives, the stimulus for adaptation in the system will be minimal at best.

The issues most significant in achieving the health objectives of the state relate to affecting the real accessibility of health services for all who need them and to seeking equal access relative to those needs rather than some uniform physical distribution of providers. That search requires the state's direct involvement in the operation of health services through the area in which its influence is most significant—that is, in the financing of care—and the formalization of planning responsibility so that it utilizes that influence to stimulate changes in health care that will serve the public interest. It is that objective which must be paramount, and toward which the following recommendations are directed:

1. *At the vital state level, specific commitment to improving equity of access and adequacy of health care services is essential.* Since problems in the distribution of health care services are generic to the system rather than unique to the poor, at the level of state-wide comprehensive health planning, the commitment to equity of access as a general objective and *as a criterion for evaluating proposed changes in the system* would best serve the public interest. The Division of Medical Care is the appropriate agency to be responsible for serving as advocate for better health services for the poor. Formal commitment to such a responsibility within the Department of Public Health is needed.

2. *The state*, through its training capabilites and the mechanisms with which it is directly providing services, *must move into the forefront in demonstrating that institutionally based services are not second-class medical care and that new methods for providing and distributing health services can provide effective, high-quality health care.* Internally operated demonstration programs are a potential benefit to all, both in increasing the supply of services throughout the state and in shaping the form of the inevitable movement toward institutionalization of health care services. If those institutions are to remain functional and able to meet the increasing demands to be made upon them, some experimentation must be undertaken with new forms in organizational structures within an institutional setting.

3. *Encouragement of consolidation and merger of existing facilities and development of additional distinctions among facilities with regard to the breadth of service for which payment will be made by the state*

is essential. Such activities are already underway within the Division of Medical Care and ought also to be incorporated in the Comprehensive Health Planning view. This would require the development of incentives for the merger of institutions, the sharing of staff, and indeed, perhaps, the acquisition of staff privileges to a group of hospitals rather than to an individual institution.

4. *All activities of the state that involve licensing and approval of new facilities should require evidence of increased access to services for such proposed expansions.* In the event of approval of a new activity, followup demonstration of impact on access to new users must be required as a condition of approval. If changes turn out not to yield anticipated increases in access on which approval was contigent, the appropriate Health Planning Office should have authority to reduce reimbursement levels of Medicaid and, perhaps, Medicare and Blue Cross for services of that institution. The reduction should be consistent with the expected increase of costs in the system as a result of having a new or expanded facility with no increase in access to service.[4]

5. *With regard to Medicaid, it seems appropriate that the Welfare Department continue to be responsible both for the eligibility determination and perhaps even for the fiscal payment; however, the authorization for such payment should be linked to the qualitative performance of the providers and should be a health department function.* In addition, functions such as utilization review and medical audits, as estimators of the quality of the services being provided for the funds expended, also belongs appropriately in the Department of Public Health. The Health Planning Office should have the responsibility for authorizing reimbursement and for identifying potential points of observation or conditional certifications for reimbursement.

The existing authority under federal legislation to apply the qualitative standards of the Crippled Children's Programs to the certification of providers of Medicaid services must be effectively implemented. Written standards for providers must be developed to allow for adequate

[4]The authority suggested here to be held by either the State Health Department or the Comprehensive Health Planning Office is similar to that in the recently enacted New York state and California legislation, where the planning authority for approval and disapproval was linked to the continued eligibility for reimbursement on the part of the institutions. Indeed, that legislation was born as a response to the proliferation of services, the lack of restraint, the lack of collective access improvements by the individual providers. The situation is no different in Massachusetts and the actual operational impact of that legislation merits further study and examination.

quality assurance and differences among providers that should be linked to their reimbursement levels. The certification process must seek a mix of quality of providers consistent with the objective of equity of access and adequacy of care for all.

6. *While the achievement of these goals will require additional expenditures, the state must work to establish a system that makes such expenditures contribute most effectively to these ends.* Efforts within the state must be matched by efforts to stimulate changes in the federal programs to support these state objectives and to respond to the needs of the citizens of Massachusetts.

Unlike many areas of state activity with respect to the poor, dealing with deficiencies in health services for the poor obviously would represent a considerable upgrading of the quality of health care services for all of the citizens of the state. There is probably no way to deal with them solely for the poor. Nevertheless, the emphasis on adequacy and equity of distribution, the differential needs, and the serious constraints on access in a system where all have some constraints on access make this focus an appropriate one. The state has a unique potential for utilizing its current fiscal involvement and its current commitment to health care planning within the existing structure of service provision in the state in a way that will stimulate movement toward these objectives.

DAVID K. COHEN AND TYLL R. VAN GEEL

public
education

This chapter examines problems of poverty in education. It is concerned with poverty at the individual level and with the fiscal problems of school districts. In Massachusetts the state is seriously involved in only one educational program for poor children—Title I of the 1965 ESEA, a federally financed compensatory education program. The chapter concludes that the program's effectiveness in Massachusetts cannot be estimated because of deficiencies in the state's evaluation and reporting system. Improvements in the evaluation system are recommended; they include addition of staff in the state Department of Education, wider dissemination of information, technical assistance to local districts, and coordination of evaluation with program planning and budgeting.

The problems of poor districts are associated with

David K. Cohen is executive director of the Center for Educational Policy Research and associate professor in the Harvard Graduate School of Education. Tyll R. Van Geel is a lawyer and a doctoral candidate in the Administrative Career Program of the Harvard Graduate School of Education. The research for this chapter was supported partly by the Harvard Center for Law and Education.

differences in educational expenditures among districts which arise from variations in taxable wealth. The state's efforts to equalize these differences have failed to remove most of them; there are two possible remedies. One, in which state school finance would be centralized under a fully equalized statewide property tax, would eliminate inequality; it would, however, also reduce the potential scope for diversity. Another would revise the state equalization formula to reimburse districts so that expenditures would always be equal when effort (proportion of wealth sacrificed to education) was equal. Since this also would provide equality, but would leave more room for diversity, we conclude it would be the better approach.

Introduction

State governments have broad responsibility for education. They set jurisdictional boundaries for schools, and they have a large role in financing them. These instances of state involvement are not recent or isolated. Schooling—as the state constitutions show quite clearly—has been a major concern of state government since the mid-nineteenth century. The state's response to problems of poverty, however, has not been more consistent or satisfactory in education than in other areas. In this paper we review state programs aimed at poverty—including the poverty of families and of school districts—and attempt to assess their adequacy. (Constraints of space and time made it impossible to explore other important issues, such as the relation between poverty and educational attainment.) We suggest several changes in the state's school policies and programs and some new directions for state school policy.

Defining poverty: institutional and individual

The first issues are ones of definition: Who are the poor?

POOR CHILDREN

How many poor children are there in Massachusetts? What is the universe of need for programs designed to combat the educational effects of poverty? The absence of much evidence on these points means that we can make only the roughest approximations. The most direct approach, of course, involves counting the number of children who receive some form of public assistance. There were 117,571 such children in the state's 351 cities and towns in 1968.[1] It is worth noting that welfare is almost exclusively urban; 93 percent of these children lived in fourteen cities,[2] and nearly half of those lived in Boston. Of course, public assistance does not cover all children, who by any general income standard, are poor. Unfortunately, the only income data derive from the 1960 census, and they are bound to be out of date; but since none other exist, we have no choice. In Massachusetts, about 155,000 children between the ages of five and nineteen are poor. Of these, about 130,000 (,roughly 80 percent) are in urban areas.[3]

There are two chief difficulties with this approach. The first is that it assumes that a uniform condition—signaled by low family income—produces uniform educational disadvantages. Yet, though all measures of children's school success are positively correlated with their parents' social and economic status, these correlations nowhere approach unity. Indeed, for individuals they hover between about .2 and .4, whether we consider achievement, IQ, or years of school completed. This suggests an important relationship, but one which is far from uniform.

Were the cognitive and affective mechanisms by which poor performance in school occurs well-known, it might seem more efficient to simply address categorical programs to the children who fail rather than those whose probability of failing is greatest. But a compelling reason urges us not to use such a direct measure. The categorical programs aimed at children whose families are poor are designed, not to eliminate educational failure (if one can conceive that), but to so increase opportunity that there will be no correlation between social class and educational failure. The programs are not concerned with schooling in itself; it was not the existence of educational failure which offended the Congress and produced the 1965 ESEA and Headstart, but its maldistribution among social, economic and racial groups.

This implies that the object of antipoverty programs in education is

---

[1]*Statistical Report of the Bureau of Research and Statistics, Massachusetts Department of Public Welfare*, 25, No. 2 (April, 1968).

[2]Boston, Brockton, Cambridge, Fall River, Haverhill, Lawrence, Lowell, Lynn, Malden, Medford, New Bedford, Somerville, Springfield, and Worcester reported a total of 109,224 children on welfare. Boston alone had 40,937 children on welfare. (*ibid.*).

[3]Derived from *Massachusetts Teacher Association Research Bulletin*, vol. 62, revised April 12, 1963, which in turn was based on the 1960 U.S. Census. In 1960 there were 1,064,488 urban school-age children and 232,719 rural children in Massachusetts (1960 U.S. Census).

not simply to eliminate poverty, but to eliminate it by providing equality. Their object is to eliminate the differences in school performance between poor children and everyone else. Thus, antipoverty programs in education are by definition geared not to providing some desirable minimum of resources to the poor—as in an income-maintenance program, for example—but to equalizing school failure rates.

From this point of view, it is sensible to use a criterion of personal wealth, such as family income, to define poverty and program eligibility, as long as one assumes: (1) that increased amounts (or different and more costly kinds) of schooling will produce lower rates of educational failure for the poor, and (2) that the school system has the diagnostic and treatment capacity to accept such categorical funds en bloc (for *all* children who fall below a given cutoff point on the criterion), but to expend them selectively on only that group of poor children which fails, not on *all* children of poor families. Although it is not clear that either is true, we will accept these ideas provisionally for the purposes of this chapter.

Poverty, however, is not simply a characteristic of some children's families—it also is an attribute of communities and the institutions which exist within them. If this were not the case, remedial strategies could be addressed equally to all poor children, no matter whether they attended school in, say, Boston or Brookline. But the educational institutions in these two places are dissimilar in several important respects, some of which can be summed up in their relative fiscal position. It takes no great effort to see that Boston's is worse than Brookline's. As a result, our view of the universe of need must be broadened: it is a question not just of how many poor children there are, but also of how many poor districts, and how poor they are.

POOR DISTRICTS

Poverty is a relative condition, not an absolute one: we cannot identify it without a criterion that tells us what nonpoverty is. In the case of school districts there is no such commonly accepted standard. Nor is it easy to settle on one. The first problem, in fact, is not what separates poverty from nonpoverty, but on what dimension this dividing line should be established. Annual per-pupil revenue or expenditure would hardly be proper, since it measures only what districts choose to raise and spend; some wealthy and exclusive districts may choose to spend as little as those in impoverished circumstances. The crucial element is not choice but the fiscal constraints on school districts' potential for producing revenue. Unlike individiuals, school jurisdictions can increase their "income" simply by collective decision (voting to raise the property tax rate). Therefore, any criterion of district poverty should comprehend the main financial constraints upon such decisions.

These constraints can be summarized in the wealth districts have available for taxation. Since property taxes are paid out of current income, one measure is average family income. By itself, of course, family income is not an entirely satisfactory measure of community wealth; it is necessary to also include equalized property valuation, if only because property taxation is the sole source of local school revenues.

These two measures of community wealth are not unrelated; among Massachusetts school districts in 1968,[4] their correlation was about .6. This tells us that communities with higher family income have more

[4]The data underlying this estimate—and all the analyses which follow, dealing with *Chapter 70*—come from a study of Massachusetts school finance, conducted with the assistance of Norton Grubb, which employed data from 157 of the 350 school districts in Massachusetts, with each school district comprising one observation. The selection of school districts was based strictly on data limitations. All consolidated school districts—that is, those whose boundaries are not contiguous with town or city boundaries—were eliminated, as well as all those for which published socio-economic data from the 1960 Census was not available. The first group of districts are largely small, rural ones which have consolidated for reasons of size, or perhaps because of better treatment under the Massachusetts school-aid statutes. The second group are those which had less than 10,000 population in 1960 *and* were not near an SMSA (hence not reported in tract data); these too are therefore both small and rural. The result is that the universe of observations underrepresents small, rural districts. But while it does not cover a majority of school districts, it does include a majority— 85.5%—of public school-attending children in Massachusetts. Previous regression-using samples of 150 and 225 school districts—the second sample containing all but consolidated districts—indicated that results differ only slightly with varying concentrations of rural districts. The only important differences are restricted to those parameters which vary wildly from rural to non-rural districts, such as transportation costs and the proportion of children from AFDC homes, but major conclusions for the two samples did not differ. We found the results to be generally descriptive of school finance in Massachusetts.

The variables included fall roughly into two categories: data relating to fiscal characteristics of a school district, for 1967–68; and socio-economic characteristics of the district, taken from the 1960 Census of the Population. The use of 1960 background data assumes that the *pattern* of community characteristics has not changed from 1960 to 1967–68. Although there is no empirical data to substantiate this assumption, it does accord with our intuition that community characteristics change only slowly.

equalized assessed valuation per student, but it also shows that the
relationship is far from perfect. Wealth measured by either criterion
explains less than 40 percent of the variation in wealth measured by
the other one. This relatively modest association is a good argument for
using both family income and property valuation in any effort to define
school district poverty.

Table 9-1 *Local revenue per pupil in NAM and tax rates by median family
income and equalized assessed valuation, Massachusetts, 1968*

Median family income (quartiles)		Valuation [A] (quintiles)				
		less than 18,860	18,860 to 22,570	22,570 to 26,990	26,990 to 36,400	More than $36,400
(Less than) $5,569	local rev.	$349	413	524	549	642
	tax rate	20.9 [b]	17.2	21.9	14.7	6.2
	(District)	(3) [c]	(4)	(1)	(3)	(2)
5,569 to 5,860	Local rev.	414	432	531	532	648
	Tax rate	22.0	20.2	17.7	16.1	10.4
	(District)	(1)	(6)	(5)	(5)	(2)
5,860 to 6,149	Local rev.	433	442	475	575	607
	Tax rate	24.7	19.9	16.9	14.7	11.4
	(District)	(4)	(3)	(7)	(5)	(6)
More than 6,149	Local rev.	429	501	583	597	726
	Tax rate	24.0	20.6	20.9	17.7	16.0
	(District)	(12)	(17)	(22)	(24)	(18)

Do districts which are low on both criteria really have less "income"?
This issue is addressed, in a rough way, in Table 9-1: here each district's average local revenue for education is cross-classified by the two
poverty criteria. The table reveals that districts at the lower end of both
scales do indeed raise less money for public education. The figures for
average property tax rate also reveal that less money raised is not a
consequence of less taxes applied. The rates are no lower in the poor
districts than in the wealthy ones; in fact, quite the reverse is the case.
Districts with greater fiscal resources need not try as hard to raise
money for education as those with less resources. Thus, if we take as
an example all the communities which had an average family income of
less than $5,569 (row one), the effect of variations in property wealth
can be seem simply by scanning across the row. The mean tax rate for
the poorest communities (the first column) is nearly 21 mills per thou-

sand, and the average local revenue per pupil is about $350; the wealthiest communities in this income quartile (the far right-hand column) tax themselves at less than one-third the rate of the poorest districts, yet they raise nearly twice the revenue per pupil. These comparisons hold for every row in the table. Wealthy communities raise more money than poor ones, and they do so with less taxation.

Thus, there is little question that districts at the lower end of both distributions are not well off. But how low should a district be on these distributions for it to be classified as poor? The only rationale for a fixed cutoff—analogous to the $3,000 family income line—is the existence of a clear minimum standard of community wealth, widely acknowledged to mark the bottom of any acceptable distribution. The literature on school finance does contain the idea of such a minimum. It is embodied in the "foundation" programs, which establish a basic state grant to all districts, so that none will provide an education less than what the state deems adequate. But there is no uniformity of practice on this point—one state's minimum is another's maximum. This leaves only Massachusetts' past practice as precedent, and the evidence we presented in Table 9-1 does not encourage acceptance of the results. The absence of any sensible minimum standard automatically turns the discussion away from eliminating poverty toward providing greater equality. While we recognize that this deviates from the theme of this book somewhat, it seems unavoidable.

There is, then, great variation among Massachusetts school districts with respect to the wealth they have available to devote to education. Even if poor children in Massachusetts were distributed at random across school districts, therefore, some districts would have a more difficult time than others in providing the extra educational services which family poverty is generally thought to require. Poor children are not randomly distributed, however: a fairly strong relationship exists between the poverty of school districts and the concentration of poor children. Moreover, these districts face other barriers in efforts to improve the quality of education for poor children. Almost all of them are older cites: they have fewer professionals in the labor force, high population densities, and old housing. In a word, they do not offer the advantages generally thought to be available in newer, suburban communities. Apart from salary considerations, these districts would have great difficulty attracting the most desirable candidates for teaching positions. Poverty in education is not a simple or single-purpose notion.

Existing state programs

PROGRAMS FOR POOR CHILDREN

Massachusetts does not fund any educational programs directed exclusively at poor children. The only such programs in the state are funded by the federal government—Title I of the 1965 Elementary and Secondary Education Act, and Headstart. Although the funds come from the U.S. Office of Education and the Office of Economic Opportunity, these programs are not independent of the state government. In fact, in some respects they might be regarded as state programs. This is especially the case with Title I, a program of categorical grants to state education agencies. Subject to federal review, the states are completely responsible for administering the title and evaluating its impact.[5] Headstart does not have nearly the same degree of state involvement, although its operation is not entirely independent. We will concentrate attention on Title I of ESEA.

The title has a variety of purposes, among which are improving the quality of education in poor schools, relieving the fiscal burdens of city school districts, raising educational achievement for poor children, and improving education for disadvantaged nonpublic-school students. Ideally, one should be able to collect evidence relevant to these program aims and determine the extent to which each purpose had been satisfied. In most cases, however, such information simply has not been gathered. The reasons involve constraints in the legislation, the administrative capacity of the State Education Department, and the character of state-federal relations. Although ESEA requires state governments to conduct evaluations and report to the U.S. Commissioner of Education, the Office of Education has not pressed this requirement, partly because it recognizes the low research capacities of most state education departments, partly because the pressure might raise the political specter of federal control, and partly because the federal agency has little real power or administrative capacity to enforce the requirement.

[5]Save, of course, allocating funds; the Title is a formula grant, and given any level of funding, each district's share is fixed.

The Massachusetts Department of Education has not carried out the evaluation requirement. The federal government allows the state a maximum of one percent of total Title I grants for all administration, including evaluation. In 1968, this amounted to about $160,000, hardly enough for both administration and a vigorous evaluation program.[6] Furthermore, in pressing the local districts to fulfill the evaluation requirement, the state must take cognizance of their slight expertise and the political barriers to asserting state control. Finally, good evaluation would make it possible to determine whether Title I funds are used to meet the priorities identified by the federal legislation or to meet state and local priorities.

Simply to identify these issues is to suggest why state and local educational authorities might have little enthusiasm for searching evaluation. It is unlikely that state or locality priorities would be nicely congruent with those of the federal government, and when the federal programs seek to correct state and local problems, we can hardly wonder that priorities conflict.

The main practical consequence of this is that the state cannot determine whether any particular Title I project—or, for that matter, the entire program—met any of its goals. The absence of such data is reflected both in the evaluation forms used by the state and in the evaluation reports themselves. Although the 1968 annual report touches on many of program goals (aid to parochial students, raising achievement, improving the quality of school offerings in poor schools), it does not provide information that would allow a decision on how well a given project, or the program as a whole, met any of the goals.

For example, the report shows achievement test scores computed before and after particular projects for several groups of children, by grade and test used; but since we do not know whether the results come from two districts or two hundred, we cannot gauge the meaning of the findings. Furthermore, the data are presented for individual students averaged over the state, rather than for schools or school districts; this removes any chance of comparing the relative efficacy of different approaches to improving the achievement of disadvantaged children.Moreover, the data on which the report is based cannot be made to yield any more useful information. Aggregate test scores are reported to the state for entire projects; since they are not identified

---

[6]The state still turns back between five and ten thousand unspent evaluation dollars, however.

with particular students, individual schools, or identifiable program activities, there is no way in which the scores could be used to evaluate project, school, or program effectiveness. The analysis in the state report is meaningless, then, because the data it collected could serve no conceivable evaluative purpose. Collecting this information was, in the strict sense of the words, futile.[7]

The same thing is true of other aspects of the program covered in the annual report. One portion of the document, for example, deals with efforts to improve the quality of teachers, through in-service training programs of various sorts. It catalogs the number of districts that had such programs, the number of people who participated in them, and whether they were teachers, counselors, or administrators. It also identifies the broad types of programs districts operated and reports the proportion of districts that used each type. The report then lists several characteristics of what it terms "the most successful programs." How success was judged, what criteria were used, and what populations were served all are questions which never are raised, let alone answered.

These two examples have one important common element: data on the satisfaction of program goals are not consistently reported by school, remedial activity, or project. The reporting varies between the general (statewide averages of individuals) and the particular (examples of one aspect of a single project the evaluators found particularly appealing). As a result the state lacks information on the basis of which it can conduct comparative studies (based on either schools or Title I projects) of program effectiveness. There is no way of determining which approach to improving achievement or training teachers produces the biggest improvements or the cheapest ones.[8]

Clearly, the state is not carrying out an effective program of evaluation for Title I of ESEA. In itself, of course, this means nothing, because evaluation is not an end in itself. It is a means to another end—improved allocation of resources. In the case of Title I, evaluation is a way to determine the relative effectiveness of different strategies for achiev-

---

[7]The futility extends a good deal beyond the evaluation form. The evaluation report schedule is not articulated with the budgeting cycle, with the result that budgets are decided *before* the evaluation of Title I programs is complete.

[8]One potential bright spot in this otherwise rather bleak landscape is a study now underway of Title I and its evaluation conducted by the School of Education at the University of Massachusetts and supported by the Massachusetts Advisory Council on Education.

ing the same end (improved achievement, better trained teachers, etc.) As such, evaluation provides a basis for improving and correcting the entire program. The present system of evaluation means that the state education department has less rational grounds for influencing the allocation of resources than need be the case. In fact, it is difficult to see what purpose the state evaluation effort presently serves.[9]

The difficulties with Title I, however, extend beyond improving either the quality of teaching in poor schools or the level of their students' achievement. Additional program purposes, which reach beyond achievement and school quality, should be evaluated more thoroughly by the state. These have to do with the relationship between Title I funds and state and local monies: the state education agency seems to make no systematic effort to determine whether Title I equalizes disparities among rich and poor schools.

This is no mere nicety of auditing. Whatever purpose of Title I we might seize on, its satisfaction within any given school district requires that the educational services it provides be *additive* to an existing equality between Title I and non-Title I schools. Were this not the case, the program would serve chiefly to provide an equality which localities had failed to offer: the program would not be compensatory. The Title I regulations make this requirement clear, and state officials are not unaware of the problem. But the state does not have staff to monitor fund allocation within districts; thus it cannot determine if Title I does in fact provide better-than-equal schooling. In fact, it appears that the state is unable to regularly audit local school systems, or even to audit when an issue arises with regard to the substitution of Title I funds. It is forced to rely on ad hoc checks when it suspects there has been substitution. Even then, state officials must depend on a financial report written by the suspect district itself, which state officials then check for accuracy. This is the main means of determining if substitution has

[9]State officials do maintain that, by means of observations and reports, they have identified the characteristics of successful Title I programs. They are reported in the state evaluation report for 1968, and apparently state officials try to promote them among the LEA's. The state urges that the local agencies consider these attributes of success, but it does not feel it can force them upon the local school districts, and it does not accept or reject project applications on the basis of these criteria. State officials do not feel secure about the criteria, which are not based on hard data. In addition, they are reluctant to encourage too much uniformity in projects, believing that it would stifle initiative and useful experiments. State officials seem as cautious in their handling of local educational agencies as federal officials are in dealing with state educational agencies.

taken place, but it is hardly a sound basis for proceeding; it is particularly distressing in view of the fact that most recent comparisons of resources allocated to affluent and poor schools reveal consistent inequalities.[10]

These examples do not exhaust the problems with Title I, but they do offer some idea of how things presently stand. In general, the state operates the program by relating to localities in much the same way that the Office of Education relates to the states. Little attention is given to monitoring performance or to weeding out useless practices and encouraging those that satisfy the program's aims. Only a handful of state personnel are assigned to such activities (less than five full-time staff members in 1968, for more than 440 Title I projects); virtually no applications from local districts have ever been turned down, and only a small number have been rewritten; Title I funds have never been withheld from any local district by the state, and there is little evidence of much effort to change this pattern. Finally, little effort is made to see to it that Title I funds are used to accomplish their main purpose—providing better-than-equal education in poor schools.

It is not hard to see how this situation arose, considering that Title I is a formula grant program and considering the gingerly attitude with which state education departments traditionally approach local school districts. Nor is it easy to see how it can be made to improve. Rapid change would require a program of systematic experimentation with alternative strategies for improving achievement, teaching, and so on, which in turn would require greatly increased state authority to manipulate local programs and more financial flexibility than the formula grant system permits. Lacking the funds and authority for this approach, the state must move at a much slower pace, persuading districts to adopt improved evaluation procedures, and on the basis of results encourage the more successful approaches. Considerable administrative lattitude exists for the state to influence the use of Title I funds within the present legislation and guidelines.

Two major barriers block this slower approach, aside from the relatively weak political and administrative position of the state department. First, at least a ten- or fifteen-fold increase in the state staff

[10]The most recent and systematic evidence on this point comes from work which Stephan Michelson has underway at the Center for Educational Policy Research, at Harvard. For a summary of earlier work, see D. Cohen, "School Resources and Racial Equality," *Education and Urban Society*, I, No. 2 (February 1969), 121–139.

allocated to Title I evaluation would be required. Since the work would be in the nature of technical assistance;[11] this would require either reallocating the state's share of Title I money, or reserving local evaluation money to the state (a difficult or impossible task), or using other federal funds (some of which are available under ESEA Title V). Short of these measures, state funds would have to be used, and they are not in abundant supply.

Second, most Massachusetts Title I projects do not add a great deal to per-pupil expenditures; the mean is $170, and 70 percent of the projects spend less than $200 per pupil. All the evidence from basic research and other program evaluation suggests that a higher level of expenditure on compensatory education is required before much change will be observed in any school performance criterion. This cannot be remedied without either more concentration of existing funds or more money. Political pressures at the local level make the first difficult (though it has been done), and national, political priorities make the second extremely unlikely for some time. Thus, while there is room for a larger state role, it depends on a substantial increase in state revenues. At a minimum, improving the state department's evaluation capacity would add between $150,000 and $200,000 a year to the budget. And supporting the experiments required for effective research and development (assuming no reallocation of funds within the Title I budget), would require a huge increase in that budget. If state education revenues are the sole source, neither step will be easy to arrange.

Other problems exist, of course. The state's deficiencies in evaluating Title I of ESEA are symptomatic of the state's generally underdeveloped capacity to provide quality control and evaluation for local educational agencies. Nor is there much evidence that the state has tried to use the evaluation of Title I as a means of stimulating citizen's interest in the program and its results. And the state has not tried to develop the capacity of other institutions within its borders, especially universities, to provide evaluation and program planning services to local school jurisdictions.

Despite these problems, change is possible. Although the recommendations set out below call for some additional funds, the amount is not

---

[11]The estimate of staff additions is based on the impression that there is little more than one full time equivalent staff member working in this area—although some consultants are employed. Technical assistance in evaluation is difficult and time-consuming; fifteen people would be enormously overworked in very short order.

large; the sine qua non is state educational leadership, and the recruitment of able staff. The following steps would be helpful:

*Increase the staff devoted to evaluation and quality control for Title I to
at least 15 full-time persons.*

Use ESEA Title V and Title I funds to finance part of this. Whatever
remains should be paid by the state.

Develop—perhaps on the basis of a contract—*systematic, long-range
state program for evaluation, technical assistance, and quality control.*

*Ensure that the state effort include attention to stimulating community
interest in program content and effectiveness.*

*Use the evaluation effort as a step in building the state's capacity for
program planning and evaluation, across the board.*

*Integrate the budgeting and evaluation systems, and schedule evalua-
tion so that it can be used in the development of budget and program.*[12]

PROGRAMS FOR POOR DISTRICTS

Like most states, Massachusetts operates a school aid equalization
program (Chapter 70 of the Acts of 1966); this statute seeks to alleviate
the consequences of variations among communities in school revenue tax
base by providing more state aid for the poorer districts. The chapter
begins:

> *The purpose of the financial assistance provided by this chapter
> shall be to promote the equalization of educational opportunity in
> the public schools of the commonwealth and the equalization of the
> burden of the cost of school support to the respective cities and
> towns.*

To what extent does the chapter achieve this goal? The answer involves
two distinct issues. One is whether equalization occurs, given the terms in
which the state defines the issue: does it eliminate the particular form of
school district poverty it identifies? The other is whether the state has
properly identified the character of school districts' poverty.[13]

[12]D. Jordan, and K. Speiss, in *Compensatory Education in Massachusetts: An Evaluation
and Recommendations,* (Boston: Massachusetts Advisory Commission on Education,
1969), come to many of the same conclusions, on the basis of a much more detailed
study.

[13]A. Danière, *Cost-Benefit Analysis of General Purpose State School Aid Formulas in
Massachusetts,* (Boston: Massachusetts Advisory Council on Education, 1968), pre-

Defining poverty

The second issue is the simpler, and we will consider it first. The legislation is so written as to make equalized assessed property valuation the sole fiscal dimension on which districts' wealth is measured. The formula prescribed in Chapter 70 provides that the criterion of community wealth is the proportion which the assessed valuation per net average membership of each school district constitutes of the state average assessed valuation per NAM. The smaller and more negative that number is (the further any given district's assessed valuation falls below the state average), the greater will be its reimbursement from the state.[14] In one sense it seems perfectly just that equalized assessed property valuation is the exclusive criterion of poverty. The property tax, after all, is the sole instrument for raising local school revenues. Yet assessed valuation is hardly an exhaustive measure of the capacity to raise money for education. As we pointed out earlier in this chapter, a district's capacity in this regard is conditioned by several other factors, chief among them the personal income available to be sacrificed to schooling. In addition only 35 percent of the variation among school districts' property valuation is accounted for by variation in their average family income. Thus the Chapter 70 criterion of community wealth is not much of a proxy for an income criterion of community wealth. Since average family income correlates more than .6 with local revenues, it should be considered in any effort to equalize.

Nor does the formula recognize other constraints on school jurisdictions' capacity to produce school revenue. The proportion of disadvantaged children is one case in point: most educators believe that schooling poor children is more costly than schooling "average" pupils; the greater the proportion of poor children, the greater the fiscal burden. If this is true, the resulting burden is not taken into account in the Chapter 70 formula, and it is not proxied by assessed valuation per NAM; the correlation between this and the proportion of children receiving AFDC among Massachusetts districts is minus .05. The correlation between proportion on AFDC and mean family income, of course, is higher—almost .5.

Such examples could be multiplied at some length (intrastate varia-

---

sents an extensive treatment of the existing Chapter 70 state aid formula and detailed recommendations for improving it.

[14]The rate of reimbursement is figured by subtracting this percentage from 100; the resulting number is the rate of state aid.

tions in the cost of school resources and municipal overburden are other possibilities), but this hardly seems necessary. Our point is simply that the present Chapter 70 criterion of poverty hardly reaches all the fiscal factors that influence local revenue-producing ability. It therefore underestimates poverty and produces less than adequate remedy.

The extent of equalization

Given this limitation, however, it still makes sense to ask how well the formula works. To what extent does Chapter 70 equalize tax-base disparities in the ability of Massachusetts districts to raise money for public education?

The answer is pretty much given in the terms of the formula itself. Although it is so written as to reward districts that have less taxable wealth, it contains several major constraints. One is the stipulation that no district can receive less than 15 percent of its local budget in state aid. The effect of this is to restrict equalization by guaranteeing even the wealthiest districts some state aid. Consider a district, for example, whose assessed valuation was so far above the state average that its reimbursable expenditures were zero. Under the Chapter 70 formula as now written, the zero is automatically replaced with 15, and the state provides that percentage of the district's reimbursable expenditures. In 1968, 28 such jurisdictions were included in the group of districts we analyzed.

Another restriction operates to much the same effect. Once the rate of state reimbursement is determined, the amount of total reimbursement is determined by multiplying total local expenditure by the rate.[15] The result is to make state reimbursement a function of local revenues; the more money a district raises, the more it gets from the state. This would pose no problems if assessed valuation were an equitable standard for state reimbursement, but we have seen that it is not. It doesn't adequately measure variations in community fiscal resources, and it is constrained by the 15 percent floor. Therefore, the formula's failure to equalize districts on grounds of wealth is compounded by making reimbursable expenditures a function of local expenditure rather than of effort.

A rough notion of the formula's effect can be gotten from Table 9–2. Massachusetts districts have been cross-classified by assessed valuation per NAM and property tax rate quintiles; the first row of cell entries

---

[15]Subject to the restriction that non-Title I federal aid is not considered reimburseable.

Table 9-2 Local revenue per pupil in NAM, and state Chapter 70 aid, by equalized assessed valuation and property tax rate, Massachusetts, 1968

property tax rate (quintiles)	$18,860	Assessed valuation per NAM (quintiles)				
		18,860 22,560	22,560 26,980	26,980 36,390	More than 36,390	Total
Less than 14.17		$408	434	496	641	568
	—	$118	121	88	49	70
		(2)	(1)	(8)	(14)	(25)
14.18 to 17.43	430	398	483	584	671	542
	147	109	104	87	55	90
	(1)	(6)	(8)	(13)	(7)	(35)
17.43 to 20.31	306	471	536	582	715	523
	96	134	102	84	72	102
	(3)	(7)	(13)	(8)	(2)	(33)
20.31 to 23.53	407	484	594	677	693	537
	129	126	107	82	96	113
	(9)	(9)	(9)	(6)	(2)	(35)
More than 23.53	452	542	683	729	1031	545
	129	137	104	85	49	123
	(13)	(7)	(4)	(1)	(1)	(26)

Average local = $546

Average local + Ch. 70 = $645

in each tax rate quintile shows the average local revenues per pupil and the second row contains the average Chapter 70 aid per pupil. Thus, the table provides a rough overview of the relation between Chapter 70 aid and local expenditures at various levels of community wealth and tax effort. The column of totals reveals a few important things. For one, a slightly negative relation exists between property tax rates and local revenues; districts that make less tax effort raise slightly more money (overall, the correlation between revenue and property tax rate is minus .16). At the same time, the districts that tax themselves more heavily receive higher average aid from Chapter 70.

This is because the districts that tax themselves more heavily tend to have lower assessed valuations, and the Chapter 70 formula rests on assessed valuation. Overall, the correlation between these two variables is minus .50—the higher tax assessment, the lower tax rate. For this reason, the table roughly controls for tax rate and assessed valuation by categorizing districts into assessment and tax rate fifths. As a result, by reading down the columns we can inspect the relationship between tax effort, local revenue, and Chapter 70 aid at any one of five levels of community wealth; by reading across the rows, we can inspect the relationship between community wealth, local revenue, and state aid at any one of five levels of tax effort. Although the controls are rough, they are enough to let us discern major trends.

The main question is whether Chapter 70 makes up for the differences among school districts owing to variations in property tax wealth; for this purpose, we want to hold variation in tax rates constant, so as not to confuse differences attributable to greater effort with differences attributable to greater wealth. Reading across the rows, we see that at each level of taxation, local school revenues rise with assessed valuation. This is the situation Chapter 70 is designed to correct. Does it?

In general, districts with higher assessed valuations receive less Chapter 70 aid per pupil at each level of taxation. As assessed valuation rises local revenue climbs and Chapter 70 aid falls. Thus, the Chapter 70 program has some equalizing effect. The next things we want to know is just *how strong* the effect is: how much easier does it make things for the poorer districts?

This question is answered—in a rough way—in Table 9–3. Once again, we don't want to confuse the effects of tax rate variation with variation in taxable wealth, so the effects of Chapter 70 have been estimated within each tax rate quintile. We computed the average local, Chapter 70, and total revenue for each tax rate quintile. Then we estimated the relation of districts in each assessed valuation quintile to those averages by computing the percentage each column subgroup was of its taxation quintile average. The percentage local revenue of average local revenue (the first row of numbers), tells us how far above or below the average each valuation quintile stood *before* the effect of Chapter 70 was felt. The percentage which local plus Chapter 70 aid is of average local plus Chapter 70 (the second row) indicates how far above or below the average each assessed valuation fifth stood *after* the effect of Chapter 70 was felt.

In general, the effect of Chapter 70 (reading across the rows) is to somewhat reduce the distance of all districts from the average for their

Table 9-3 *Percentage local revenue of tax rate quintile average revenue, Chapter 70, by equalized assessed valuation and property tax rate, Massachusetts, 1968*

Assessed valuation per NAM

Property tax rate	Less than $18,860	18,860– 22,560	22,560– 26,980	26,980– 36,390	More than 36,390
Less than 14.17	—	71.8[a] / 82.4[b]	76.4 / 86.9	87.3 / 91.5	112 / 108
14.18 to 17.43	80 / 91	73 / 80	89 / 92	107 / 106	123 / 114
17.43 to 20.31	58 / 64	90 / 96	102 / 103	111 / 107	137 / 126
20.31 to 23.53	76 / 82	90 / 94	111 / 108	126 / 117	129 / 121
More than 23.53	83 / 87	99 / 102	125 / 118	134 / 122	189 / 162

[a] Top figure is percentage local revenue of tax rate quintile average local revenue.
[b] Bottom figure is percentage local revenue plus Chapter 70 of tax rate quintile average local revenue plus Chapter 70.

tax rate quintile, but not to change the rank order of district outlays for education. Chapter 70 reduces some of the differences among districts attributable to wealth, but it does not remove all of them. A very rough idea of the effect can be formed by comparing the changes on the right side of the dotted line running through the table, in which Chapter 70 raises local outlays relative to the average, with the changes on the left side, in which Chapter 70 lowers local outlays relative to the quintile average. Most of the percentage changes do not exceed ten points on the right side—the "rich" districts, where the district position is lowered —and on the left side roughly the same condition holds. The table suggest, then, that the degree of equalization is modest.

Two other summary measures of the Chapter's effect help illustrate this point. First, in Table 9-4, we present the proportion of the difference between local expenditures and average local expenditures in that tax rate quintile for which Chapter 70 accounts. In effect, the table estimates how much closer to the tax rate quintile average Chapter 70 moves each subgroup of districts. While this is a rough and ready measure, it does give us some idea of the degree to which the statute

Table 9–4 Percentage of gap between local revenue and tax rate quintile
average local revenue closed by Chapter 70 aid, by equalized
assessed valuation and property tax rate, Massachusetts, 1968

Property tax rate	Assessed valuation per NAM				
	Less than $18,860	18,860– 22,560	22,560– 26,980	26,980– 36,390	More than 36,390
less than 14.17	—	+32	+33	+11	-58
14.18 to 17.43	+50	+27	+16	-16	-32
17.43 to 20.31	+15	+64	+20	-83	-30
20.31 to 23.53	+30	+50	0	-91	-13
More than 23.53	+44	+60	-12	-21	-23

equalizes wealth disparities within groups of districts that make about
the same tax effort. Scanning the table reveals a few cases in which
Chapter 70 closes more than half the distance between a given subgroup of districts and the average (seven out of a possible 24), but in
most cases (15) the degree of change is less than 33 percent. Thus,
for most of the subgroups of districts, Chapter 70 somewhat improves
their condition, but it does not eliminate most of the disparitites in
question. If our criterion of equalization is the distance between any
subgroup of districts defined by the valuation quintiles, and the average
for all those districts in the same tax rate range, then the equalizing
effect of Chapter 70 is moderate. For most of the districts, less than
one-third of the gap is closed by Chapter 70. Furthermore, it does not
change their rank order in terms of expenditures per pupil.

In a sense, however, this is a deceiving way of presenting the results.
The problem that poor districts have does not arise when they compare
themselves to the "average" of all districts making the same tax effort.
That average, after all, is something cooked up by analysts who want
to see how the formula works. The problem of poor districts arises from
comparisons between themselves and districts which make the same
tax effort but have much more property tax wealth per pupil. Thus, the
question is, How much does Chapter 70 reduce the distance between
rich and poor districts that make the same tax effort? Table 9–5 pro-

vides a rough answer to this question. Comparing the first and second columns shows how much of the gap between the poorest and the wealthiest districts (at each tax rate fifth) Chapter 70 closed. It is never more than 40 percent of the difference, and in most cases it is much less. The state equalization program, then, does a relatively ineffective job of eliminating expenditure differences among school districts that tax themselves at the same rate but vary in property tax base.

Table 9–5 *Effect of Chapter 70 aid on Gap between richest and poorest assessed valuation quintile, for each tax rate quintile*

Property tax rate	% lowest of highest before Chapter 70	% lowest of highest after Chapter 70
Less than 14.17	62%	76%
14.18 to 17.43	67	79
17.43 to 20.31	42	51
20.31 to 23.53	59	67
More than 23.53	43	53

Alternative schemes

Can the state aid program be refashioned so it has a more complete equalizing effect? Any serious change in the program whether through Chapter 70 or some new instrument, would involve redistribution. In some way, money would have to be taken from wealthy communities and applied to the cost of schooling in less advantaged districts. There seem to be two main ways in which this could be accomplished.

State takeover of school finance

One approach which has received a good deal of attention lately involves abandoning local property taxation as the basis of school support. School revenues would then be made to depend on some other statewide taxation and distribution scheme, either a fully equalized statewide property tax or an income or sales tax. A statewide per-pupil minimum for every district could be established, with all aid over that amount to be conditioned on need, as determined by such things as variations in the cost of education, municipal overburden, poverty, and so on. By itself, however, such an arrangement would eliminate variations in local expenditures based on taste: how could districts which valued education more highly spend more on it? One way to arrange this would be through supplementary local taxation; were this uncorrected for variations in local wealth, however, the state would be back to the same problem with which we began. Thus, in order to allow room for the expression of variation in local values, some sort of state equalization arrangement would have to be worked out on top of the basic grant system.

Although this may seem conceptually cumbersome, a state system of revenue collection and distribution would almost surely be more efficient than the present arrangement, if efficiency is measured by the cost of collecting and distributing money. There are, however, other relevant values; chief among them are equality, diversity, and governmental responsiveness.

Centralizing the responsibility for taxation and distribution would significantly weaken the connection between decisions to tax for education and the quality of local education. Voter preference on basic school expenditures under a statewide system of taxation could be made only through the legislature and any of these expressions would affect only statwide expenditures. As a result, local values on basic expenditures could not affect local policy unless they affected *all* districts in the state. Direct relationships between voter expression and local education would arise only under a system of supplemental local taxation.

What is more, centralization would probably reduce diversity in pedagogical and cultural style and the organization and administration of schools. Displacing fiscal authority to the state would shift the center of political and administrative power to the legislature and the state education department. By virtue of their statewide responsibilities and the general identification of good government with efficiency and rationality, we suspect that the more effective the centralization of fiscal authority was, the less room there would be for administrative and organizational variety among schools and districts. Similar reasoning probably applies to the question of cultural and pedagogical styles. The tendency of centralized school bureaucracies in the large cities certainly has not been to strengthen such diversity, and there is little evidence that state administrations differ in any fundamental respect from their local counterparts.

A centralized system of taxation and distribution, then, would not lead inevitably to either greater actual uniformity or less potential for diversity, although these do seem the likely results. It is undeniable, however, that such a scheme would increase equality. A statewide system of taxation and distribution could equalize wealth-related variations in local outlays for schooling, as proposals now under consideration in Michigan make clear. In our view, the value of equality is sufficiently great that a statewide scheme should be implemented in Massachusetts, unless some means can be found to provide equality under conditions more responsive to local differences.

Equality with diversity

The question then, is, whether equality could be provided in some way less likely to discourage variety. The foundation of such a remedy is not hard to identify; it consists of little more than carrying the principle of the existing state equalization scheme to its logical conclusion. The basis of the formula is that expenditures on education should be a function not of wealth but of effort. By making the reimbursement percentage an inverse function of assessed valuation, the state seeks to reward the poor; by applying that percentage to local expenditures when the amount of state aid is computed, it seeks to reward those who try harder. The difficulties we have identified in the formula are:

1. It measures wealth inadequately.
2. It measures effort inadequately.
3. It does not allow the principle that expenditures should be a function of effort, not wealth, to operate freely.

The first two difficulties are relatively easy to correct. A more adequate measure of community wealth might be expressed in an index that summarized the position of each district relative to the state averages of assessed valuation and median family income. A similar measure of effort could be based on property tax rates and the proportion of personal income sacrificed to public education. The formula would be based on the relationship between a district's position on the two indices and that level of expenditures which the state decided should be the norm; this could be the state average, but if higher or lower spending were desired, the norm could be set up or down accordingly. The formula should not, however, contain absolute disincentives to spend for education. That is, it should be no harder for wealthy districts than for poor districts to raise a given dollar for education at a given level of taxation. The idea is not to penalize wealthy communities but to eliminate community wealth as a basis for variation in educational expenditures. Thus, the main constraint would be that effort could never produce less revenue at one point on the scale of district wealth than on the other. Such a scheme also would require a program of uniform statewide property assessment.

The issues that such a distribution scheme raises, then, have to do with its merit and feasibility. They arise as we imagine the consequences that might be thought to flow from implementing the sort of scheme we suggest:

1. Reduction in state average expenditures for education due to a general reduction of tax rates in wealthy districts
2. Slowdown in the growth rate of state average expenitures due to greater difficulty in raising local revenues
3. Creation of relative disincentives for spending on education (as a result of penalties for raising more than average expenditures with less than average effort), with a consequent leveling in the quality of education among districts within the state

The first consequence rests on the assumption that wealthier districts would reduce their own educational expenditures to lessen the cost to them of equalization. Although conceivable, this is extraordinarily difficult to imagine, for it would require a drop in the level of educational services.

At first glance, at least, the second contingency does not seem so remote. If the formula had the effect of taxing wealthy districts for raising more than the state average with less effort than average, it seems reasonable to suppose their incentive to spend might be somewhat reduced. Suppose for example, that on the average 50 percent of all the "surplus" revenue from wealthy districts were turned back to the state. Suppose also that most districts would choose not to substantially reduce existing levels of educational services, therefore making only what tax increases were required to maintain existing services under the full equalization system. It is not hard to foresee a general reluctance among the wealthy districts to increase expenditures by very much.

If this were to occur, would the rate of educational growth—if such a thing can be expressed in terms of average expenditures—be slowed? In itself, of course, there is nothing wrong with slowing down educational growth. It is undesirable only if growth in school expenditures is economically essential, or has a positive impact on students, or has a benign effect on the health of the body politic. We know of no evidence relating these phenomena to school expenditures. Moreover, the possible negative consequences of slowdown in expenditure growth would have to be weighed against the value of equality. But to answer the question, it is not self-evident that expenditures for education would fail to grow under full equalizing. After all, the existing system provides at least as many disincentives for poor communities to increase spending on education as the proposed system would provide for wealthy ones. Since the movement of any average has as much to do with change in the units underneath as with those on top, it can hardly be argued that slower average educational growth would be an inevitable consequence of equalization.

Whether full equalization would reduce variation in educational quality is a different aspect of the same problem. In effect, the view that existing differences in expenditure and quality would disappear with full equalization reduces to the idea that rich communities do not differ from poor ones with respect to their desire for education. In fact, this is not far from the mark—the correlation between communities' mean family income and their effort (the proportion of income sacrificed to education is the measure of community desire for education we have devised), is only about .3; wealthy communities sacrifice only a slightly larger proportion of income to schooling than poor ones. And when wealth is measured by assessed valuation, the correlation slips to minus .1; communities with higher assessed valuations sacrifice a slightly smaller proportion of their mean family income to education than communities with low valuations. However wealth is measured, it seems that effort is not strongly related to it.

This does not mean that full equalization would produce leveling, or that there is no variation in community values concerning education. It means only that there is little relation between wealth and our measure of community values. Whether there is much variation in the desire for education is a separate issue. We can get some notion of the extent to which it varies by looking at the mean and standard deviation for effort over all districts in the state. On the average, slightly more than nine percent of family income is sacrificed to public education in Massachusetts, and the average deviation from that is just about half the mean—slightly more than four percent. Although the absolute sacrifice may not seem large, when translated into per-pupil expenditure it would produce considerable variation. Under a system of full equalization, if the standard deviation of effort were half the mean and the state mean per-pupil outlay were what it is today ($540), the standard deviation of district expenditures would be about $270. That is just precisely twice the current standard deviation for local expenditures. This little exercise suggests that if our tax effort variable is a decent measure of community values (in principle it should be, since it is hard to imagine any more stringent test of the desire for education than the proportion of income spent on it), then there is no need to fear that absolute equalization would reduce variation in educational quality. It would change the distribution as respects wealth, but there is no evidence that the size of deviations around the average would shrink.

Of course, this is hardly conclusive. For one thing, our measure of effort is far from perfect, and for another (even if the measure is valid), efforts are not carved in stone. Things might change under a fully equalized system for one reason or another, and produce less variation among districts. But even if this were true, full equalization would be desirable. For one thing, there is some evidence that the existing situation may violate the Constitution. Finance arrangements that make the quality of education a function of community wealth imply that the state has adopted community wealth as a system of education classification. The effect of this classification system is well known to make it easier for wealthy communities to provide education than for poor ones. A growing number of students argue that wealth is an irrational and discriminatory basis for classifying public institutions and distributing public money.[16] It is not hard to see why this view has gained some currency. Education, after all, is a state function, and under a great variety of conditions, state and federal courts have held local districts to be only the creatures of state government. In addition, federal and state courts tend to regard education as a specially protected activity —the federal courts because they believe it crucial to individuals' opportunity and citizenship, and the state courts because they believe an educated citizenry is an important political resource.

Although we have no way of predicting the outcome of litigation on this issue, we find the arguments compelling. It is extremely difficult to produce a convincing rationale for a governmental finance scheme which discriminates on the basis of wealth. This view is reinforced by the absence of any evidence that the discrimination has any redeeming

[16]The best discussion is in J. Coons, W. Clune, and S. Sugarman, *Private Wealth and Public Education* (Cambridge, Mass.: Harvard University Press, 1970), forthcoming.

features. There is no clear reason to believe that variability in educational expenditures or in school quality would be eliminated by full equalization. The evidence suggests that equalization would eliminate diversity resulting from variations in community wealth and replace it with diversity arising from variation in taste. Although the information on these points is hardly conclusive, it suggests that equalizing on the basis of local effort will probably not produce educational monotony.

For these reasons it is of great importance that the state move rapidly toward a nondiscriminatory system of school finance. We have summarized the main problems with the existing system, suggested the principles on which a nondiscriminatory system might work, and concluded that equality probably is not inconsistent with diversity. Yet, if no further research is needed to demonstrate that the present scheme works badly, more work is needed to clarify the fiscal and educational implications of alternative remedies and to work out the details of one best suited to conditions here. There is no reason why a proposal could not be ready for the legislature within a year.

Conclusion

We have suggested two steps that would somewhat improve the system of schooling in Massachusetts: strengthening state administration and evaluation of Title I ESEA and improving the school aid equalization formula. Although the exact degree of improvement in each case is open to debate, education for poor children in the state would be somewhat better as a result.

Yet these efforts would be limited. First, this chapter has dealt only with a very narrow range of problems in education and restricted itself to existing programs. Yet a range of other issues concerns increasing the power families or communities have over their children's public education: decentralization, tuition voucher schemes, and diversification of schooling—each would affect antipoverty efforts in education. Limitations of space, and the fact that attention in this book has been focused on improvements over the short run, simply forbade consideration of such measures. Second, even the advances we have suggested probably would require a good deal of money, and major progress toward equalizing the burden of education within the state would require serious redistribution. In education, at least, significant strengthening of the state government's antipoverty efforts will be costly, both fiscally and politically. And the problems would not be solved by vastly increased infusions of federal dollars. Although more money is a necessary condition of redistributing the benefits of schooling, it is far from sufficient. The money must be used wisely, effectively, and with clear purpose. Such use implies a changed relationship between the state education department and local school jurisdictions, in which the state assumes a much more active leadership and regulatory role. That is a question of the balance of political forces within Massachusetts between the localities and the state: at the moment it is not clear whether the state has either the desire to shift the balance or the political and administrative resources required to do so.

BASIL J. F. MOTT

state
planning

Recent years have seen a remarkable growth of
planning in state governments. Not only is this development one of the most promising of contemporary efforts to make states more effective
instruments for meeting public needs, including the
needs of the poor, but the very viability of state
governments may hinge upon successful development of state planning. Indeed, it is doubtful
whether any state can keep abreast of public expectations, which seem to be ever expanding, let alone
mount a successful attack on such a complex problem as poverty, without benefit of a well-developed
planning capacity.

State governments have become so large and
complex that they have outgrown the ability of their
key officials, in particular governors, legislators, and
agency heads, to perform responsibly. The recent
growth of state governments has produced a proliferation of agencies, most of which are nearly au-

*Basil J.F. Mott is associate professor of health services
administration at the Harvard University School of Public
Health. He is pleased to express his appreciation of the
exceedingly able and invaluable assistance of Joanne P.
McGeary in the preparation of this chapter.*

tonomous, and most of which are slow to change because of organizational rigidities and political inertia. Governors and legislators have enormous difficulty in making the multitude of agencies account to them and respond to their direction. They also are finding it increasingly difficult to decide how best to serve public needs, for they have woefully inadequate knowledge of the nature of the problems involved, which are increasingly complex, and of the impact of state programs upon these problems. Typically, too, they are heavily dependent for information upon the agencies themselves or upon interest groups. Yet, difficult as it may be to believe, agency heads and their staffs usually have little knowledge of how their agencies' resources are utilized and of the effectiveness of their programs. Agency executives tend to be so bogged down in day-to-day operations that they lack time to develop adequate information systems and mechanisms for evaluating their programs, let alone look ahead and develop more effective programs for future implementation. Without planning, therefore, it is hard to imagine how state governments can rise above stultifying inertia and often ineffective responses to crises.

Whether state planning will become an effective force in the performance of state governments, and thus whether our states will be able to rise to the challanges facing them, is problematic. State planning has an uncertain future, for it is a new and frail species seeking to become established in an unfamiliar and often unfriendly environment. Morever, those who would nurture state planning have little to guide them; there are few precedents and much difference of opinion among its proponents about what its functions should be and how best to develop them.[1]

The crux of the problem impeding the development of state planning is that state planning means changing the behavior of state officials and institutions in many fundamental and different ways, which is bound to evoke controversy and resistance. A broad range of things is being undertaken in the name of state planning, and states vary widely in what are they are doing. There is even disagreement whether all of the activities involved are really planning. The basic issue is not, however, what the activities are called, but what they can contribute to the effectiveness of state government.

[1]See *Report of the Committee on State Planning in the 60s*, American Institute of Planners, mimeograph reprint, 1969; *State Planning: A Quest for Relevance*, Institute of State Programming for the 70s (Chapel Hill: University of North Carolina, 1968); and T. Beyle, S. Seligson, and D. Wright, "New Directions in State Planning," *Journal of the American Institute of Planners*, September 1969.

The view taken here is that there are two basic ways in which state planning can contribute to the effectiveness of state government in meeting the needs of its citizens, including those of the poor. First, *state planning can make state government more responsive to the needs of the people by helping it to do relevant things*. This is a question of the appropriateness of present policies and programs and the need for different ones. Second, *state planning can contribute to effective execution of the responsibilities that a state undertakes*. This is a question of how well state government performs its functions, of efficiency—getting the greatest impact from present programs and doing so with the most economic use of resources. Both dimensions are essential to full effectiveness.

This chapter will examine the development of state planning in Massachusetts and consider its implications for meeting the problems of poverty in the state. Following a brief description of the background of state planning nationally and in Massachusetts, four questions will be discussed. First, I shall consider how state planning can benefit the poor. Second, the character and status of state planning in Massachusetts will be described, including how what is now being done affects the poor. Third, I shall consider means of increasing the benefits of planning to Massachusetts, particularly with regard to planning's impact upon the poor, and suggest ways in which the state can do more through planning to help the poor than it presently does. Finally, I shall discuss the prospects for realizing the full benefits of state planning in Massachusetts.

Background of state planning

NATIONAL DEVELOPMENTS

State planning was born during the New Deal and was largely a child of federal interest and monies.[2] The Public Works Administration stimulated the development of state planning agencies to parallel the formation of the National Planning Board in 1933.[3] As part of the national

---

[2] See the Council of State Governments, *State Planning and Federal Grants* (Chicago, 1969); and the Council of State Governments, *A Framework for Planning in State Government* (Chicago, 1968).

[3] See National Industrial Recovery Act, 1933, and the Council of State Governments, *Planning Services for State Government* (Chicago, 1956).

effort to overcome the Depression, these bodies focused upon the conservation of natural resources and development of physical facilities. These early agencies, which were dependent largely upon federal support, did not, however, take root within the states. Thus state planning declined in the late 1930s and early 1940s, when federal public works programs tapered off, and when federal priorities changed with the advent of World War II. The isolation of these early state planning bodies from politics and the influence of elected officials was also an important factor in the decline of state planning.

During the past ten years state planning has begun to enjoy a renaissance.[4] Again, federal initiatives and financing are playing a major part in the development and character of state planning: reemergence was initiated in 1959 by the National Housing Act, which was amended to provide federal matching funds for state planning.[5] But now, for the first time, the potential of planning within the states is gaining recognition. The astronomical growth of federal grants-in-aid to the states in the last decade, now exceeding 500 separate programs, has created serious problems of coordinating these federally supported activities and integrating them with state programs, and thus of coherent utilization of federal and state funds. Moreover, the highly fragmented nature of most state governments, which are characterized by multitudes of separate and often autonomous agencies and weak central authority, is causing increasing concern about the capacity of the states to respond to the needs of the time. As a consequence, there is renewed interest in state planning at the federal level, where it is viewed primarily as a means of achieving more effective utilization of federal grants-in-aid, and in the states, especially at the gubernatorial level, where planning is seen as strengthening the capacity of the chief executive to direct state affairs.

State planning is also making new headway because it is conceived in far more realistic and broader terms than was done in the past. Most advocates of state planning—the Department of Housing and Urban Development (HUD), which is the chief federal patron of state planning, and the National Governor's Conference, for example—take the posi-

---

[4] I am not talking about planning as required under federal formula grants, or special planning projects like mental health, mental retardation, or vocational rehabilitation. My concern is with planning as a permanently organized function.

[5] Public Law 86-372 "Housing Act of 1959" 73 STAT. 654. In 1954, under Section 701 of the Act, federal funds were first made available to the states for the support of regional (intra-state) planning efforts.

tion that state planning should be tied closely to decision-makers who have authority and power, in particular, the governor. Moreover, unlike the narrow view of state planning held during the New Deal, the new interest is increasingly in comprehensive planning, both within and across functional areas of state responsibility. As in the past, however, there is no special emphasis upon the problems of poverty.

REBIRTH IN MASSACHUSETTS

The rebirth of state planning in Massachusetts is the product of both state and national developments. Although a few state agencies have had planning units for a number of years, and governors have occasionally appointed planners to their staffs, the reemergence of planning in the state is intimately connected with the gubernatorial politics of the second administration of Governor John Volpe and his successor, Governor Francis Sargent. Volpe, a Republican, was reelected in 1966 in a sweeping victory over his Democratic opponent that was viewed as a vindication of his successful and bitter struggle, before the election, to obtain enactment of a state sales tax from a Democratic legislature. Shortly after his reelection the Governor sought a new issue that would maintain the momentum of his leadership and obviate further personal and partisan conflict with the legislature. He and his aides settled upon reorganization of state government, later to be called "modernization" mainly because of its broader appeal. This issue had the advantage of being susceptible to nonpartisan treatment, and it had become known to the Governor and his staff that federal funds were available for state planning, including reorganization of the executive branch. It was not felt propitious to seek a state appropriation in view of the strained relations between the Governor and the General Court.

Having embarked on this course, the Governor assigned a key member of his staff, the Director of Program Planning and Research in the Executive Office of Administration and Finance, the task of securing federal funds to develop a central planning unit. This official was interested in several aspects of planning, though the Governor's interest was primarily in reorganization; but both sought to improve the general effectiveness of the executive branch. After successfully negotiating with HUD, in August 1967 Massachusetts was awarded almost a half million dollars, which was matched by a commitment of a quarter of a million dollars in staff time solicited from several state agencies by the Governor's staff. The undertaking's importance to the principals was underlined when the Governor met with federal officials during the negotiations, including President Johnson, and when Secretary Weaver presented the award.

The benefits of planning

State planning has the potential of helping states to overcome what is probably the most critical problem facing them: their inability to deal effectively with many vital problems of their citizens, especially poverty. The significance of state planning is that it is an instrument by which elected officials, the representatives of the people, can give meaningful policy direction to the multitude of agencies making up the executive branch, and thereby increase their state's effectiveness. In most states, the number of agencies has become so large, and operations of the agencies so complex, that the governor and the legislature lack means of giving appropriate policy direction to them or ensuring implementation of their policy decisions. Even the heads of departments composing the state bureaucracy are severely limited in what they can do to move their agencies along new and desired paths. Individual state agencies are usually able to perpetuate themselves within their special and frequently narrow spheres of responsibility with minimal consideration of broad and changing needs. Comfortable in established ways of doing things and protected by the ignorance of key officials and the fear of change held by many of the special interests it serves, the bureaucracy has become almost sovereign, with the result that its own interests frequently take precedence over the interests of the public. This problem, which affects all citizens and not merely the poor, accounts for the widespread dissatisfaction with state government. But the poor suffer disproportionately from the situation.

In this section, which considers how state planning can benefit the poor, I shall look at this question within a larger context: the role of state planning in making a state more effective in meeting the needs of all its citizens. Many benefits of state planning are not divisible and cannot be distributed among particular population groups. But the benefits from planning that flow from general improvements in the effectiveness of state government are not in themselves adequate for meeting the needs of the poor. The poor have special problems that must be taken into account in planning, if a state is to deal effectively with the problems of poverty.

GREATER RESPONSIVENESS

The most important way in which state planning can benefit the poor and other citizens is by making state policies and programs more responsive to their needs. This is a question of whether present policies and programs do, in fact, meet the needs of the poor, and a question of what different ones would be more beneficial. A planning staff can help determine the nature of present and future public needs, assess the adequacy of the existing policies and programs in meeting these needs, formulate alternative courses of action, and evaluate their advantages and disadvantages. State planning of this kind can increase the effectiveness of state government by bringing to key decision-makers the information and assistance they require to make policy and program decisions that are truly responsive to public needs.

State planning can play a vital role in opening up state government to citizens' needs and translating them into proposals for action in both executive and legislative branches. But the functions of planning vary with the responsibilites and circumstances of the officials involved. In the case of the governor, a central planning office can enable him to give relevant and unified policy direction to the many agencies in the executive branch. This is a matter of determining priorities and developing a coordinated approach. A planning staff can, for example, inform the governor of the relative effectiveness of an agency's programs for meeting its major responsibilities, and suggest what efforts by the state will have the greatest impact in dealing with the problems involved. Since the governor is expected in turn to bring basic problems to the attention of the legislature and propose legislature solutions, the information provided him by a central planning staff is invaluable to his role as leader.

State planning has a distinctive and much needed contribution to make to the responsiveness of state government at the departmental level. It is critical that the appropriateness of present policies and programs be questioned at the departmental level, for it is within the agencies of the executive branch that the purpose and relevance of state action become lost in activities and procedures that tend to become ends in themselves. Departmental planning staffs are a vehicle for questioning the purpose of ongoing operating activities and assisting in the formulation of appropriate objectives and programs within the constraints of gubernatorial and legislative policy directives and resource allocations. Such planning is essential to the responsiveness of state government, for it is at the departmental level that key officials must eventually place responsibility for the substance of state programs. In being close to those served by state government, departmental planning staffs also have an important role to play in generating proposals for new and better programs for gubernatorial and legislative consideration. Moreover, they are an essential source of information to the governor and legislature, including their planners, in giving overall direction to state government.

The responsiveness of the legislature process to citizen's needs can be greatly aided by state planning. In order to function effectively, legislators must know the nature of the complex problems facing state government and the short- and long-range implications of the courses of action open to them. They particularly need the assistance that planners can provide in evaluating proposals for action from the many individuals, groups, and agencies that seek legislation, including those emanating from the executive branch, in particular from the governor. They must necessarily rely to an important extent upon information provided by interest groups, and by the executive branch, including planning units, but legislators also require their sources of information and independent evaluation of problems and proposals, which can be provided only by legislative staffs.

The development of planning units serving each of the principal elements of state government—the governor, the legislature, and the departments—can contribute to their taking more responsive joint action in meeting citizen needs. State planning can produce greater common understanding of the nature of state problems and what the state needs to do about them. Such understanding can be encouraged by having the planning units develop, under the leadership of the central planning office, common definitions of terms and comparable presentations of data. Since planning units are necessarily influenced by the conflicts inherent in the relationships among the elements of state government, the debate among those influencing the direction of state government would be more productive if based on common language and common information.

Increasing the responsiveness of key decision-makers to the needs of the poor requires, however, that the poor be given special consideration in the structuring of state planning. While it is important to all citizens that methods of consumer representation, such as task forces and advisory committees, be created to enlarge the understanding and widen the vision of planners, there is yet a special need to ensure that the planning process incorporate the particular needs of the poor. People who are not poor themselves find it very hard to identify with and understand those who live in poverty. Unless a special effort is made to reflect their problems and outlook in the planning process, the interests of the poor will surely be eclipsed by those of the more powerful and the more articulate. This requires building into the planning process mechanisms by which planning staffs are made directly aware of the views and circumstances of poor people and the urgings of their advocates. No panaceas are offered and no sure ways exist for doing this, but conscientious efforts must be made to give force to familiar methods, such as hearings, ad hoc committees, and task forces, and to experiment with new or untried ones, such as citizen's boards and advocates for the poor. Unless workable mechanisms are created, the contribution state planning can make to the eradication of poverty will be lost.

State planning can make a major contribution to state government's responsiveness to the people by helping to inform public opinion on the nature of public needs and the effectivenss of present state efforts to deal with these needs. By developing more meaningful debate and consensus among the groups and organizations that influence legislative and executive policy-making, planning can produce more responsive as well as more concerted action by the state. With regard to the poor, state planning could well become a moral force in bringing home to a wide range of influential individuals and groups, as well as to key decision-makers, the desperate needs of the poor. The state could inform public opinion regarding poverty by providing technical planning assistance to community groups interested in examining problems and bringing their findings and recommendations to the attention of responsible officials.

GREATER EFFICIENCY

The second fundamental way in which state planning can contribute to the effectiveness of state government is by improving the execution of policies and programs undertaken. This is a question of how efficiently state government performs its functions. It is not enough that a state decide upon policies and programs that are responsive to the needs of the people, poor and nonpoor alike. It is also important for the state to achieve the objectives it has set for itself and to do so economically. State planning can contribute to the efficiency of state government by increasing the capacity of executives to manage and coordinate their areas of responsibility. For the governor a planning staff can be a powerful tool for managing the executive branch. This staff can develop management information systems for measuring and following up on implementation of his decisions, or it can be used to study the adequacy of the organization of the executive branch and develop proposals for making this branch a more effective instrument in carrying out its programs. The governor can also utilize a planning staff to coordinate the operations of state agencies by assigning it responsibility for reviewing major departmental programs and plans, taking into consideration the relations among state programs in making policy decisions. Increasing the efficiency of state government through planning is particularly important at the departmental level where programs are carried out, if programs are to achieve their intended objectives. Some benefit also accrues to the legislature from increased efficiency through planning. For example, improved management information systems may provide legislators with valuable information for making budget decisions.

The poor, however, are unlikely to benefit from general improvements in the efficiency of state government unless their needs are taken into account in the development and implementation of such improvements. Improving the decision-making capacity of responsible officials, whether through managerial systems or reorganizations, does not necessarily produce better policies and programs for the poor. It may even have the opposite consequences, as managerial improvements may make the bureaucracy more effective in serving its own interests, or those of the middle class, rather than in responding to the needs of the poor. A singular emphasis upon efficiency often overrides human considerations that are essential to serving citizens who feel alienated from society, including state government. Similarly, reorganizations that change the accessibility of state agencies may leave the people, especially the poor, less well represented in the decision-making process. To ensure that efforts to improve efficiency do not interfere with a state's responsiveness to public needs, it must be determined how such efforts affect the play of interests upon decision-makers. This is particularly necessary in the case of the poor, who are weak politically and poorly represented by officials of the executive branch, most of whom come from different backgrounds and are more insulated than legislators from individuals and groups representing the poor. How much the poor actually benefit from improvements in the efficiency of state government, then, depends upon how these changes affect the policies and programs that impinge upon their lives.

Whether a state realizes the potential of planning as an instrument for overcoming the problems of poverty, however, depends ultimately upon the commitment of the governor and legislature. Success requires developing a state planning structure that opens state government to the needs of the poor, in particular establishing special mechanisms that will ensure accurate and influential expression and representation of the needs of the poor at all levels of decision-making. Such an approach holds promise, not only of eradicating a human problem that weakens our moral fiber and tarnishes our achievements, but of making state government a truly effective partner in a federal system adjusting to a rapidly changing society.

Character and status of planning [6]

State planning in Massachusetts is entirely an activity of the executive branch, for it has grown from the interest and initiative of the present governor and his predecessor. Most of what is being done in the name of planning is the work of the Office of Program Planning and Coordination (OPPC), which was established by Governor Volpe and placed under the direct supervision of his chief executive officer, the Commissioner of Administration. The central planning office is responsible for all comprehensive planning, which attempts to integrate all policy sectors. Moreover, it conducts almost all the state's functional planning, which focuses upon particular policy sectors. OPPC is the administrative home of several functional planning efforts, including the state's Comprehensive Health Planning agency, the Bureau of Retardation, a day-care project, and the federal-state manpower project, known as CAMPS, all of which have been assigned to OPPC for development and coordination. The central planning office is also the principal source of contact between the state and other governmental planning endeavors, such as the New England Regional Commission.[7]

The only other planning to be found at the state level is departmental

---

[6] The findings in this section are based upon interviews, reports, and memoranda, and other written materials provided by state officials, in particular by the staff of OPPC.

[7] The Department of Community Affairs presently is the main contact with the intrastate regional planning agencies, sponsored originally by Federal funds. See Public Law 86–372, "Housing Act of 1959" 73 STAT 654, Section 701.

planning, which is conducted by individual operating agencies in respect to their particular functions. Departmental planning is rather varied. In the Department of Natural Resources, with the exception of a special, federally funded unit that is engaged in preparing a state plan (outdoor recreation) under federal grants-in-aid requirements, planning is decentralized to the agency's operating units and is a part of the budgetary process. By comparison, in the Department of Community Affairs planning is highly centralized and is focused upon formulating departmental and state urban policy. Both these departments also are the sites of several OPPC pilot projects for the "modernization" of state government. But in general, the extent of departmental planning is very limited, according to OPPC data. For example, these data reveal that of 11 major agencies only two had identifiable planning units. The planning done in these agencies is largely the work of the regular administrative staff.

A description of present planning efforts in Massachusetts, then, must necesarily focus upon the activities of the central planning office. State planning in Massachusetts consists of a wide range of activities, as it does in most other states, but most things being undertaken can be described under four categories: modernization of state government, policy and program formulation, coordination, and trouble-shooting.

MODERNIZATION OF STATE GOVERNMENT

Improved "manageability" of the executive branch, or "modernization," has been the principal, if not the dominant, objective of state planning in Massachusetts, so much so that in the minds of many, including legislators and agency officials, state planning and modernization tend to be synonymous. Originally, before the term "modernization" was used by OPPC, the task was seen primarily as one of reorganizing the structure of the executive branch. But with time it has come to be viewed by OPPC as one requiring structural changes and development and installation of systems for improved decision-making—for example, management information systems. The potential benefits of modernizing the executive branch have been the major source of gubernatorial support for state planning and have played a major part in the creation and development of the central planning office. The planners at OPPC have also grown deeply committed to reorganization. As a result of their first exposure to the myriad of state agencies, they have come to view modernization as a necessary precondition of other kinds of planning.

The reorganizational aspect of modernization calls for broad and fundamental changes in the structure of the executive branch, which has not
experienced a major reorganization since 1918. The approach being
taken is to consolidate along functional lines all 176 state agencies that
report to the governor into nine cabinet offices, which will be headed by
secretaries having broad authority and serving at the pleasure of the governor. Legislation implementing this approach was submitted to the legislature by Governor Sargent in May 1969, and after two days of searching
hearings was approved with only minor substantive changes and a politically significant change in the date of implementation.

Reorganization is being carried out in two phases. The first, which
was completed with passage of the enabling act in August 1969,[8]
assigned the state agencies to their respective cabinet offices. As originally proposed, the first phase authorized immediate establishment of
the new cabinet offices and appointment of the secretaries and their
staffs. Governor Sargent, however, deferred to the wishes of the Demo-
crat-controlled legislature that the cabinet offices not be activated, and
thus the secretaries not be appointed, until after the 1970 gubernatorial election, which would allow a Democrat to implement the reorganization if that party should gain control of the governorship. The
legislature, however, appropriated $600,000 for fiscal year 1970 to
be used during the interim period to develop and test managerial techniques and systems that OPPC feels will be required by the secretaries
to function effectively. A special Modernization Systems Unit (MSU) has
been established within OPPC to do this work. It is staffed mainly by the
personnel who have been most active in developing the modernization
proposals.

The second phase will begin with appointment of the secretaries. The
enabling act devolves to each secretary broad executive powers, now
exercised by the Commissioner of Administration, including budgetary
approval and authorization to undertake planning, making each secretary, in effect, a deputy commissioner of administration witin his functional area. Phase two calls for each secretary to develop an
appropriate organization of his area and, within two years of his appointment, recommend to the governor changes in laws relating to
agencies in his office that he believes are necessary to achieve an
effective structure.

The more typically managerial aspects of modernization, such as the

---

[8]Chapter 704, The Acts of 1969, Massachusetts General Court.

development of management information systems, may be distinguished from the reorganizational aspects. They are, however, viewed by OPPC staff not as two separate efforts but as two closely interrelated aspects of a single effort to improve the manageability of the executive branch. The objective is to improve the quality of decision-making at all levels of state government, gubernatorial, secretarial, and departmental, by increasing the discretion of decision-makers at each level. Reorganizational changes accomplish this through changes in formal structure and authority, mainly by bringing all state agencies together into nine cabinet groupings, whereas managerial efforts do so by improving systems of control and information.

In seeking to improve the managerial capacity of decision-makers, the major focus is upon development and installation of programing and budgeting systems, information systems, and data banks. Early in the process, the central planning office attempted to encourage the state's operating agencies to define their goals and program objectives. The underlying intent was to have the agencies organize their own operations along program lines and thereby establish a more rational basis for their operations. This effort was also viewed as laying a foundation for future installation of a statewide program budgeting system (PPBS). However, as OPPC staff learned more about the primitive state of departmental operations, they decided it would be fruitless to deal with the problem directly, at the departmental level, because the task was so great and the central planning office so far from the agencies' operations. For the same reasons they had become convinced of the need for state reorganization, they decided that the task of improving decision-making at the departmental level must be approached within the new cabinet structures. Having recommended establishment of a new level of organization in the cabinets, they also felt that priority must be given to making the new secretaries effective; consequently, most of the managerial activities of OPPC have been directed to this level of decision-making.

How modernization of the state government affects the poor, whether through reorganization or managerial improvements, is very difficult to determine. Modernization is still in its very early stages, and its effects are largely indirect. Any benefits the poor might receive from modernization can be expected to flow largely from general improvements in the efficiency of state operations. But whether the poor will actually benefit from such improvements, and the extent to which they do, depends upon how the benefits of modernization are distributed. Insofar as modernization changes the balance of forces that impinge upon policy-making and the delivery of services, disadvantaged citizens may gain or lose disproportionately compared with other groups. In the final analysis, whether the poor benefit from modernization will depend upon whether organizational and managerial remedies lead to better policies and programs.

POLICY AND PROGRAM FORMULATION

As distinguished from other kinds of planning activities, policy-or program-oriented planning studies and analyzes problems that may require new policies and programs or changes in existing ones. These are the activities that have the most to contribute to the responsiveness of state government to public needs. Policy- and program-oriented planning includes such activities as projecting trends (e.g., economic and social); identifying and defining needs and problems (e.g., of population groups—for example, the poor); evaluating the appropriateness and effectiveness of existing state programs; appraising the advantages and disadvantages of alternative courses of action; and recommending new or improved ones. In contrast with modernization, it is primarily substantive, not procedural.

Policy-oriented planning in Massachusetts has been primarily an OPPC effort and, with the exception of several special functional projects, has been limited to preliminary steps. It has been involved in projecting trends, collecting demographic data, and identifying needs and problems. No attempt has been made to evaluate existing state programs or make programatic recommendations. On the whole, the effort has been modest and based upon secondary data, and the emphasis has been primarily economic.

Several functional planning efforts having a policy orientation, including the state's Comprehensive Health Planning Agency, a day-care project, and the federal-state manpower project (CAMPS), are located within OPPC. These activities have been assigned to OPPC because they cut across agency lines and are related to other OPPC efforts. However, it is envisioned that they may be assigned in whole or in part to the appropriate cabinets after modernization enters its second phase. Much of the energy of the Comprehensive Health Planning agency has been devoted to organizing its program, including the development of regional planning units, which are required under the federal legislation establishing the agency. But the agency has also developed a state plan for the use of the federal formula project grants covered under the program. The purpose of the day-care project is to find an appropriate state role in fostering the establishment of day-care facilities throughout the state in connection with the federal 4-C program. In the CAMPS project, OPPC is engaged in increasing the impact, upon the chronic unemployed, of federal and state programs aimed at training and job placement.

Policy-oriented planning can have a very significant effect upon the poor. Being substantive in nature and concerned with the relevance of state action, it can aid the poor by identifying and defining their needs (e.g., employment, education, and health); by assessing the impact upon poverty of existing programs (e.g., public assistance and transportation); and by evaluating alternative programs and recommending better ones. Such planning is, for example, essential to assessing the feasibility of particular policy proposals and determining whether they can be combined into a concerted state attack upon poverty, as in the case of Rosenthal's proposal to make health services "indifferent to the economic circumstance of the individual . . . ," and Wofford's suggestion that relocation policy be revised to "cover more of the 'social costs' of transportation construction, particularly highways."[9] So far, however, policy-oriented planning being conducted within Massachusetts has had little impact upon the problems of poverty. Such planning in the state is in its infancy, and with the exception of isolated departmental efforts and the few special projects being conducted under the aegis of OPPC, in particular the day-care and CAMPS efforts, the planners have not focused specifically upon the problems of the poor.

COORDINATION

Another principal thrust of state planning aims to obtain greater coordination among related functional areas and programs through review and clearance procedures. Such procedures are increasing the coordinative capacity of governors in two basic ways. First, they are being used to ensure that proposals for gubernatorial action meet certain policy requirements—for example, the requirement that agency proposals be consistent with agency objectives. Second, review and clearance procedures are being used to bring within the purview of the governor certain agency transactions with federal organizations that may have

[9]See the chapters in this book on health care and transportation.

implications for the programs of other agencies—for example, reviewing applications to federal agencies for grants-in-aid, which gives the governor the opportunity to shape as well as enforce consistent overall policies. A major example of this coordination through planning is OPPC's development of a capital budget system for the state, which is improving the quality of agency decisions, as well as giving the governor an opportunity to impress his policy preferences upon state agencies.

A new federal policy, emanating from the Bureau of the Budget, gives the governor new coordinative power of potentially great significance, which he has delegated to the central planning office. BOB Circular A–95, the latest of several BOB policy statements interpreting Federal laws,[10] requires that the governor be given 45 days to review state plans required as a condition of receiving federal formula grants—for example, those required under federal welfare programs. The circular also requires that the governor be given 30 days to review and comment on any federal grant application covered under the circular, before it is acted upon by the responsible federal agency. Previous circulars required only that metropolitan planning bodies be given this opportunity.

The opportunity to consider the impact upon his state of proposals for federal funds provides the chief executive with a powerful means of achieving more effective coordination of federal funds entering his state. The inability of the chief executive to coordinative the use of federal monies in the state has been widely cited as a major aspect of the ineffectiveness of state governments.

Several of the special functional projects located in OPPC likewise involve the central planning office in aspects of coordination. The Bureau of Retardation, which was created in fulfillment of recommendations made by a special mental retardation planning project, coordinates decision-making among state programs in the various agencies affecting the mentally retarded. Some activities of the Comprehensive Health Planning Agency and of the CAMPS project have a similar coordinative character.

If the state did have a broad-based antipoverty policy, review and clearance procedures would become a powerful means of ensuring that

[10]See Public Law 89–154, "Demonstration Cities and Metropolitan Development Act of 1966," 80 STAT 1255; and Public Law 90–577, "Intergovernmental Cooperation Act of 1968," 82 STAT 1098.

agency proposals conform to such a policy. Any other benefits received by the poor are likely to flow only from general improvements in the efficiency of state operations. The developments in Massachusetts are, however, at too early a stage to see any general improvement in the functioning of state government, let along determine how these benefits are utilized.

TROUBLE-SHOOTING

The central planning office in Massachusetts has done relatively little trouble-shooting, but it is increasingly being brought in on short-run projects, an involvement that reflects the growing confidence the Governor and his staff in this office and OPPC's increasing ability to be useful. That OPPC has not done more trouble-shooting probably reflects the high priority that both the Governor and OPPC have placed upon reorganization of the executive branch.

Trouble-shooting, of all planning activities, is least likely to affect the poor, unless the planners are called upon specifically to deal with problems of poverty. Trouble-shooting can also adversely affect the poor by limiting the capacity of a planning office to undertake other more important activities. There is an inherent danger that, in becoming successful, planning bodies may be diverted from more appropriate roles and thus lose some of their value. In Massachusetts this has not been the case. Although it is somewhat necessary to gain support, planners are usually reluctant to take on trouble-shooting activities. It draws them away from the long-range activities that constitute their central concern and which they are basically equipped to undertake; many of them do not consider it planning.

Improving the benefits of planning

It has not been expected that the planners would give special attention and priority to the problems of the poor. Indeed, if they had given priority to any population group, this could have impeded and distorted the development of state planning. My intention here is not to second-guess those responsible for its development. Rather, it is to consider how planning could be a major force in eradicating poverty in Massachusetts, should the state's leaders decide to pursue such a policy. In discussing how the benefits of state planning can be increased, I shall

consider the contribution that planning can make to both the responsiveness and the efficiency of the state government. The first deals with
what is being done; the second, with how these things are being done.

EMPHASIS ON MANAGEABILITY

As is true of most human endeavors, state planning in Massachusetts
has the defects of its virtues. In focusing upon modernization, those
responsible for the development of state planning are addressing themselves to a valid problem: the almost desperate need of state officials
to obtain some measure of control over a fragmented administrative
landscape in which close to 200 agencies go their own ways. One
cannot, therefore, question the importance of improving the manageability of the executive branch through modernization. But there are
serious limitations in this approach, for it is mainly concerned with the
efficiency dimension of effectiveness.

A major characteristic of the modernization approach is that it does
not deal with the substantive issues of policy. The objectives of modernization are all designed to increase the manageability of the machinery
of government. The goal is basically efficiency. In the words of OPPC,
modernization is guided by three basic questions:

1. Are the agencies in the executive branch ... sufficiently responsive to the policy direction of the *governor and of the legislature*
   to accomplish effectively the objectives of those policies? Are they
   officially accountable for their actions? ...
2. Is the present machinery of state government able to deliver to
   the public a reasonable return in terms of services received, for
   tax money invested? ...
3. Does the present machinery ... conform to those principles of
   sound management, and utilize those tools of modern management, as are pertinent and applicable to public management?[11]

The solution is twofold. On one hand, all the state agencies are to be
brought together under nine secretaries to whom substantial authority
will be delegated. On the other, agency executives, cabinet secretaries,
and the governor and his staff will be supported by new managerial
information systems that will increase their control within their sector

[11]Office of Planning and Program Coordination, *Modernization of the Government of
the Commonwealth of Massachusetts: A Report* (1968), page 4.

of responsibility, with control growing more general as one goes up the administration hierarchy. This approach attempts to correct both the fragmentation of the executive branch as a whole and the overcentralization of control of detail in the Office of Administration and Finance.

Having given priority to modernization, OPPC had little energy left to develop policy-oriented planning, which, over the long run, is probably the most necessary and important kind of planning to Massachusetts. Ultimately, it is the substance of state policy and programs that is crucial to the responsiveness of governments to citizens' needs. There is a critical need for policy-oriented planning to consider whether many of the services and programs conducted by the state really are necessary or useful. Similarly, there is a great need to determine to what extent the state may be failing to recognize and respond to much more important problems than it may presently be addressing. Modernization largely takes as given existing policy commitments, whereas substantive planning is needed to question them. In the long run, more effective government requires considering *what* the state should do, as well as how to do more efficiently what it is presently doing.

Policy-oriented planning has special significance to the poor, for in being substantive it holds the greatest promise of directly and demonstrably benefiting them. Such planning is necessary to determine their needs and develop efficient and practical approaches to the problems involved. It is, for example, essential in evaluating the proposals contained in this book, and translating them into viable and efficient programs. Poverty is a problem of many dimensions; it requires that many different programs be undertaken and coordinated toward a common end. The development of a well-functioning policy and program capacity is therefore essential to improving the effectiveness of existing state services to the poor and vital to a concerted effort to eradicate poverty.

Policy- and program-oriented planning needs to be developed at the gubernatorial, cabinet, and departmental levels, but there are differences in what it can accomplish at each level. Planning units close to the operating programs and the delivery scene, which have first-hand knowledge of the problems of poverty, are best equipped to determine the needs of the poor and evaluate the responsiveness and efficiency of existing and prospective programs. Strong direction from the governor and the secretaries is necessary if the agencies are to perform this function, for such planning threatens existing operations. Moreover, support and coordination at the top is crucial to the formulation of broad statewide and agency-wide policies. It is appropriate for the planning units higher in the governmental hierarchy to appraise the combined and relative effect of state programs upon areas of need and to advise top decision-makers on broad priorities. A fully effective attack upon the problems of poverty, and the needs of other citizens as well, therefore requires development of appropriate planning units at the cabinet and agency levels, whose functions are coordinated and guided by the central planning office.

How much will the poor actually benefit from modernization? The planners in Massachusetts feel that modernization will improve the efficiency of existing services and make it easier for decision-makers to adopt and implement new policies and programs, including those beneficial to the poor. But one cannot conclude that the poor will benefit from these improvements. Unless their needs are taken into account in the design of improvements resulting from modernization—which has not been the case—it is doubtful that the poor will benefit much, let alone receive a fair share of the fruits of modernization.

Although it is difficult to predict the effect of regrouping all state agencies into cabinet structures, there are indications that the poor may not be well represented in the changes. The reorganizational aspects of modernization are likely to change the relative influence of interest groups on decision-makers—for example, by altering the hierarchical position of service programs through functional consolidation. Then, too, they are likely to affect the degree and kind of access to policy-making officials of such groups as client groups, professional associations, and representatives of the poor. Being generally ineffective in the struggle for influence, disadvantaged people are likely to fare badly from changes affecting the forces at play on state decision-makers. Similarly, the poor are likely to bear, in the short run at least, a disproportionate share of the disruptions that typically accompany reorganizations, such as delays in service and unsatisfactory performance by unsettled and untrained personnel.

Another serious question is: How will the poor be affected by the managerial improvements associated with modernization, especially those of a technological character? Such approaches often place high value upon administrative efficiency, and thus may override human considerations. Much of the difficulty that the poor experience in encountering government services, such as impersonality, officiousness, and perennial "red tape," is associated with services in which administrative requirements are paramount and have become an end in themselves. A case in point is the tendency of PPB systems to encourage service-rendering personnel to concentrate their efforts upon easily measurable activities—for example, by choosing cases in which progress is easy to show. Yet, the poor have problems in which it is often difficult to demonstrate progress. Real danger exists that the needs of the poor will not receive adequate consideration, unless means are developed to mitigate the undesirable consequences of managerial and technological efficiency.

If the poor are to share significantly in the benefits of modernization, let alone avoid an unfair share of the disruptions, it is essential that their needs be given special attention. Since the poor will experience the impact of state modernization mainly through the cabinet offices responsible for the programs most relevant to their needs, attention should be focused upon these cabinets. Those responsible for modernization should assess the impact upon the poor of the new cabinet offices, in particular the effect of plans for internal reorganization and management of these offices, to ensure that the interests of the poor are well represented. An effort should be made to establish at the central planning level and within the cabinet planning units, including agency planning units, specific mechanisms to accomplish this end: special advisory groups, appointed advocates of the poor, and task forces. The process will also be helped by having state planning units recruit personnel from minority groups. There are no tried and proven ways to ensure the opening of the planning process to consumer needs, and in particular to those of the poor, but unless efforts are made to experiment and to continue experimenting until satisfactory means are achieved, it is doubtful that modernization will benefit the poor.

AN EXECUTIVE FOCUS

Another problem in the development of state planning in Massachusetts is its focus upon the executive branch. Increasing the manageability of state government largely means increasing the capacity of governors to make and implement decisions. Although the proponents of modernization view it as also serving the needs of state legislators, it is largely assumed that their needs will be met by improving the effectiveness of the executive branch, especially the effectiveness of the governor.

But this can be true only to a limited extent, for governors and legislators often have conflicting interests, and governors are, to an important extent, accountable to the legislature. The legislature also has a need for planning that goes beyond simply increasing its ability to hold the state's agencies accountable for their use of state funds and to determine the efficiency of individual programs. The General Court has requirements of its own, and they do not always coincide with those of the governor. The size and increasing complexity of the state government, and the growing pressures to which legislators are being subjected, are making it more difficult for them to meet their responsibilities. Legislators greatly need means to evaluate proposals for legislative action, including those recommended by the governor and individual agencies, in particular, means to determine the future implication of the actions they might take. To do this well, legislators have a strong need for planning, especially policy-oriented planning, for the responsiveness of state government to the needs of people is reflected most directly in the legislative process.

State planning should therefore be structured to meet legislative as well as executive needs. What is needed is for the planning units in the executive branch, under the general supervision of the central planning office, to provide both branches of government with a broad and common fund of information on the nature of state problems, so that executive and legislative officials will be better informed and the dialogue between them more likely to lead to desirable action. In this way, state planning can make a very significant contribution to the responsiveness of state government. There are, of course, limitations on how far a central planning office can go in performing this function, because it is supposed to given priority to gubernatorial needs, but there is precedent for state planning of this kind and increasing interest in advancing it.[12]

The legislature cannot realize the full potential of state planning without development of a staff capacity of its own that can make use of and appraise the output of the planners in the executive branch. As matters now stand, the General Court and its committees are understaffed; so

---

[12]"There is ever-increasing evidence that interest in the potential advantage of state planning is developing in the legislative branch of state government. A number of the newer state planning acts carry sections requiring that planning agencies provide information for the use of legislative committees and to report to the General Assembly at each legislative session as to the performance of its duties. Some observers are even beginning to express thoughts regarding the necessity of a separate planning function for the legislative branch. ... " The Report of the Committee on State Planning October, 1969, American Institute of Planners, 1917 Fifteenth Street, N.W., Washington, D.C.

is the legislative research bureau, which serves as a special study arm of the legislative. But much more is called for than development by the General Court of a vitally needed staff capacity. The legislature has a role to play in determining in what ways the executive branch can serve the legislature more effectively. The state should therefore consider establishing formal and informal means of bringing together, in ongoing dialogue, legislative staff members and members of the central planning office. There might be established, for example, an advisory committee to OPPC composed of legislative staff personnel. Another mechanism worth considering, which might bring the two branches together in realizing the potential of planning, is a joint legislative committee on state planning.

State planning in Massachusetts has yet to become a source of information on state problems to other units of government and to individuals and groups outside state government that have a stake in what the state does, such as opinion molders, interest groups, and regional planning units. State planning, however, can play a significant role both in raising the level of discussion of important problems and in helping to develop consensus leading to more responsive and effective action by the governor and the legislature.

The development of a broad scope for state planning has particular significance for the poor. It is not enough for the executive branch to develop an understanding of the problems of poverty and the impact of state programs. If the state is to make a truly effective attack upon the problems of the poor, it will require basic changes in present operations and a broader and deeper state commitment to face very unpleasant realities. This will require action of the legislature as well as of the executive branch, and thus the development of broad political support. State planning, by increasing understanding of the needs of the poor and of the inadequacy, if not actual harmfulness, of existing efforts, can contribute to the development of vitally needed support.

Other considerations

The state planners should develop close links between their efforts and those of regional planning agencies. It is important that state plans be closely coordinated with regional planning to ensure consistency of efforts and maximum effectiveness. Since the regional planning bodies are much closer to the local scene, they offer an important avenue by which citizens' needs may reach the state level.

Similarly, they can become an important resource to state planners for developing plans that are responsive to local, as well as state-wide, conditions.

In these ways, coordination of state planning with regional planning can help to create a more effective statewide attack upon the problems of poverty. The regional planning bodies should be encouraged by the state to establish special mechanisms for seeing that the interests of the poor are given appropriate consideration in their own decision-making. The state could, for example, provide technical assistance to the regional planning bodies in dealing with problems of poverty. It could even provide financial support to these planning agencies for use by community groups concerned with issues of poverty and alternative ways of dealing with them.

The effectiveness of state planning is also vitally dependent upon the link between planning and budgeting. A major need is to inform the budget process with the long-run implications of short-run (usually annual) budget decisions. And it is essential that planning be closely related to budgeting so that decision-makers may know the financial implications of alternative courses of action, such as different proposals to eradicate poverty. Planners need to be close to the budgetary process in order to produce realistic proposals, and budgeters require inputs from planners in order to ascertain the policy implications of financial decisions.

Typically, planners and budgeters have operated in separate spheres. The bringing together of planning and budgeting is a very difficult task. Each has particular perspectives, and this fact increases the difficulty of communication; moreover, budgeters are suspicious of planners, for planners intrude into an established process. But, it is this difference in perspective which each contributes to decision-making that makes it important to bring them together. To maintain these differences in perspectives, the two functions must be kept distinct, and thus organizationally separate, though responsible to a common superior. This strategy is also likely to reduce undesirable conflict between planners and budgeters and to encourage cooperation. Since the establishment of the central planning office, planning and budgeting have been moving closer together, but they still have a long way to go. Thus far, they have been brought together in the area of capital budgeting, and in several PPB projects being conducted by OPPC as part of its modernization thrusts. Linking budgeting to planning, in particular to policy-oriented planning, will make planning far more realistic in attacking the problems of poverty. The joining of planning to the anti-poverty budget proposed by Friedlaender is an example of how planning could gain in power by linking itself to the reality of finance.

Prospects for planning

WHO CALLS THE TUNE?

Who calls the tune has profoundly shaped the character of state planning. Having once failed to make planning valuable to chief executives and legislators, largely because of the early insulation of planning from elected officials, proponents of state planning are now encouraging its linkage to key decision-makers. The predominant view is that state planning should be attached to the governor's office. This has been the major thrust of recent federal stimulation and financial support of state planning, as in the case of the HUD grants to Massachusetts to get OPPC off the ground.

The future development of state planning will, however, require more than an executive orientation if it is to develop permanent roots. The reemergence of state planning in the last decade is attributable largely to federal initiatives and depends mainly upon federal financing; thus, withdrawal of federal support may again lead to the demise of state planning, unless state legislators and private interests are persuaded that planning is valuable to them. The central planning office in Massachusetts depends almost entirely upon funds from sources outside the state, except for funds appropriated to the present administration to prepare for implementation of the new cabinet system. Although the legislature has enacted the governor's reorganization plan, it would be risky to interpret the action as a commitment to underwrite the future development of planning in the state. The legislature is hardly aware of the other planning activities of OPPC, or of their implications for executive-legislative relations.

THE POWER OF PLANNING

The effectiveness of state planning is seriously constrained by contingencies inherent in the nature of planning and in the situations in which planning staffs operate. Planning is necessarily threatening to those whom it affects, for planners are engaged in evaluating the performance of others and suggesting changes in their behavior. If planning is to have any impact at all, and thus be effective, it must necessarily cause changes in the operations of state agencies—for example, in their objectives, resources, and organizational arrangements. A central planning agency is potentially threatening to all the organizational elements of state government, including the many client and constituent groups that have a vested interest in state operations. Needless to say, those affected by state planning resist efforts to implement the recommendations of planning bodies not in accord with their view of the problem at hand and threatening to their interests.

The effectiveness of state planning, therefore, is dependent largely upon the capacity of state planning units to do controversial things and to survive the consequences. Hence, they must be closely attached to centers of power like the governor and the legislature. The recent trend of tying state planning staffs to key decision-makers is therefore breathing new life into state planning. However, this union—or, more properly, courtship—is so new that the planners have not yet had time to determine the extent of their newly won influence, and those to whom they are accountable are uncertain how far they should go with the planners. Whether this new relationship becomes permanent, therefore, will depend upon the capacity of planning staffs to appreciate the power dimensions of their position and activities and the ability of their superiors to make appropriate use of them.

Although the central planning office has great influence because of its location in the governor's office, its use by Massachusetts governors to spearhead state modernization may soon involve OPPC in controversy that could seriously impair the development of state planning. Since modernization calls for sweeping changes in the structure of the executive branch, there is great danger that OPPC may become implicated in the struggles among state agencies for position and survival within the new cabinet offices. It is, for example, likely that OPPC will be blamed for many of the "evils" with which reorganization will be charged by those who are adversely affected by it.

Much of the controversy of state reorganization has been avoided to date by the two-phase strategy of modernization. Since phase one does not change the internal structure of the agencies, or make any personnel changes, opposition so far has been limited largely to objecting to the functional location of individual agencies within the cabinet structures. It has not been profitable to oppose reorganization in principle, as all state agencies are affected. There has been little open resistance to the functional location of the agencies, partly because OPPC has done its staff work carefully and consulted the agencies with regard to their location in the cabinet structures. But there is just as much, if not more, reason to believe that that the lack of conflict is due to postponement of phase two and thus that the agencies and their constituents feel that is not yet time to fight; that time may come in 1971, when the next governor assumes office.

There is some possibility that the two-phase approach of modernization will reduce the scope and intensity of the forthcoming struggles over reorganization, in that the nine cabinet offices create nine separate arenas of controversy and thus fragment the conflict. Yet no matter how successful the modernization strategy proves to be, there is bound to be considerable conflect and adverse reaction to state planning. Many in OPPC feel that the heat will be focused upon the new cabinet offices, not on OPPC. But whether or not this proves to be the case, state planning cannot escape some of the costs at one level or another. As a result of the emphasis upon modernization, there already appears to be lack of understanding and appreciation, in the legislature and other state circles, of the potential range of planning activities, in particular of policy-oriented planning. After the cabinet offices are established, it might therefore be desirable to create within the Office of Administration and Finance a separate unit to handle the reorganizational aspects of modernization. A similar approach might also be taken at the cabinet level in handling the structuring of the cabinets. If planning in Massachusetts is to attain its full potential, it will need understanding and support for all its major functions at both the gubernatorial and the legislative levels. Because of its newness and frailty, state planning must be carefully nurtured.

ANN F. FRIEDLAENDER

fiscal
prospects

In order to place the discussion of the state and the poor in perspective, it is important to determine the fiscal effort currently made by the state to alleviate poverty, the fiscal capabilities of the state to adopt additional antipoverty programs, and the fiscal constraints under which such programs must operate. Thus the purpose of this chapter is to quantify and evaluate the impact of the state's fiscal structure upon the poor and near-poor and to analyze its potential for adopting additional antipoverty programs.

The first part of this chapter quantifies the effort currently being made to alleviate poverty in the state and evaluates the fiscal effort implied by these expenditures. The second part views the entire fiscal structure to determine its overall progressiveness or regressiveness. Because new programs can

Ann F. Friedlaender is professor of economics at Boston College. Conversations with Richard A. Musgrave contributed to the conception and execution of this paper. Sumner Hoisington and Charles M. Cobb were most generous in providing data for the poverty budget and tax and expenditure projections. Ahmet Tekiner and Ataman Aksoy gathered the data and performed the calculations on which this chapter is based.

be adopted only if funds are available or can be made available, part three discusses the capabilities of the revenue structure. The final part discusses how the fiscal structure could be changed to permit the financing of antipoverty programs.

The major conclusions of this chapter are:

Antipoverty expenditures in Massachusetts total something more than $1 billion. Approximately 40 percent of these funds are allocated to direct income transfers, with the remainder being spent to subsidize socially desirable services. Since the welfare reorganization, the role of the cities and towns has become negligible. The federal government provides the major share of these funds, with the state providing the remainder.

By all measures, the state's effort to alleviate poverty compares favorably with that of the federal government.

The state's tax structure is regressive for lower levels of income, but somewhat progressive at the upper end of the income scale. Its tax structure is generally more progressive than that of other states, but less so than that of the federal government. When transfers and other expenditures are taken into account, the state's entire fiscal structure is somewhat progressive.

The introduction of an annual poverty budget should be an issue of high priority for the state. Such a budget should itemize the different kinds of antipoverty expenditures by different types of the poor to enable the policy-maker to assess the impact of existing antipoverty expenditures.

An increase of $100–$150 million in expenditures on antipoverty programs is called for by the other proposals of this book. This could be financed by a combination of taxes: increasing the base and rate of the sales tax; increasing the base or rate on a range of miscellaneous taxes; adopting the federal personal income tax base while maintaining the existing rates on different kinds of income.

Because of the magnitude of other revenue needs, it is probably unrealistic to finance a poverty program alone. The state and local governments are currently facing a revenue gap of approximately $125 million. Additional expenditures in the field of local aid, environment, transportation, and the like, on the order of $200 million are probably desirable. If antipoverty programs are to be financed in conjunction with other revenue needs, a tax program raising an additional $500 million should be developed.

Tax programs generating the desired amounts of money can be constructed using a combination of sales, income, and miscellaneous taxes. The adoption of a progressive income tax is highly desirable and should probably be used in conjunction with tightening miscellaneous taxes, rather than broadening the scope of the sales tax on a large scale.

Fiscal effort and antipoverty expenditures

This section outlines the magnitude and nature of antipoverty expenditures in Massachusetts and attempts to develop some criteria by which the fiscal effort implied by these expenditures can be evaluated.

POVERTY EXPENDITURES IN MASSACHUSETTS

Like most states, Massachusetts presents its budget in terms of departments or agencies rather than functions. Consequently, it is extremely difficult to determine the total resources devoted to antipoverty purposes. A shift in state budgeting methods toward a plannning-pro-graming-budgeting system (PPBS) would make such an antipoverty budget feasible. Such a budget would cut across departmental lines, picking out those activities constituting the antipoverty effort. While it would not supplant the ordinary budget, it could be used as a control on the allocation of resources within the antipoverty effort and between it and other objects of public policy.

Ideally, a poverty budget should outline the resources that go to different categories of the poor. Thus expenditures on housing, health, welfare, and so on should be broken down to show the amounts spent on different kinds of poor: the elderly, the young, the disabled, the chronic, the transient, the marginally employed. At present data are unavailable to permit the construction of a poverty budget in the desired detail. Nevertheless, sufficient data are available to outline different types of antipoverty expenditures by different sources of funds. Table 11–1 contains the summary figures of this budget.[1]

Tables 11–1, 11–2, and 11–3 provide data to analyze the nature of

[1]These figures are based on data compiled by the OEO, *Federal Outlays in Massachusetts, Fiscal 1968,* 2 vols. (Washington, D.C.: U.S. Government Printing Office, 1969), and the Federal Information Exchange System, *State-Federal Outlay Reports: Massachusetts,* June 30, 1968. In constructing this budget, Social Security payments were classified under welfare, while Medicaid and Medicare were classified under health. A poverty budget, which outlines the specific programs within the

Table 11-1 Poverty expenditures in Massachusetts, by type of program, source of funds, fiscal 1968 (millions of dollars)

		Federal outlays				State outlays			Local outlays	
	Total	State expend.	Local expend.	Other expend.	Total	State expend.	Local expend.	Total	Local expend.	Total
Housing	108.5	—	47.4	48.2	95.6	—	6.8	6.8	6.1	6.1
Urban environment	8.8	—	8.8	—	8.8	—	—	—	—	—
Criminal justice	10.2	—	1.2	0.7	1.9	2.1	—	2.1	6.2	6.2
Health	376.8	91.5	7.4	81.2	180.1	183.9	1.2	185.1	11.6	11.6
Education	61.5	0.7	41.7	12.3	54.7	0.1	—	0.1	6.7	6.7
Manpower	152.1	8.9	33.8	14.9	57.6	94.5	—	94.5	—	—
Welfare	436.2	83.7	—	218.2	301.9	134.3	—	134.3	—	—
Food assistance	22.2	7.8	8.9	0.3	17.0	4.6	0.6	5.2	—	—
Asst. to business	1.5	—	0.1	1.4	1.5	—	—	—	—	—
Total	1177.8	192.6	149.3	377.2	719.1	419.5	8.6	428.1	30.6	30.6

Source: Friedlaender poverty budget (see appendix to this chapter). These estimates assume that the welfare reorganization, which actually took place in fiscal 1969, occurred in fiscal 1968. Thus all Medicaid and specific welfare program payments that are attributed to the cities and towns in the poverty budget appended to this chapter are attributed to the state in Table 11-1.

Table 11-2 Distribution of poverty expenditures in Massachusetts, by type of program, fiscal 1968

	Federal outlays					State outlays		Local outlays	
	Total	State expend.	Local expend.	Other expend.	Total	State expend.	Local expend.	Local expend.	Total
Housing	13.3%	—	31.7%	12.7%	1.6%	—	79.1%	70.9%	9.4%
Urban environment	1.2	—	5.9	—	—	—	—	—	0.7
Criminal justice	0.2	—	0.8	0.2	0.5	0.5	—	2.3	0.4
Health	25.1	47.5	5.0	21.5	42.0	42.8	—	18.6	31.6
Education	7.6	0.4	27.9	3.2	0.3	—	14.0	8.0	4.9
Manpower	8.0	4.6	22.6	3.9	22.1	22.1	—	—	13.2
Welfare	42.0	43.5	—	57.8	31.4	31.3	—	—	37.7
Food assistance	2.3	4.0	6.0	0.1	1.2	1.1	7.0	—	1.9
Asst. to Business	0.2	—	0.1	0.4	—	—	—	—	1.5
Total	100.0%	100.0%	100.0%	100.0%	100.0%	100.0%	100.0%	100.0%	100.0%

Source: Table 11–1. Totals may not sum to 100% because of rounding.

Table 11-3 Distribution of poverty expenditures in Massachusetts, by source of fund, fiscal 1968

	Federal outlays				State outlays			Local outlays	
	Total	State expend.	Local expend.	Other expend.	Total	State expend.	Local expend.	Local expend.	Total
Housing	88.1%	—	43.7%	44.4%	6.3%	—	6.3%	5.6%	100.0%
Urban environment	100.0	—	100.0	—	—	—	—	—	100.0
Criminal justice	45.2	—	28.6	16.7	50.0	50.0	—	4.8	100.0
Health	49.3	25.0	2.0	22.2	50.2	50.2	—	0.4	100.0
Education	96.4	1.2	73.6	21.7	2.3	0.2	2.1	1.2	100.0
Manpower	37.9	5.9	22.2	9.8	62.1	62.1	—	—	100.0
Welfare	64.2	19.2	—	50.0	30.8	30.8	—	—	100.0
Food assistance	76.6	35.1	40.1	1.4	23.4	20.7	2.7	—	100.0
Asst. to business	100.0	—	6.7	93.3	—	—	—	—	100.0
Total	62.2	16.7	12.9	32.6	37.0	36.6	0.7	0.7	100.0

Source: Table 11-1. Totals may not sum to 100.0% because of rounding

antipoverty expenditures in Massachusetts in fiscal 1968. Table 11-1 gives the absolute magnitude of these expenditures, while Tables 11-2 and 11-3 give the percentage breakdown of these expenditures by program and source.

Table 11-1 indicates that these expenditures were substantial in fiscal 1968. The total of $1.156 billion was more than five percent of the 1968 personal income in Massachusetts of $19.315 billion. The amount spent on antipoverty purposes by all governments was equivalent to 70 percent of the total state budget of $1.704 billion in fiscal 1968. Of this total, the largest amount, (45 percent) was spent on youth, while the remainder was spent on the general poor and the elderly poor (30 percent and 25 percent, respectively).

The breakdown by function gives some indication of the preferences of the various levels of government regarding income redistribution. Approximately 40 percent of all antipoverty expenditures were composed of direct income transfers through welfare payments. The remaining 60 percent were divided among specific programs aimed at improving health (32 percent), job capabilities (13 percent), housing and environment (10 percent), education (5 percent), etc., of the poor and near-poor. However, within those categories, the expenditures on different types of poor people varied widely. For example, most health, education, and food assistance payments went to the youth, while most welfare payments went to the elderly.

By granting direct income transfers, the government indicates that it is willing to ensure that families and individuals receive some minimum level of income. Beyond that level, however, income is granted only in kind through the subsidization of socially desirable services—housing, education, job training, and the like. These services are usually called "merit wants,"[2] a phrase which indicates that society views their provision as meritorious enough that it is willing to subsidize their consumption by specific groups. However, in most cases it can be shown that the private market mechanism would undervalue these services and produce them in insufficient amounts in the absence of governmental intervention. If the government were to substitute direct income transfers for merit want programs, the resulting consumption and production

broader categories given in Table 11-1, appears at the end of this chapter.

[2]Richard A. Musgrave, *The Theory of Public Finance* (New York: McGraw-Hill, 1959), pp. 13-14.

patterns would consist of less than the socially desirable amounts of these merit wants because of the private market's inability to value them adequately. Direct governmental intervention is needed to make the social and private valuations coincide.

Table 11-3 gives the percentage distribution of expenditures by source of government and dispensing level of government. In fiscal 1968, the federal government provided some 62 percent of the total poverty outlays. However, one-half of federal outlays—for example, Social Security payments—went directly to individuals or private organizations and were not channeled through state or local agencies. Under the welfare reorganization, which went into effect in fiscal 1969, the state has taken over all the direct welfare programs from the cities and towns. Consequently, their share of antipoverty expenditures has become negligible. For example, if the welfare reorganization had gone into effect in fiscal 1968, the state would have accounted for 37 percent of the antipoverty outlays, whereas the local governments would have accounted for less than one percent of the antipoverty outlays.

EVALUATING FISCAL EFFORT

Measuring fiscal effort is difficult. Ideally, measures of fiscal effort should reflect the effectiveness of the government's programs aimed at alleviating poverty in the context of its fiscal capabilities and the magnitude of the problem facing it. Unfortunately, no summary measure seems capable of encompassing all these dimensions. Consequently, it is necessary to utilize several measures:

1 The share of the budget devoted to alleviating poverty on the national, state, and local levels
2. The share of personal income devoted to alleviating poverty on the national, state, and local levels
3. Poverty expenditures per poor family on the national, state, and local levels
4. The ratio of poverty expenditures per poor family to the total budget expenditures per family on the national, state, and local levels.

The first and second measures indicate what percentage of available resources is devoted to alleviating poverty, whereas the third estimates the magnitude of the effort relative to the problem. The fourth measure indicates the weight given to antipoverty expenditures per poor family relative to total governmental expenditures per family; as such it is a crude measure of the redistribution of income that is made through the government budget.

Table 11–4 summarizes the fiscal effort made by state and local governments under various measures of poverty expenditures in fiscal 1968, assuming that the welfare reorganization actually took place in this year. The state performs quite well with respect to antipoverty expenditures, whereas the cities and towns perform quite badly. Whereas the federal government allocates 11.9 percent of its budgetary resources to the poor, the state allocates 26.2 percent of its own budgetary resources, and the cities and towns allocate less than one percent of their own budgetary resources to the poor. Similarly, whereas the federal government spends a total of $1,609 per poor family, the state spends a total of $1,707 per poor family, and the cities and towns spend only $42 per poor family. Finally, the state's ratio of total poverty expenditures per poor family to total expenditures per family is much higher than that of the federal government, but that of the cities and towns is much lower. Thus the welfare reorganization has removed virtually all of the responsibility of caring for the poor from the cities and towns and placed it with the state, which is presumably better equipped to carry out antipoverty programs.

Incidence of the fiscal structure

Having considered the expenditures made to alleviate poverty in Massachusetts, we should analyze the progressivity or regressivity of the state's fiscal structure. In this connection, it is useful to distinguish between the impact of the total fiscal structure, which includes taxes and expenditures, and the impact of taxes and expenditures separately. Whereas incidence usually refers to tax incidence alone, total incidence is the more relevant concept. To analyze total incidence, however, it is necessary to determine the incidence of the tax and expenditure programs separately.

TAXES

The progressivity of the tax structure can best be measured by the percentage of total money income paid in taxes by different income classes. The measurement of the incidence of taxation is well estab-

Table 11-4. Estimated fiscal effort devoted to alleviation of poverty, 1968, assuming that welfare reorganization took place in fiscal 1968

| | Poverty expend. as % of | | | | | Poverty expend. per poor family[a] $ | Budget expend. per family $ | Pov. exp. per poor family / Budget exp. per family |
	Total budget %	Budget less fed. funds %	Budget less fed. and state funds %	Inter-govern-mental transfers %	Personal income %			
Federal in U.S.	11.9	—	—	—	3.2	1609	3772	.425
Mass. state govt.	31.0	—	—	—	2.9	2488	1452	1.713
State less federal	—	26.2	—	—	2.0	1707	1180	1.445
Federal in Mass.	—	—	—	51.8	—	—	—	—
Local Mass. govts.	10.2	—	—	—	1.0	815	1436	.568
Local less federal	—	1.2	—	—	0.1	83	1224	.068
Local less federal less state	—	—	0.7	—	0.05	42	1020	.040
Fed. in cities and towns	—	—	—	100.0	—	—	—	—
State in cities and towns	—	—	—	3.7	—	—	—	—

a "Poor" are defined here according to Birch's definition: the lower 20% of the Northeast's population. If the Orshanky definition were used, the poverty expenditures per poor family would rise proportionately.

lished.[3] Briefly, it involves estimating the distribution of different types of income and expenditures by income classes and allocating taxes to these income classes by the appropriate series. Once the total taxes paid by income class are known and the amount of income accruing to each class is known, the tax burden is simply expressed as the percentage of total income accruing to each class that is paid in taxes.[4]

Table 11–5 gives the tax incidence in Massachusetts by type of tax; Figure 11–1 shows the tax incidence for the major categories of tax. In general, families with incomes less than $1,000 pay a disproportionate amount of their income in tax. It is interesting to note, however, that their direct tax payments are negligible. Thus the poor people's payments of business, property, and consumption taxes are generally hidden in their expenditures on goods and services.[5]

Between the ranges of income between $1,000 and $4,000 the tax structure is generally progressive. However, the tax structure is generally regressive after this. While the tax burden increases somewhat for families whose income exceeds $15,000, the total tax burden of families whose income exceeds $15,000 is somewhat less than that of families whose income lies between $3,000 and $4,000. Since families with incomes less than $4,000 are generally classified as poor or near-poor, this implies that the overall tax structure is quite regressive.

The tax burden for different types of taxes generally follows the total tax burden. While the property tax is regressive for the lowest and highest income brackets, it is mildly progressive for intermediate income levels. Business taxes and consumption taxes follow the same pattern as the total tax burden.

It is interesting to compare Massachusetts' tax structure with that of the federal government and other states. These comparisons are also shown in Figure 11–1. While Massachusetts' tax structure may be regressive, it is somewhat less regressive than that of other states. In particular, Massachusetts' tax burden is lower for low-income groups and higher for high-income groups than that of other states. However,

[3]See W. Irwin Gillespie, "Effect of Public Expenditures on the Distribution of Income," in R.A. Musgrave (ed.), *Essays in Fiscal Federalism* (Washington, D.C.: The Brookings Institution, 1965), pp. 122–186.

[4]The specific methodology and assumptions followed in this analysis will be made available upon request.

[5]The extent to which these taxes are actually shifted is a source of considerable controversy in the economics profession. For a good discussion, see Gillespie, "Effect of Public Expenditures."

Table 11-5. Incidence of state and local fiscal programs, by income class, Massachusetts, 1967

	Fiscal burden or gain as % of family income when family income is								
	under $1000	$1000–$1999	$2000–$2999	$3000–$3999	$4000–$4999	$5000–$5999	$6000–$9999	$10,000–$14,999	over $15,000
Total state and local taxes	21.5%	11.5%	13.7%	15.4%	15.1%	14.7%	14.1%	14.0%	14.3%
Total state taxes	10.4	6.3	8.0	9.5	9.1	8.5	7.9	7.7	9.0
Income taxes	0.3	0.7	1.0	1.3	1.3	1.3	1.3	1.3	2.1
Business taxes	8.0	4.3	5.1	5.7	5.3	4.9	4.5	4.9	5.4
Consumption taxes	2.1	1.2	1.9	2.5	2.5	2.3	2.1	1.9	1.5
Total property taxes	11.1	5.2	5.7	5.9	6.0	6.2	6.2	6.3	5.3
Total transfers [a]	68.3	56.2	0.8	0.7	0.4	0.3	0.2	0.3	1.4
Total specific services [b]	61.7	8.3	9.3	10.3	10.4	10.0	7.7	5.4	3.1
Total public goods (allocation A) [c]	208.2	23.0	13.8	9.9	7.7	6.3	4.5	3.7	1.5
Total public goods (allocation B) [c]	9.0	4.1	4.4	4.3	4.2	4.2	4.4	4.5	4.0
Transfers less taxes	46.8	44.6	-12.9	-14.7	-14.7	-14.3	-13.9	-13.1	-12.9
Transfers and special services less taxes	108.5		-3.7	-4.4	-4.3	-4.4	-6.2	-7.8	-9.9
Transfers and special services and public goods (A) less taxes	316.7	75.9	-10.2	5.5	3.4	1.9	-1.7	-4.1	-8.3
Transfers and special services and public goods (B) less taxes	117.5	57.0	0.7	-0.1	-0.1	-0.2	-1.8	-3.3	-5.9

[a] Transfers include all direct welfare payments plus interest.

[b] Specific service includes expenditures on the following: education, highways, welfare, health and hospitals, interest.

[c] Public goods include expenditures on the following: fire and police, parks, sanitation, sewerage, general government etc. Under allocation A, these goods are allocated according to the distribution of population; under allocation B they are distributed according to the distribution of property.

middle-income groups in Massachusetts, with incomes between $4,000 and $6,000, bear a substantially higher tax burden than their counterparts in other states.

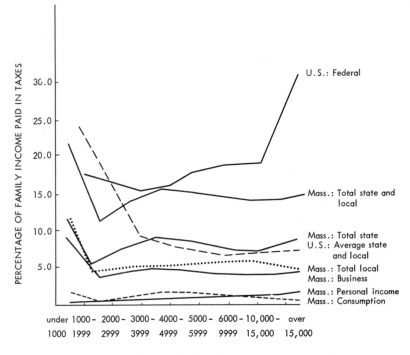

ANNUAL FAMILY INCOME

Figure 11–1 Percentage of family income paid in taxes by type of tax

The federal tax burden is generally higher than that of the state and local governments and is considerably more progressive. Except for the lowest income bracket, the federal tax structure is progressive throughout, with a high degree of progressiveness for families whose income is over $15,000. This constrasts sharply with the behavior of state and local governments, where the highest-income groups pay a smaller proportion of their income in taxes than the lower-income groups.

EXPENDITURES

Discussion of tax incidence is somewhat misleading because it neglects the allocation of benefits. Thus, to get a true picture of the impact of Massachusetts' fiscal structure upon the distribution of income, we must determine the incidence of expenditures as well as that of taxes.

Whereas the allocation of taxes is, conceptually, relatively straightforward, the allocation of benefits is not. This arises from the "public good" nature of most expenditures. In its purest form, a public good is something that must be consumed equally by all. National defense is the classic example of a public good. Once it has been provided by the government, all citizens share equally in its protection. However, most services that are provided by the government have a public good quality. Fire and police protection, parks, sanitation and sewerage, expenditures or general government, and the like have the common characteristic of being provided for all. Once the decision has been made to provide these services, it is virtually impossible to exclude anyone from enjoying their benefits.

Because public goods can be consumed equally by all, there is no obvious way to allocate their benefits among individuals or among income classes. If, in fact, the benefits from expenditures on public goods are evenly distributed, a per-capita allocation will have a certain intuitive appeal. However, one cannot help but have a lingering suspicion that the benefits are not evenly distributed, that the poor are not sharing as fully in the benefits as the nonpoor. Unfortunately, no hard information bears on this question. But it may well be that the benefits are distributed more in accordance with property than on the basis of families and individuals. Thus two allocations should be made for public goods: one with respect to population and one with respect to property.

Although a large number of state and local services fall in the realm of public goods, certain services are directly used by certain types of families, individuals, or activities. In particular, expenditures on education, highways, welfare, health and hospitals, and interest can probably be allocated directly to different types of individuals.

Table 11–5 gives the allocation of benefits for various types of state and local expenditures under various assumptions about the allocation of public goods. The distribution of transfer payments (which consist of welfare and interest payments) is highly progressive. The distribution of specific government service is also generally progressive.

The progressivity of the distribution of public goods depends heavily upon the assumptions made about the allocation of these goods. If they are distributed on a per-capita basis, they are extremely progressive. This follows because of the inequality of the income distribution: the poor have a large proportion of the population and a small proportion of the income. However, when benefits are allocated on the basis of property the distribution changes dramatically. The very poor still receive the largest share of benefits relative to their income, but beyond incomes of $1,000, the distribution becomes slightly regressive until incomes over $15,000 are reached. Thus the distribution of benefits from public goods depends very heavily on the assumption made concerning their allocation.

NET INCIDENCE

In analyzing the impact of government upon the income distribution, total or net incidence is probably more relevant than the incidence of taxation or expenditures alone. However, the measurement of total incidence must be somewhat suspect because of the arbitrary nature of the assumption about the allocation of public goods. From the viewpoint of the individual, taxes paid less transfers is probably the most relevant measure, since this reflects the net impact of monetary transfers made between him and the government. However, from the point of view of society, the net incidence or the difference between total taxes paid and total benefits received is the most relevant.

Table 11–5 gives the net incidence of state and local governmental activities by income class under varying assumptions about the distribution of the benefits. The net incidence of the monetary payments transfers less taxes is very progressive for incomes less than $2,000, slightly progressive for incomes $2,000 and $5,000, and then somewhat regressive. Families with incomes over $15,000 have the same net burden as those with an income between $2,000 and $3,000. When, however, the distribution of the benefits of specific programs is taken into account, the net burden is clearly progressive. The inclusion of public goods increases the degree of progression of the net burden whether these goods are allocated on a per-capita basis or on a property basis. However, the net burden is considerably more progressive if these goods are allocated according to the distribution of families than if they are allocated according to the distribution of property.

To summarize, although the distribution of the burden of state and local taxes is generally regressive, the distribution of the expenditures of state and local governments is generally progressive. Thus while the poor and near-poor may pay a higher percentage of their income in taxes than the well-to-do, they also receive a higher percentage of their incomes in benefits—both direct and indirect. On balance, there is a definite redistribution of income on the state and local level. However, in terms of monetary payments, there seems to be relatively little redistribution with respect to the near-poor. Families with incomes under $6,000 have a higher net burden than those with incomes over $15,000. Since people are aware of their monetary burden and generally do not consider the indirect, nonmonetary benefits they receive from governmental programs, the distribution of the monetary burden may well raise some difficult political problems. In particular, it probably is desirable to increase the observable progressivity in the tax structure. The ways in which this could be done will be discussed in the concluding section.

Fiscal opportunities and constraints

If Massachusetts is to increase its antipoverty outlays, it is important to understand the fiscal constraints under which the state is operating. Since tax and expenditure elasticities measure the percentage change in revenues and expenditures resulting from a given percentage change in economic activity, they are probably the best summary measure of the long-term forces acting upon the state's fiscal structure. These are given in Table 11–6, along with the estimated annual rate of growth of taxes and expenditures. These estimates form the basis of determining the fiscal constraints facing state and local governments in Massachusetts.

THE STATE GOVERNMENT

On the state level, total expenditures and total revenues (the sum of revenues from income, business, consumption, and miscellaneous taxes) are not sensitive to population and thus are related to personal income alone. Because the elasticity of expenditures is greater with respect to income than that of taxes and because the expenditure base is larger than the tax revenue base,[6] any given increase in income will generate a larger increase in expenditures than in tax revenues. For example, if personal income grows at six percent,[7] expenditures will increase by approximately $150 million while revenues will increase by approximately $75 million. Thus, even in the absence of increased

---

[6]Tax revenues finance approximately two-thirds of expenditures on the state level.
[7]This represents the average of the ten-year period 1958–1968.

Table 11-6.   *Tax and expenditure elasticities and projected annual growth rates, state and local governments, Massachusetts, 1968*

| | Elasticity[1] with respect to | | Annual percentage rate of growth if population grows annually at 1% and personal income grows annually at | | |
	Income	Population	4.5%	6.0%	7.5%
State government					
Expenditures	1.417	—	6.37	8.50	10.63
Taxes	1.121		5.04	6.73	8.40
Local governments					
Expenditures	1.123	—	5.05	6.74	8.42
Taxes	0.898	1.347	4.17	6.74	6.89

[1] The elasticities were estimated by regressing the appropriate tax and expenditure categories upon personal income and population and then by making appropriate transformations of the estimated coefficients. If the population variable was found to be statistically insignificant, taxes and expenditures were related to personal income alone. A full description of the regression analysis employed will be made available upon request.

antipoverty programs, this "revenue gap" must be financed. This could be done by increased revenues from nontax revenues, bond finance, federal funds, or changes in the tax structure.

Nontax revenue consists of various fees, licenses, rents, motor vehicles licenses and registrations, and so on. In 1968, this revenue of $146 million accounted for some nine percent of state revenues. Since, however, the elasticity of nontax revenue is somewhat less than that of tax revenue with respect to income, nontax revenue cannot be expected to fill the revenue gap.

Because bond financing is limited to financing capital expenditures, it cannot be used to close the revenue gap that exists with regard to current operating expenses. Moreover, because of high interest rates and uncertainty in the money market, bond financing is not likely to be used for any large-scale capital expansion program.

The $365 million which Massachusetts currently receives from the federal government represents more than 20 percent of its revenues. While pure conjecture, two potential sources of additional federal funds present themselves.

First, Nixon's proposed welfare program would introduce a federally financed minimal family income of $1,600, with any excess to be paid by the state. By estimating the current federal welfare payments per family and then determining the additional federal welfare payments per family needed to reach the proposed federal minimum, it is possible to obtain a crude measure of the additional federal funds potentially available. Calculations of this type indicate that an additional $15 million would be forthcoming under this proposal. However, if the federal government introduced a broader-based program that ensured a $1,600 minimum for all families and individuals, the state would be a net recipient of some $65 million.

In addition, Nixon's welfare proposal mentioned the possibility of giving additional bloc grants to the states.[8] Most proposals postulate federal outlays of $2 billion, to be allocated on an adjusted per-capita basis that takes into account the relative wealth of the states and their current fiscal effort. Most programs estimate that Massachusetts would receive between $40 and $50 million under block grants of this type.[9]

Thus Massachusetts might receive $100 million, at most, if the federal government adopted broad-based welfare program; under current proposals it would receive closer to $60 million.

LOCAL GOVERNMENTS

Since property tax revenues largely reflect the demand for public services, they should grow at roughly the same rate as expenditures. Nevertheless, because property taxes account for only about 60 percent of local revenues, a given percentage increase in expenditures and revenues would give rise to a larger amount of expenditures than property tax revenues. The gap between increased revenues and expenditures is currently at least $50 million a year.

The ability of the cities and towns to finance this gap in the absence of increased property taxes is limited. Bond financing suffers from the same defects on the local level that it does on the state level. This

[8] In recent years, a substantial number of revenue sharing plans have been proposed. For a full discussion of these see U.S. Congress, Joint Economic Committee, *Revenue Sharing and Its Alternatives: What Future for Fiscal Federalism?* (Washington, D.C.:U.S. Government Printing Office, 1967), Vols. 1–3.

[9] See C. Lowell Harriss, *Federal Revenue Sharing with the States,* Tax Foundation, Inc., Government Finance Brief No. 9, March 1967; George F. Break, *Intergovernmental Fiscal Relations in the United States* (Washington, D.C.: The Brookings Institution, 1967).

leaves federal and state aid as the alternative revenue sources in the absence of increased property tax rates.

While the attitude of the Nixon Administration toward the cities and towns is not entirely clear, one gets the impression that its fiscal federalism is aimed more at the states than at the localities. Moreover, there is some evidence that the administration will cut back on the OEO programs that have typically been channeled through the cities and towns and local action agencies. Thus, the cities and towns may well find themselves receiving reduced rather than increased federal funds.

There are strong political pressures for increased state aid. Currently Massachusetts has one of the highest property tax burdens in the nation. Costs are rising in all areas and property tax levies are rising with them. These levies rose by 14 percent between 1968 and 1969 despite the state's takeover of welfare, which made some $200 million available to the cities and towns. The central cities, particularly, are in a budget squeeze since they provide a broad range of services to the suburbanites who work and play in the city but pay taxes in their own communities. Because the residents of the central cities are generally poorer than those of the suburbs, efforts to finance what are essentially metropolitan services through local property taxes represent a redistribution of income from the poor to the nonpoor. Consequently a restructuring, if not an increase, in local aid is desirable.

Because of the pressures imposed upon the state by the welfare reorganization, Massachusetts has recently restructured and reduced its local aid. Starting in fiscal 1970, the state will allocate $240 million to the cities and towns, exclusive of specific reimbursement programs, which are unaffected by the change.[10] This sum will grow at the same rate as sales tax revenue. Data are not available to calculate the net gain or loss in state aid resulting from the welfare reorganization and the change in the local aid distribution, but on balance the cities and towns should have gained. For example, if the welfare reorganization and local aid distribution had gone into effect in fiscal 1968, the cities and towns would have gained $194 million from the welfare takeover, but lost only $33 million from the general distribution.

As presently structured, local aid is heavily oriented toward education. Under the current local aid distribution, aid to education takes

---

[10]These include school and library construction, school lunch programs, veterans benefits, expenditures on the Youth Services Board, etc. In 1969 these amounted to some $87 million, exclusive of welfare payments.

precedence; only funds remaining after the education distribution will be allocated as a bloc grant. However, because education expenditures tend to rise faster than sales tax revenues, the entire local aid program should take the form of a reimbursement program for education in the fairly near future.

The education distribution is inversely related to the ratio of the equalized valuation per pupil in the city or town to the equalized valuation per pupil in the state; the general aid distribution is directly related to the equalized valuation of the cities and towns. Thus the education distribution is probably somewhat more progressive than the general distribution. However, in view of the pressing needs facing the cities and towns in areas other than education, some question arises whether local aid should be as oriented exclusively toward education as it is.

This raises the question whether local aid could be structured to increase the role of the cities and towns in fighting poverty. Under the current distribution formulas, increases in state aid would probably go to the cities and towns as a bloc grant if education had not preempted all the available funds. In view of the small effort currently made by the cities and towns to alleviate poverty, it is doubtful that any of these funds would go to antipoverty programs as such. Similarly, even if increased state aid went to education, its impact on poverty would be only indirect. Thus, without a restructuring of state aid, any increases in its magnitudes should have only an indirect impact on the poor through relative reductions in property taxes and an improvement in education and other services.

However, restructuring the local aid distribution has considerable merit. On the federal level, many revenue-sharing plans have been developed that would allocate federal aid to the states in such a way that the poor states and those making relatively more fiscal effort would receive relatively more funds. There is no reason why comparable allocation procedures could not be applied on the state level. For example, an allocation of funds on a per-capita basis, adjusted for per-capita income and fiscal effort would increase the levels of state aid to the cities. Since the cities house the bulk of the poor, changes in the local aid distribution in this direction not only would ease the pressures emanating from the heavy reliance on the property tax, but also would lead to an increase of expenditures on the poor and near-poor.

However, it should be stressed, local aid is no substitute for antipoverty programs. Increased local aid would tend to act as a bloc grant that would only stimulate antipoverty expenditures through a general revenue effect. Poverty would only be one of the many competing claims on these funds. In contrast, specific antipoverty programs would affect poverty directly. Thus while local aid could and should be restructured to have a more progressive impact, if poverty is to be alleviated in Massachusetts, additional antipoverty programs will have to be introduced.

Fiscal programs for the state

The main question facing Massachusetts is whether a fiscal structure can be constructed that will permit an efficient and equitable allocation of resources among the competing claims, while at the same time generating sufficient revenues to finance the normal growth of expenditures and needed new programs in poverty and other areas.

THE ROLE OF PROGRAM BUDGETING

The introduction of program budgeting in Massachusetts represents an important step toward rationalizing the decision-making process. Currently, it is virtually impossible to know what funds are actually being spent in the area of health, education, environment, poverty, and so on. However, efforts are being made to correct this, and program budgeting is being introduced in the areas of health, community affairs, natural resources, and human services.

The introduction of a poverty budget would be highly desirable. Without one, it is impossible to know the magnitude of the state's effort to alleviate poverty, much less to assess it. The budget presented in the appendix to this paper is indicative of the direction such a budget should take, but it does not cut the poverty profile sufficiently. In addition to allocating expenditures by age, a poverty budget should allocate expenditures by other categories: chronic poor versus temporary poor versus working poor; suburban poor versus urban poor, and so on.

However, program budgeting is only a first step in rationalizing the decision-making process. In view of the size and growth of the state budget, it is important to ensure that existing programs actually achieve their stated goals. Unfortunately, considerable evidence shows that currently they do not. For example, in both the health and education fields, funds that are ostensibly supposed to reach the poor generally go elsewhere. Thus, if existing funds are to be used as efficiently as possible, some means of controlling them must be developed. Program budgeting in conjunction with a cost-effectiveness analysis is generally thought to be the means of achieving this control.

REVENUE NEEDS

The magnitude of additional antipoverty funds depends upon several variables: can existing programs be restructured to serve the needs of the poor better without increased expenditures? Will more federal aid be made available? What will be the actual costs associated with the programs proposed in this book?

While a more efficient utilization of funds currently allocated to alleviating poverty could have considerable impact, this alone will not solve the poverty problem in Massachusetts. More housing units should be built; welfare standards should be raised; more appropriate transportation facilities should be built, and so on. The costs of these programs to the state vary depending upon the scope of the program and the extent of federal aid.

The question of federal aid is a difficult one because it depends on so many imponderables. Optimistic views of revenue-sharing and increased federal responsibility for welfare indicate that the state could receive an additional $100 million. However, in view of the recent tax cut and the Administration's commitment to fight inflation, it is more reasonable to postulate no significant increases in federal aid accruing to Massachusetts.

Housing and welfare are the main areas in which additional antipoverty expenditures should be made. Without a substantial increase in federal or private-market activity, the housing proposals would entail initial expenditures of $20 million, rising to $150 million at the end of ten years. Increases in welfare payments of 30 to 50 percent have been recommended. If the welfare population remained stable, this would entail increases in welfare expenditures of some $75 to $125 million. However, because new families would be attracted to welfare as the payments rose, the actual costs of introducing these increases would be substantially greater than estimated. While the expenditures involved with other antipoverty programs have not been estimated, total additional expenditures of $50 million are probably not unrealistic.

Obviously, the size of an antipoverty program is a political decision that must be determined in the context of the competing claims on the budget. In this respect, an antipoverty program ranging between $100 and $150 million does not seem unreasonable. Expenditures of this magnitude in conjunction with better utilization of the existing funds could have a substantial impact upon the state's poor people.

Additional expenditures of this magnitude would not be difficult to finance. Expanding the sales tax base to include services and raising the rate to 3.5 percent would yield approximately $75 million. Increasing the rate or expanding the base on cigarets, alcohol, motor fuel, insurance companies, and inheritances could generate another $50 million. The substitution of the federal personal tax base for the current Massachusetts personal tax base, while keeping the rates on different kinds of income constant, would yield about $75 million more. Although the taxation of food and clothing is generally regressive, introduction of these items into the sales tax could generate $125 million.

However, it is not entirely reasonable to propose and finance an antipoverty program alone. The state and local governments face a combined revenue gap of some $125 million. There are strong pressures for increasing local aid, or for having the state take over all education expenses, or for both. Environmental control will doubtless call for increased resources. Unless the federal government increases its share of mass transit expenses, transportation will require additional funds.

Table 11–7 outlines the total revenue needs for fiscal 1971. This indicates that the state would need an additional $475 million: $150 million for poverty, $125 million for the combined revenue gap, and $200 million for the introduction of new programs in other areas (local aid, environment, transportation,). While federal revenue-sharing and increased federal activity in the field of welfare could reduce this figure by $50 to $100 million, such activity seems unlikely for the time being. Thus, the state should try to devise tax programs that would yield approximately $500 million initially, with an adequate growth potential to finance normal expenditure growth.

ALTERNATIVE TAX PROGRAMS FOR THE STATE

Table 11–8 outlines three such tax programs for the state. Each program was devised to yield $500 million in fiscal 1969, the last year for which data are available to make the necessary calculations. Thus each program should generate more than sufficient revenue to finance the outlined expenditure programs.

Basically there are three sources of revenues: (1) minor increases in

Table 11-7 *Additional revenue needs facing Massachusetts, fiscal 1971*

Revenue gap	
State	75
Local	50
Specific Program Increase	
(local aid, environment, etc.)	200
Antipoverty program	
Housing	20
Welfare	80
Other	50
Total	475
Possible federal aid	
Small welfare program	15
($1,600 min. for AFDC)	
Medium welfare program	65
($1,600 min. to all welfare	
recipients)	
Progressive block grant	40
($2 billion program)	

the rate and base of a wide range of taxes; (2) introduction of a graduated income tax;[11] (3) broadening the base and increasing the rates of the sales tax. All three tax sources are included in the proposed tax programs.

Plan A relies on several sources: (1) broadening the base and increasing the rate on a range of taxes (reducing the tax-exempt status of nonprofit institutions; bringing insurance company incomes into the tax base; making the Massachusetts inheritance tax base conform to the federal base; increasing rates on cigarets, alcohol, and motor fuels); (2) expanding the sales tax base to include services, food, and clothing; (3) modeling the Massachusetts personal income tax on the federal income tax and imposing a 20 percent surcharge on the federal tax liabilities.

Plan B relies on increases in the sales and income tax revenues. Specifically, it envisages taxing services and retail purchases on the part of businesses while leaving purchases of food and clothing exempt. In this case the seven percent tax on manufacturing tangible property

[11]Graduated income taxes would need a constitutional amendment; proposals for such an amendment are currently under consideration in the General Court and should go before the public in 1972. However, a similar proposal was voted down four to one by the electorate in 1962.

Table 11-8. *Alternative tax programs for Massachusetts, potential yield,*
fiscal 1969

I.	Plan A	
	Sales tax: Base includes services, food,	
	clothing; rate raised to 3.5%	200
	Income tax: 20% rate applied to federal	
	tax liability	600
	less current yield	−450
	Miscellaneous taxes:	
	Some taxation of exempt property	100
	Taxation of insurance company income	20
	Inheritance tax base broadened	10
	Cigarette and alcohol excises raised	10
	Motor fuel excise raised	10
	Total	500
II.	Plan B	
	Sales tax: Base includes services and	
	business purchases from retailers; 3.5% rate	170
	Corporate tax: Taxation of manufacturing	
	machinery eliminated	−70
	Income tax: New York base and rates adopted;	850
	less current yield	−450
	Total	500
III.	Plan C	
	Sales tax: no change	—
	Income tax: 30% rate applied to federal	
	tax liability	800
	less current yield	−450
	Miscellaneous taxes: Same as Plan A	150
	Total	500

would be removed. Instead of piggybacking on the federal income
taxes, this plan envisages the same rate structure as that used in New
York.

Finally, Plan C does not entail an increase in sales tax revenues, but
would impose a 30 percent piggybacking rate on the federal tax liabilities. In addition it would impose the same increases in miscellaneous
taxes outlined in Plan A.

Three criteria can be used to evaluate tax programs: economic efficiency; elasticity of tax yield; and progressivity. In general, if the existing situation is thought to be satisfactory, tax programs that would
generate considerable changes in relative product or factor prices are

less desirable than those that would not. Large changes in relative prices would tend to distort consumption, production, and locational decisions and are consequently viewed with suspicion by economists. The elasticity of the tax yield refers to the sensitivity of yield with respect to changes in economic variables. The higher the elasticity, the greater the response of yield to a given change in economic activity. Tax programs with high yield elasticity are desirable for two reasons: first, they enable the growth of expenditures to be financed without changes in rates; second, they tend to stabilize the economy by taking relatively more funds out of the income stream in an upswing and placing relatively more in the income stream in a downswing. Finally, the more progressive the tax program, the more the burden falls on the high income groups, who are presumably more able to finance additional expenditures.

Of the three plans outlined here, no plan dominates the others. Plan B is probably inferior to the others with respect to efficiency. By substituting a tax on business purchases from retailers for the existing tax on tangible manufacturing property, this program would introduce unpredictable and capricious pricing effects that might adversely affect industrial location in Massachusetts. However, Table 11–9 indicates that Plan B is the most progressive of the tax plans. Insofar as elasticity of yield is apt to be closely related to progressivity, this plan is also likely to be the most elastic with respect to revenue.

Plan C relies on income taxes somewhat less heavily than Plan B and is therefore somewhat less progressive. Nevertheless, because it does not introduce the distortions inherent in the taxation of business purchases from retailers, it is probably preferable to Plan B on balance.

Finally, Plan A is the least progressive tax plan because of its heavy reliance on increasing the sales tax base. Because Massachusetts has a relatively low sales tax burden and a relatively high income tax burden, this plan may well have the most political appeal.

Basically, the questions of how much, in what way, and for what purposes taxes should be raised are political decisions. However, this book contends that Massachusetts can and should do more to alleviate poverty. This brief discussion has indicated that funds can not only be made available to finance an antipoverty program alone, but also in conjunction with other programs that might compete for the

Table 11-9 Incidence of alternative tax programs

				Percent of income paid in tax when income is					
	under $1000	$1000–$1999	$2000–$2999	$3000–$3999	$4000–$4999	$5000–$5999	$6000–$9999	$10,000–$14,999	over $15,000
Plan A									
Miscellaneous Taxes	0.52	0.51	0.57	0.65	0.67	0.66	0.69	0.64	.74
Sales Tax	1.58	0.81	.97	1.16	1.08	1.00	.93	.92	0.80
Net Income Tax	−0.15	0.26	0.58	0.60	1.12	0.58	0.39	0.31	.91
Total	1.95	1.58	2.12	2.41	2.87	2.24	2.01	1.87	2.45
Plan B									
Sales Tax	1.01	0.36	0.48	0.61	0.66	0.62	0.62	0.59	0.19
Net Income Tax	−0.30	−0.12	0.0	.25	.66	.65	.85	1.51	3.23
Total	.71	.24	.48	.86	1.32	1.27	1.47	2.10	3.42
Plan C									
Miscellaneous Taxes	0.52	0.51	0.57	0.65	0.67	0.66	0.69	0.64	.74
Net Income Tax	−0.07	0.69	1.27	1.42	2.09	1.35	1.11	1.02	2.21
Total	0.45	1.20	1.84	2.07	2.76	2.01	1.80	1.66	2.95

available revenues. Thus, if the General Court has the will, it appears that there are any number of ways.

Appendix: A poverty budget for Massachusetts in fiscal 1968 (in millions of dollars)

	Federal outlays				State outlays			Local outlays	
	Total	State expend.	Local expend.	Other expend.	Total	State expend.	Local expend.	Loc. expend.	Total
I. Housing	95.6	—	47.4	48.2	6.8	—	6.8	6.1	108.5
Elderly	10.3	—	10.3	—	2.7	—	2.7	—	13.0
Housing for elderly and handicapped	10.3	—	10.3	—	2.7	—	2.7	—	13.0
Other	85.3	—	37.1	48.2	4.1	—	4.1	6.1	95.5
Housing for low-mod. income-below mkt. int. rates	72.2	—	30.3	41.9	—	—	—	6.1[a]	78.3
Housing for low-mod. income-market int. rates	6.3	—	—	6.3	—	—	—	—	6.3
Rehabilitation grants	0.1	—	0.1	—	—	—	—	—	0.1
Low Rent Public Housing	6.7	—	6.7	—	—	—	—	—	6.7
Housing not financed with fed. funds	—	—	—	—	4.1	—	4.1	—	4.1
II. Urban Environment	8.9	—	8.9	—	—	—	—	0.1	9.0
Urban mass transit grants	8.8	—	8.8	—	—	—	—	—	8.8[b]
Neighborhood facilities	0.1	—	0.1	—	—	—	—	0.1[c]	0.2

III. Criminal Justice	1.9	—	1.2	0.7	2.1	2.1	—	0.2	4.2
Youth	—	—	—	—	1.8	1.8	—	—	1.8
Youth Services Board	—	—	—	—	1.8	1.8	—	—	1.8
Other	1.9	—	1.2	0.7	0.3	0.3	—	0.2	2.4
Mass. Commission Against Discrimination	—	—	—	—	0.3	0.3	—	0.2[a]	0.3
Legal Services	1.5	—	0.8	0.7	—	—	—	—	1.7
Community Relations	ins	—	—	—	—	—	—	—	ins
Law Enforcement Assistance	0.4	—	0.4	—	—	—	—	—	0.4[d]
IV. Health	180.1	91.5	7.4	81.2	74.2	18.8	55.4	111.3	365.6
Youth	141.6	90.6	4.3	46.7	56.6	1.2	55.4	110.7	308.9
NTH—Human Development and Child Health	3.6	0.2	1.2	2.4	—	—	—	—	3.6[d]
Maternal and Child Health	1.8	0.7	1.0	0.1	0.4	0.4	—	0.5[c]	2.7
Grants for Mother and Child Welfare Service	1.7	1.0	0.7	—	0.3	0.3	—	0.2[e]	2.2
Health - School and Pre-School Children	1.3	—	1.3	—	—	—	—	0.3[e]	1.6
Maternity and Infant Care	1.2	1.1	0.1	—	0.3	0.3	—	ins[e]	1.5

	Federal outlays				State outlays			Local outlays	
	Total	State expend.	Local expend.	Other expend.	Total	State expend.	Local expend.	Loc. expend.	Total
Crippled Children's Service	0.7	0.5	—	0.2	0.2	0.2	—	—	0.9
Medicaid	131.3	87.1	—	44.2	55.4	—	55.4	109.7	296.4
Elderly	30.4	—	—	30.4	17.4	17.4	—	—	47.8
Federal Supplement. Med.-Ins. Trust Fund	6.5	—	—	6.5	—	—	—	—	6.5[g]
Federal Hosp. Ins. Trust Fund	23.9	—	—	23.9	—	—	—	—	23.9[g]
Care of Aged — Mental Health	—	—	—	—	17.4	17.4	—	—	17.4
Other	8.1	0.9	3.1	4.1	0.2	0.2	—	0.6	8.9
Community Health Grants	1.2	—	0.5	0.7	—	—	—	—	1.2[d]
Community Health Planning Service	3.3	0.9	2.4	—	0.2	0.2	—	0.6	4.1[e]
Neighborhood Health Centers	3.4	—	—	3.4	—	—	—	—	3.4[d]
Mental Retardation — Rehab. Service	0.2	—	0.2	—	—	—	—	ins	0.2[e]
V. Education	54.7	0.7	41.7	12.3	1.3	6.1	1.2	0.7	56.7
Youth	53.1	—	40.8	12.3	1.2	—	1.2	0.6	54.9

Education of Deprived Children —ESEA, Title I	36.1	—	36.1	—	—	—	—	—	36.1[d]
Supp. Ed. Centers— ESEA Title III	3.7	—	—	3.7	—	—	—	—	3.7[d]
Teacher Corps	0.4	—	0.4	—	—	—	—	—	0.4
Head Start	5.6	—	3.1	2.5	—	—	—	0.6	6.2[a]
Follow Through	0.4	—	0.4	—	—	—	—	—	0.4
Upward Bound	1.7	—	0.5	1.2	—	—	—	—	1.7
Disadvantaged Students - tuition and transport	—	—	—	—	1.2	—	1.2	—	1.2
Pre-School and School Program	0.3	—	0.3	—	—	—	—	—	0.3
Education Opp. Grants	4.9	—	—	4.9	—	—	—	—	4.9
Other	1.6	0.7	0.9	—	0.1	0.1	—	0.1	1.8
Adult Basic Education	1.6	0.7	0.9	—	0.1	0.1	—	0.1	1.8[h]
VI. Manpower	57.6	8.9	33.8	14.9	94.5	94.5	—	—	152.1
Youth	9.9	—	4.2	5.7	—	—	—	—	9.9
Neighborhood Youth Corps	3.6	—	—	3.6	—	—	—	—	3.6
Job Corps	6.3	—	4.2	2.1	—	—	—	—	6.3
Other	47.9	8.9	29.6	9.2	94.5	94.5	—	—	142.2

	Federal outlays				State outlays			Local outlays	
	Total	State expend.	Local expend.	Other expend.	Total	State expend.	Local expend.	Loc. expend.	Total
Federal Employee Injury Compensation	3.2	—	1.6	1.6	—	—	—	—	3.2
Unemployment Insurance	11.6	—	9.0	2.6	93.1	93.1	—	—	104.7
MDTA—Research, Pilots and Demonstrat.	1.6	1.2	0.4	—	—	—	—	—	1.6
MDTA—Institute Training	5.0	—	5.0	—	—	—	—	—	5.0
Tech. Asst.	0.3	—	—	0.3	—	—	—	—	0.3
On the Job Training	5.8	—	5.2	0.6	—	—	—	—	5.8^d
Vocational Training	—	—	—	—	0.8	0.8	—	—	0.8
Concentrated Employment Program	1.7	—	1.7	—	—	—	—	—	1.7
Vocational Rehab. Service	5.4	5.1	—	0.3	—	—	—	—	5.4
Community Achievement Program	11.2	2.5	6.3	2.4	—	—	—	—	11.2
Work Experience Program	0.4	—	—	0.4	—	—	—	—	0.4

Job Opportunities in Private Business	1.4	—	0.1	1.3	—	—	—	—	1.4[d]
Vista	0.4	0.1	0.3	—	—	—	—	—	0.4[d]
Mass. Rehab. Commission	—	—	—	—	0.6	0.6	—	—	0.6
VII. Welfare	301.9	83.7	—	218.2	82.8	16.3	66.5	51.5	436.2
Youth	48.3	44.1	—	4.2	44.3	0.4	43.9	25.4	118.0
Aid to Dependent Children	47.3	43.1	—	4.2	32.0	—	32.0	24.9	104.2
Child Welfare Service	1.0	1.0	—	—	12.3	0.4	11.9	0.5	13.8
Elderly	202.9	29.5	—	173.4	17.0	1.2	15.8	19.6	239.5
Medical and Old Age Assistance Administration	—	—	—	—	1.2	1.2	—	—	1.2
Old Age Assistance	35.5	29.5	—	6.0	15.8	—	15.8	19.6	70.9
Fed. Old Age Survivors Ins.	137.8	—	—	137.8	—	—	—	—	137.8[g]
Civil Service Retirement Board	22.4	—	—	22.4	—	—	—	—	22.4[g]
Soc. Ins. for R.R. Workers	7.2	—	—	7.2	—	—	—	—	7.2[g]
Other	50.7	10.1	—	40.6	21.5	14.7	6.8	6.5	78.7
General Administration	—	—	—	—	5.7	5.7	—	—	5.7
Aid to the Blind	1.4	—	—	1.4	—	—	—	0.7	1.4

| | Federal outlays | | | | State outlays | | | Local outlays | |
	Total	State expend.	Local expend.	Other expend.	Total	State expend.	Local expend.	Loc. expend.	Total
Aid to the Totally and Permanently Disabled	10.6	9.9	—	0.7	6.0	2.7	3.3	6.8	22.4
General Relief	—	—	—	—	9.8	6.3	3.5	—	9.8
Asst. to Migrant Workers	0.3	0.2	—	0.1	—	—	—	—	0.3
Disability Ins. Trust Fund	38.4	—	—	38.4	—	—	—	—	38.4
VIII. Food Assistance	17.0	7.8	8.9	0.3	5.2	4.6	0.6	—	22.2
Youth	15.2	7.8	7.4	—	5.2	4.6	0.6	—	20.4
Food Dist. to Schools	6.6	—	3.0	—					
Payment to State for School Lunch	3.6	7.8	1.7	—	5.2	4.6	0.6	—	20.4
Payment to State for School Milk	3.6		2.0	—					
Donation of Commod. to School Lunch	1.4		0.7	—					
Other	1.8	1.5	0.3	—	—	—	—	—	1.8
Food Dist. to Families	1.1	—	1.1	—	—	—	—	—	1.1
Food Dist. to Institutions	0.7	—	0.4	0.3	—	—	—	—	0.7

IX.	Assistance to Business	1.5	—	—	0.1	1.4	—	—	1.5
	Economic Opp. to Small Bus.	1.0	—	—	0.1	0.9	—	—	1.0
	Small Bus. Investment Program	0.5	—	—	—	0.5	—	—	0.5

Source: Prepared by Ann F. Friedlaender with the assistance of Ataman Aksoy and Ahmet Tekiner.

[a] Assumes state or local governments contribute 20%.
[b] Assumes 50% of mass transit expenditures go to poor.
[c] Assumes state or local governments contribute 50%.
[d] Assumes federal share is 100%.
[e] Assumes state or local governments contribute 25%.
[f] Assumes state or local governments contribute 33.3%.
[g] Assumes that 1/3 of these expenditures go to Poor.
[h] Assumes state or local governments contribute 10%.

Sources: The proportions noted in notes a–h come from OEO, *Catalog of Federal Domestic Assistance.* Data in the appendix come from: OEO, *Federal Outlays in Massachusetts,* Fiscal year, 1968, Vols. 1 and 2; Federal information Exchange System, *State-Federal Outlays Report,* June 30, 1968; Massachusetts Office of the Comptroller, *Financial Report,* Fiscal 1968; and estimates from required matching share of federal funds (see footnotes at end of budget); 1967 *Census of Governments,* Vol. 4, No. 4, *Finances of Municipalities and Township Governments,* and Vol. 6, No. 4, *State Payments to Local Governments,* and estimates from required matching share of federal funds (see footnotes at end of budget).

RICHARD E. BARRINGER

Epilogue: poverty
and priorities

For some, poverty is merely the fact of a simple life.
To them, a life of hardship and discipline is not
necessarily objectionable; and to suggest that it is
intolerable in either personal or political terms is to
impose comfortable and pious middle-class values
upon it. For most of the "poor" in a modern society,
however, poverty is an enforced condition, a life of
deprivation and inequity. For them, poverty is properly a political issue and rightly a matter of public
policy.

As an issue of political debate and national policy,
poverty is the product of our affluence, the by-
product of the same social, political, and economic
institutions that have made general and continuing
prosperity possible. That prosperity began in the
United States during World War II, and by 1960 it
had reached a level unprecedented in human history. It was by then apparent, however, that the

*Richard E. Barringer is lecturer on public policy in the
Kennedy School of Government and research fellow in
the Institute of Politics, Harvard University. He is pleased
to acknowledge the thoughtful assistance of Ronald Simon in the conception and execution of this paper, and
of Theodore Siff in providing research materials for it.*

private institutions that produced the nation's wealth and the traditional public institutions that ministered to those excluded from it were not sufficient to meet the legitimate needs of all the people. So John F. Kennedy set in motion the public processes that culminated in Lyndon Johnson's 1964 declaration of "war on poverty," and thus began poverty's brief tenure as the overriding issue of domestic national policy.

Now we set about to turn the nation's exclusive attentions to the issues of "the environment," even before we have fully learned who in fact is poor, how to provide decent jobs and adequate shelter for all, how to make the institutions of our great wealth responsive to the needs of the least among us. For as much as we are any single thing, Americans are impatient with intractable problems: if a problem cannot be solved in the terms in which it is first formulated and attacked, we feel, it is probably not soluble at all except by natural processes.

Our society's failure to eliminate poverty, however, may well derive not from the intractability of the problem itself, but from the assumptions we have made about it and from the very fashion in which we have defined it as an issue of public policy. By now it is the conventional wisdom that "victory" in the war on poverty was lost for too much rhetoric and too little money—not because the federal government had tried too much, but because it had promised what it could not deliver. But there is an alternative explanation: the campaign foundered because the issue of poverty was never defined in terms sufficiently relevant to the lives of those with access to the political system to provide a lasting base of support for it—namely, the middle class—and because, in practice, the poverty programs of the 1960s did not provide access to the system to enough of those with the greatest stake in the issue itself—namely, the poor. Rhetoric can overcome policy inertia, and government funds can generate policy momentum. Only self-interest, built right into the fabric of free institutions, can maintain it.

Who are the poor?

Until now, poverty strategists have taken as an article of faith the assumption that poverty is primarily and most compellingly an urban-racial problem. So the federal poverty programs of the 1960s were built in overwhelming measure upon twin strategies, one urban, one racial. But poverty in Massachusetts is not primarily the problem of black residents of central cities. By whatever standard one uses, Massachusetts' poor people are primarily suburban and rural, and overwhelmingly white. They are partly urban and partly black. The 1960 census suggested that this was the case throughout the United States, and demographic trends since that time have only reinforced it—both in Massachusetts and in the nation.

To be sure, the greatest concentrations of the poor are in the same place as the greatest concentrations of the general population—the urban core. But like the rest of the population, the poor have become increasingly suburban. And while the old and the nonwhite do not participate in this trend on a proportionate basis, clearly they—and especially young families, both white and black—are doing so in ever increasing numbers. They do this seeking the same middle-class values that have traditionally drawn Americans out of their cities: more space, better housing, better schools and recreational facilities for their children, and the prospect of making some real impact on governmental institutions of manageable proportions. For two decades, this movement has been accelerated by an absolute decrease in the number of jobs available to the poor in the central cities and a proportionate increase in such jobs in the suburbs.

An antipoverty stragegy that ignores these facts contains the seeds of its own destruction. For "poverty" *is* the product of our present institutions and if it is to be eliminated, as a condition and as an issue, those institutions must change. Any exclusionary strategy, though it may work to the advantage of the few in the short run, sacrifices the broad base of political support that alone can bring about permanent and effective change in those institutions.

The urban strategy for combatting poverty was grafted onto the "urban renewal" program of the 1950s to rebuild the central business districts of the cities. It has served mainly as a holding action against economic, technological, and demographic forces acting on the urban core that are generally beyond the reach of government in a free society. Those forces can be changed only by altering their logic or, alternatively, by governmental coercion. The automobile, truck, and superhighway especially have changed forever the indispensable role of the central city in commerce, trade, industry, and low-income housing. New levels of mobility have created new opportunities for profit, pleasure, housing, and employment beyond the confines of the urban core and have permanently altered its place in society.

The racial strategy for combatting poverty was, in turn, first formulated to grease the squeaky wheel of the time, and has served to now only as a holding action against forces that afflict a far wider public than the black lower class. For there is increasing and compelling evidence that the prejudices, discrimination, and handicaps from which lower-class blacks suffer are related more strongly to income and class than to race or color. Increasingly, they are of the same kind as the obstacles to personal advancement that confront all low-income peoples. Increasingly, what differences exist between low-income blacks and whites in this regard are matters of degree.

This is not to suggest that there are no urban and racial problems among us. Such as they are, they are acute and compelling. It is only to suggest that the urban-racial strategy, even while it has made little impact on the physical decay of cities outside their central business districts, has fixed a firm and obstructive wedge between low-income whites and blacks. It is to suggest that the way in which poverty has to now now been formulated and translated into policy programs has obscured the issue of poverty itself, divided society into hostile camps of peoples with common stakes in that issue, and promoted the continuance of *all* the poor in their present state. To persist in that strategy is to admit that its purpose is *not* to eliminate poverty but to promote more limited, if sometimes worthy, interests. A new, more inclusive antipoverty strategy is required, one which will *subsume within a larger context* the urban-racial strategy of the recent past. Such a strategy must be built upon the common interests of all the poor—urban, suburban, and rural; black, brown, and white; old and young—and upon the common interests they have with the rest of society.

The poor and society

We need no longer argue that the conventional "welfare" structure and mechanisms traditionally used to cope with poverty are insufficient to their purpose. At the end of a decade in which the designation "welfare recipient" has, under the pressure of inflation, begun to lose much of its social stigma, case loads are running many times ahead of projections, costs are increasing exponentially, and the system is crumbling under its own weight. This is so, I would argue, because the welfare bureaucracy has attempted to satisfy needs that can be met for the number of people involved only through the mechanism of the private market. It is the genius of the private market mechanism, for which we pay a considerable cost in terms of resources to produce competitive goods and services, that it *is* capable of responding to individual needs when they are expressed on an organized basis. It is ironic that we should treat poverty in such fashion as to deny the poor access to the mechanism in which we so much believe as a generator of economic growth and personal progress and as a satisfier of individual wants and needs. In fact, this denial follows from the assumption upon which our traditional welfare structures have been based: if one is not "making it" economically on his own in this land of individual enterprise, it is only because of some deficiency in oneself that makes it necessary for government to "provide for" one on a semi-institutional basis. The individual, in other words, is responsible for such "failure" rather than anything in the social institutions themselves.

This assumption raises a fundamental question about how poverty is best dealt with and, if possible, eliminated. I have suggested that poverty is not intolerable in and of itself, nor even necessarily objectionable. Indeed, it has often been cited as a source of spiritual strength and salvation by the great philosophers—Socrates, Christ, and Ghandi among them. Poverty is objectionable and intolerable only in some of its more insidious contemporary effects: higher incidence of emotional debility and family disorganization, higher rates of sickness and mortality, greater incidence of criminal convictions and recidivism, and so on. Presently, then, to be poor is to be *different* from the more fortunate among us, at least in a statistical sense. The relevant question for policy is: are poor people different because they are poor, or are they poor because they are different? Do the poor demonstrate these objectionable characteristics in disproportionate fashion *because* they lack money and means? Or do they lack money and means because of their *own* characteristics? If the former is the case, policy should seek to guarantee the poor access to the normal mechanisms by which goods and services are made available to the rest of society. To the extent that the latter applies, eliminating poverty requires the prior "rehabilitation" of the poor in some sense.

The anthropologist Oscar Lewis has been the principal intellectual source of the idea that poverty is more than just an economic condition, that there is a "culture of poverty" that allows the poor to survive even while reinforcing them in their poverty. To be poor, in this view, is more than simply to lack money and means. It is to be absorbed within a way of life characterized by lack of participation in the major institutions of society and by lack of integration into the ways of the larger middle-class culture. It is to be helpless in one's own right except within the poverty culture, and dependent upon the larger culture for survival. It is, in Lewis' words, "a way of life, remarkably stable and persistent, passed down from generation to generation along family lines".[1]

Any social worker will attest to the existence of individual cases that support this view. There are, and probably always will be, individuals who are emotionally or physically dependent for survival upon semi-institutional care or intensive case work. What is not demonstrated is the general validity of the argument for a "culture of poverty," for a more or less permanent "underclass" in this nation. And what is particularly insidious about the thesis is its clear implication that only after the poor have become conventionally responsive and responsible in middle-class terms can they hope to leave poverty behind. It is too easy a rationale for blaming poverty on the poor, for avoiding the necessity for institutional change, to accept without question. (It is interesting to speculate in this connection whether the dependence of a second or third generation welfare mother represents an indictment of herself or of the institutions which fostered and perpetuated her dependence.)

Lewis' thesis is a thoughtful and useful heuristic device for examining peasant society and its relation to modern life, but it has never been put to a creditable test in American society. It is in fact an untested hypothesis, developed in a social environment that would lead one at least to question seriously its applicability to the United States: a traditional culture *not* characterized by generations of marked economic expansion, by positive attitudes toward achievement and self-denial and a malleable environment, or by more than a generation of the middle-class socializing influence of mass communications. Indeed, there is every evidence that the opportunities for upward mobility in our society continue to expand constantly for all the poor—once they have achieved access and entry to the job market. At the same time, all the evidence we have in hand, and especially the increasing amount available from experiments with the guaranteed annual wage for low-income workers, indicates that the poor have the capacity to climb out of poverty within very reasonable periods of time, given the appropriate access and means.

Access to the private market is gained by means of cash. With money, the poor tend very quickly to learn middle-class values and habits. Their problem then becomes that of the middle-class: obtaining needed goods and services even with money in hand. We need not dwell

[1]*The Children of Sanchez* (New York: Random House, 1961), p. xxiv.

on the difficulty in an inflated economy of obtaining goods at what seem to reasonable men to be reasonable prices. In an earlier economic era, the government might have applied conventional Keynesian wisdom, restricted the amount and flow of cash in the economy, encouraged the exercise of consumer sovereignty, and so reduced what is known as "demand-pull" inflation. Ours, on the other hand, is an era characterized by what J. Kenneth Galbraith has called "producer sovereignty." It is a time following upon continued inflation and concentration in industry, in which oligopolistic practices generally set the price of a consumer product and advertising creates the demand for it. Thus, "cost-push" inflation increases despite cutbacks in government spending and "tight" money, and the consumer is left without his traditional sovereign power in the market place, to await the slow development of new economic levers and antitrust devices.

At the same time, the private market is inherently unresponsive to both individual and collective demands for certain necessary services. And the difference between the poor and the nonpoor in this regard is mainly one of degree, not of kind. Simply stated, there is not sufficient profit in it—or at least we have not yet found the means to build sufficient profit into it—for the private market to produce adequate housing, transportation, health care, education, police protection, and so on, for all people. If eliminating poverty means affording the poor an income large enough to purchase such services through the private market, then it is necessary either to put them into considerably higher income brackets (even if then), or to establish institutions that will in fact be responsive to their need for such services.

Poverty, then, is a matter of both goods and services. Neither an "income" nor a "service" strategy is adequate by itself to provide the poor with effective and meaningful choices. Only a strategy that delivers both goods and services can give poor people the means to conquer their poverty. Delivering both means not only designing "delivery systems" and making programs available, but also ensuring that the poor have access to them and that they are in fact responsive to the needs of the poor themselves.

Income and services

To the extent that it represents the lack of effective choice, poverty for most of the poor is ultimately economic in origin. It is a matter of money and income. To create a foundation from which the poor can operate as effective individuals means to assure them a minimal adequate income. In practice, this means more and better jobs for the poor, and a federally supported program of family income maintenance.

So long as government does not own the means of producing most of society's goods and services, it cannot be the sole source of financial support for all its citizens. In a private economy incapable itself of generating enough of the jobs that afford a man dignity and independence, government has the responsibility of generating adequate numbers of such jobs within both the private and public sectors. This means more jobs with higher wages, greater security, and greater opportunity for advancement. At the same time, it means stronger and more effective programs of vocational education and job training, relentless application of antidiscrimination laws, and balanced transportation systems that connect poor people with existing and expanding job markets.

Jobs alone are not enough, however. Too many of those now available to the poor do not provide an adequate income, and too many of the poor are simply unable to work. The major precipitants of poverty are, in fact, old age, disability, and the absence of male heads of households. Better than half of all the poor families in Massachusetts, for example, are headed by men over 65. If we accept the standards set by the Department of Labor, a family of four presently requires *at least* $5,000 a year to live in this state. To assure every family that income is merely to accept the cost of a free enterprise system that is unable to provide every family with the minimum income necessary to survive. For government to assume responsibility for doing so is merely for it to assume the "overhead" of the economic freedoms we value. However, only a guaranteed income program containing a scale of income supplements far beyond the $5,000 level will be adequate to maintain work incentives and to build political support for the program. Such a program should therefore provide progressively decreasing salary supplements to all heads of household with incomes up to some higher figure, say the present median income of about $9,700 a year. President Nixon's proposed "family maintenance plan" of $1,600 guaranteed annual income for a family of four establishes the political and economic foundation from which to mount a program to guarantee every family a minimum adequate income geared to local living standards in each state.

But income is not enough. Services are required. In the case of the many poor who, for good reasons, cannot hold jobs and make do on their own resources, various programs of intensive services must be provided by a welfare establishment freed of its enormous case load by the guaranteed-income program. And beyond this lies the whole question of services to which the private market is not presently responsive: day-care centers, family-planning programs, housing, education, health care, police protection, consumer protection, and many others. All these services are needed by the entire population, and by the poor especially. To deliver them to the poor is to deliver them to everyone, and to assure the poor access to them. To deliver them to all is, moreover, to remove the stigma attaching to services delivered exclusively to the poor and so to make such services more accessible to all the poor.

A good example is consumer protection. The New York State Consumer Advisory Council recently concluded that "the low-income consumer lacks the power of choice, and the national interest suffers as a consequence." The low-income buyer is often forced to pay more for the same necessities than the middle-class consumer who can buy in larger quantities, obtain reasonable credit rates, and pay to protect his interests through the legal process. Presently, however, the "consumer movement" is primarily a middle-class exercise. To be effective, an antipoverty program must include a program of consumer protection and education that is available to all and especially sensitized to the needs of the poor.

This, then, raises the question of how one prevents programs designed for everybody from becoming responsive only to the values of those who already have power—the middle class—or to the values of those who run the programs—the bureaucrats. If needed services can be delivered to the poor only by delivering them first to everyone, how can one ensure that these programs are responsive, at least in part, to the needs of the poor? At least the beginning of an answer appears to lie in building access mechanisms into the institutions that deliver these services, and in fostering competition, wherever possible, among public, private, and nonprofit deliverers of services.

Let us take an example from the private sector. Given present expectations about what constitutes "satisfactory" health care, such services can no longer be dispensed by the general practitioner exclusively on his own resources, without vast and costly institutional backup. The technology involved in delivering that service to large numbers of people requires that it be institutionalized. Such is the case today with virtually all services, public and private. The public sector provides no better example than the public education system. To counter this institutional development in both the public and private sectors, access mechanisms must be established to allow consumers of services to voice their requirements and grievances effectively, and organizational mechanisms established to encourage them to voice these in a concerted fashion. In the public sector, for example, this suggests introducing the "consumer advocate" concept into the organizational structure of all large service programs. In practice, this might mean the establishment at the highest management level of an "office of consumer affairs" which would be responsible in that area both inside and outside the organization. Such an office would at least provide a point of access for dissatisfied consumers of the service and for querulous producers of it, and would encourage consumers to act on behalf of their own interests where these conflict with the institution's.

At the same time, because such voices of dissatisfaction are likely to go unheeded unless they are organized, this concept requires that effective forms of community organization be developed simultaneously and in parallel. No government can be expected to organize against itself. But it is not unreasonable to expect government to recognize how remote its large institutions are from their clients and to support new institutional forms to deal more responsively with them. From this viewpoint, it is very much in government's interest to provide seed-money for developing community organizations that can provide people with timely information on existing programs, with professional assistance in making full use of them, and with a sense of more immediate participation in the political processes that control their lives. This is not to suggest "community control" of government programs by individuals or groups not representative of their total constituencies. Community organization is not a substitute for the political processes of the larger community. It is simply a means whereby those upon whom the programs of large institutions come to bear can gain a voice in the determination of what those programs will be. It is, moreover, a structured and meaningful focus of new career options for the increasing numbers of young professionals seeking unconventional careers in the public service.

Such access mechanisms are the only means by which anyone, including the poor, can hope to introduce his own needs and values into the institutions of government. This does not mean that even with such mechanisms those institutions will necessarily serve the *poor* in any adequate or immediate fashion. If such new political forms are to be developed, they must be available to all—including the middle class. Until the poor learn that it will "pay" them to make knowledgeable and effective use of these mechanisms and become adept at doing so, such community organizations are certain to work to the advantage of middle-class persons. They are, simply, practiced and accustomed in the uses of power.

Finally, it is worth suggesting at this point in our history that both the public and private means of delivering services have become concentrated to a degree that demands a conscious governmental policy of promoting competition among various possible delivery systems and mechanisms wherever such offers the prospect of more responsive service. It is unlikely, for example, that the public education systems in virtually every city and suburban town would do anything but benefit from competing directly with alternative systems for limited, fixed sources of financial support. As we have long since learned in the private market, almost nothing is as effective as the prospect of financial failure or even diminished returns in inducing producer responsiveness to consumer demands. In recent years an increasing number of schemes have been advanced to provide the poor and non-poor alike with cash "vouchers" for services traditionally delivered or supported by government. These vouchers could be "spent" to obtain those services from any available and certified institution, public or private, profit or non-profit, that the holder feels is most responsive to his own needs, and exchanged by that institution for a cash transfer from the government. In principle, this concept might well be approved by government, and in practice, its applicability in every proposed instance fully and fairly tested by authoritative and knowledgeable professional sources. Again, the time seems upon us to accept the costs and short-term "inefficiencies" of duplication of services in the interest of introducing greater diversity, responsiveness, and personal satisfaction into our social institutions.

The state's role

Clearly, one lesson of the 1960s is that federal government and local government are, singly and in combination, inadequate to the task of eliminating poverty. This is not to say that their efforts are not both necessary and, in most cases, commendable. But neither commands the power necessary to mount and sustain a fully responsive and effective antipoverty program. This, and the facts of poverty itself, suggest a new and necessary role for state government in eliminating poverty. For poverty happens only to individuals, rather than to aggregated entities or statistical abstractions that can be generalized upon without doing violence to them. At the same time, it is widely dispersed throughout the countryside rather than concentrated exclusively or even mostly in the innermost ring of commercial and industrial development. Eliminating poverty, as I have argued, requires services that must be delivered to all our citizens if they are to be delivered to any; and state government already possesses critical powers governing the terms and conditions under which those services are delivered to any of its citizens, and therefore to all.

For its part, the federal government is too remote from the problem of poverty to cope with it directly and effectively. Nationwide generalizations are the prime movers of the federal bureaucracy. Poverty, on the other hand, both as a term and as a condition, is not to be generalized upon in easy fashion. The poor are as rich in diversity as life itself—to an extent which federal policy makers and operators have been unable to give them credit for, much less to organize for. They come in all the sizes, shapes, colors, and ages as do people of conventional means, and often with somewhat more personal resourcefulness for having had to make do without it. This richness is lost in the statistical abstractions whereby political coalitions and policy programs are organized at the federal level. "The poor" become a slogan, a cause, a myth ambiguous enough to satisfy all and to offend none. Historically, the role of national government in our cooperative federalism has comprised revenue raising, setting broad national standards, and redistributing that revenue to lower levels of government, to institutions, and to private citizens, in accordance with those standards. It is this same role that national government can best play in the poverty area, using its vast array of incentives to achieve broad objectives and to encourage the exercise of initiative and imagination in problem solving at the local and state levels. At the same time, of course, the federal government alone can assume the especially critical role in this area of judicious use of its fiscal and monetary policies to maintain a high rate of employment and a tolerable level of inflation.

At the other end of the spectrum, local government is too close to the problem of poverty and too limited in its jurisdiction and resources to deal fully with any of the problems plaguing it. A hard look at the extent of the problems of mass transportation, housing, education, sewage disposal, and so on, shows that few if any of the problems besetting city and town governments are coterminous with their own borders. Thus, in spite of the political obstacles to it, "metropolitanization" of local government and services has become practically an article of faith among those concerned with local problems. They argue essentially that metropolitanization of services will broaden the local tax base and deliver those services more efficiently. The argument, however, is not compelling; the question remains open. For the argument rests fundamentally upon the question of "efficient" organization in service delivery. It finds its fullest expression, therefore, in the full consolidation of services within a metropolitan community under an areawide political or fiscal jurisdiction. Among more than 100 attempts at full consolidation of metropolitan services over the past 40 years, only a handful have been achieved, notably in Nashville, Jacksonville, and Indianapolis. In Nashville and Jacksonville, expenditures for public services have risen at a faster rate since metropolitanization than before, with no indication that anyone is now getting any more for his money. And in all three cities, the potential for redistributing the tax burden from the inner city to the suburbs was undermined by the political price necessary to effect consolidation of services: a different tax rate for suburban and central-city landowners, rationalized in terms of a "general services rate" for the former and an "urban services rate" for the latter.

This is not to suggest that the value of local government is not great and that it does not have a vital role to play in delivering services to the poor and the nonpoor alike. Indeed, the value of a political community that is at once manageable and accessible at the local level greatly outweighs any arguments of efficiency attaching to governmental consolidation. Where the need is demonstrated for attacking problems on an areawide basis, cooperation among local governments should be encouraged and appropriate agencies developed that are directly responsible either to the governor or to the local governments they serve, and have built into them the kinds of access mechanisms I mentioned above.

This is only to say that an intermediate level of authority is already available—the state. In that position, the state is auspiciously located to perform the functions of information gathering, overall planning, goal setting, and performance evaluation in the case of services that do not correspond organizationally to local jurisdictions. More than this, however, the state already possesses powers that constitute a singularly potent and critical array of levers affecting the delivery of services to any of its citizens. As the basic unit in our federal system from which all local powers proceed, the state has major influence over the content and structure of such basic services as education, transportation, housing, health care, manpower policy, police protection, and so on. The state exercises this power by virtue of its laws creating local property tax systems, state grant-in-aid programs, zoning laws, housing codes, teacher certification requirements, public school systems, educational standards, colleges, universities, highways, transit systems, health codes, medical licensing, insurance rating systems, air and water pollution codes, the courts, police training requirements, and the like.

Until now, few of these laws have been considered to be involved directly and critically in the problem of poverty. But as we have seen, that problem is inextricably linked to the delivery of services and to the responsiveness of the institutions delivering them. If those services are to be delivered, and if a truly effective antipoverty program is to be established, the state must make *conscious and consistent* use of the leverage points it controls as antipoverty devices and as instruments of more responsive public and private institutions. The use of those powers, sanctions, and incentives in that fashion will, of course, require state government to "take on" established institutions, both public and private, and to regard itself more clearly as a purposeful agent of change in the very organization, goals, and behavior of those institutions. In no area is this more evident, for example, than that of subprofessional employment categories in various technical and service fields such as medicine, education, police work, and so on. Often the creation of such categories promises *simultaneously* to relieve the problems of poverty, racial discrimination, manpower shortages, and community alienation from remote, impersonal institutions. Yet they are just as often resisted as direct threats to professionalism and professional privilege. Whether the state will be willing to combat such professional chauvinism will be one measure of its commitment to eliminating poverty. The powers and leverage are there for the state to play its role. That the services necessary to eliminate poverty are required by all is a mandate for their delivery, as well as a promise of political advantage to the deliverer.

Finally, it is worth reminding ourselves that, in a fundamental sense, any state is its people. And among the people, those who are poor have proven to be far more heterogeneous and far more widely distributed than policy makers have heretofore given them credit for. Just as there is no "typical" American, there is no "typical" poor American. And as no state is "typical" in its poverty, no one set of policy proposals for its elimination can or should be made welcome in every state capitol. Certain facts about poverty and the poor have been found in Massachusetts that appear consistent among the several states. These facts suggest a role for state government and a strategy for combatting poverty that have not yet been fully explored. To the extent that these facts prove valid, and the strategy compelling, it is hoped that this book will serve as a useful model for other states.

The traditional value has been claimed for state government that it constitutes a viable and desirable "laboratory for experimentation" in our federal system. In other times, in the face of other compelling problems of government, such states as New York, Connecticut, Wisconsin, Minnesota, California, and Massachusetts itself have undertaken experiments in political and institutional innovation that have provided standards for application by other states and by the federal government. The present need for innovation and experimentation in arriving at an effective and lasting antipoverty strategy is manifest. Our knowledge both of poverty and of the processes of deliberate social change is still far from complete. So must and will men even fully abreast of the existing "state of the art" disagree on the specific implications of new knowledge and understanding. But to shrink from necessary action because of either the likelihood of error or the certainty of opposition becomes no man well, and ill serves the ends of democratic government.

Suggested readings

Banfield, Edward C. *The Unheavenly City: The Nature and Future of Our Urban Crisis*. Boston: Little Brown, and Company, 1970.

Bundy, McGeorge. *The Strength of Government*. Cambridge, Mass.: Harvard University Press, 1968.

Campbell, Alan K. (ed.). *The States and the Urban Crisis*. Englewood Cliffs, N.J.: Prentice-Hall, Inc., 1970.

Moynihan, Daniel P. (ed.). *On Understanding Poverty: Perspectives from the Social Sciences*. New York: Basic Books, Inc., 1969.

Sundquist, James L. (ed.). *On Fighting Poverty: Perspectives from Experience*. New York: Basic Books, Inc., 1969.

Valentine, Charles A. *Culture and Poverty: Critique and Counter-Proposals*. Chicago: The University of Chicago Press, 1968.

Vernon, Raymond. *The Myth and Reality of Our Urban Problems*. Second Edition. Cambridge, Mass: Harvard University Press, 1966.

Wilson, James Q. (ed.). *The Metropolitan Enigma: Inquiries into the Nature and Dimensions of America's "Urban Crisis."* Cambridge, Mass.: Harvard University Press, 1968.

The Study Group on *The State and The Poor*

THE INSTITUTE OF POLITICS, KENNEDY SCHOOL OF GOVERNMENT

Members

Paul Abrams
Richard E. Barringer
Samuel H. Beer
David L. Birch
David K. Cohen
David Davis
Donald R. Dwight
Rashi Fein
Bernard J. Frieden
Ann F. Friedlaender
Francis J. Larkin
Hans F. Loeser
Basil J. F. Mott
Richard A. Musgrave
John R. Myer
Michael J. Piore
Gerald Rosenthal
Charles I. Schottland
John G. Wofford
Adam Yarmolinsky

Research members

Vincent F. Ciampa
John Perkins
Richard H. Rowland
Eugene L. Saenger, Jr.
Hugh Tilson
Tyll Van Geel

Faculty associates

Alan Altshuler
Francis M. Bator
Martha Derthick
Peter Doeringer

Otto Eckstein
Nathan Glazer
Charles Harr
John F. Kain
Sidney S. Lee
Frank I. Michelman
Lloyd Ohlin
Samuel Popkin
Raymond Vernon
Alonzo S. Yerby

Research associates

M. Ataman Aksoy
Christa Carnegie
W. Norton Grubb
Cornelia Lehmann
Daniel Lidman
Joanne McGeary
Alan Rubin
Leslie Schlesinger
Bertram Schlensky
Ronald Simon
Ahmet Tekiner
Eric J. Wallach

Guest participants

David M. Bartley
Levin H. Campbell
Hale Champion
Maurice A. Donahue
Harry M. Durning, Jr.
John W. Gardner
Robert H. Marden
John F. Parker
Elliot Richardson